Canadian Guide to
PERSONAL FINANCIAL
MANAGEMENT

3rd Edition

▲ **Touche Ross**

Canadian Guide to
PERSONAL
FINANCIAL
MANAGEMENT
3rd Edition

Mary Turner
Daniel Le Rossignol
Claude Rinfret
Eric Feilden

Prentice-Hall Canada Inc., Scarborough, Ontario

Canadian Cataloguing in Publication Data

Main entry under title:

Touche Ross Canadian guide to personal financial management

3rd ed.
Includes index.
ISBN 0-13-925819-1

1. Finance, Personal. 1. Turner, Mary.
II. Touche Ross & Co. III. Title: Canadian guide to personal financial
   management.

HG179.T68 1988   332.024   C88-093330-5

Prentice-Hall Inc., Englewood Cliffs, *New Jersey*
Prentice-Hall International, Inc., *London*
Prentice-Hall of Australia, Pty., *Sydney*
Prentice-Hall of India Pvt., Ltd., *New Delhi*
Prentice-Hall of Japan, Inc., *Tokyo*
Prentice-Hall of Southeast Asia (Pte.) Ltd., *Singapore*
Editora Prentice-Hall do Brasil Ltda., *Rio de Janeiro*
Prentice-Hall Hispanoamericana, S.A., *Mexico*

Production Editor: Sharyn Rosart
Design: Gail Ferreira Ng-A-Kien
Manufacturing Buyer: Don Blair
Composition: CompuScreen Typesetting Ltd.

ISBN: 0-13-925819-1

Printed and bound in Canada by Alger Press

1 2 3 4 5   AP   92 91 90 89 88

Table of Contents

About The Authors

Mary Turner, B.Sc., C.A., is a partner in the Toronto office of Touche Ross, one of Canada's "Big Eight" accounting firms. She specializes in corporate and personal tax planning and is in charge of the group which provides personal financial management services to clients of the Toronto office. She is a frequent author and lecturer on personal financial management and various tax areas.

Daniel Le Rossignol, B.Comm., C.A., is a partner in the Montreal office of Touche Ross. Since joining Touche Ross he has had extensive experience in all areas of personal financial planning and management. He has been a lecturer at McGill University since 1977 and has taught a number of tax courses offered by the Canadian Institute of Chartered Accountants. He has written numerous articles and presented several papers on tax and financial planning.

Claude Rinfret, B.Comm., C.A., is a partner in the Vancouver office of Touche Ross. He specializes principally in personal and corporate income tax planning, Canada/U.S. cross-border tax planning and estate planning. He was co-author and lecturer for the B.C. Institute of Chartered Accountants' Introductory Income Tax Course. Mr. Rinfret has presented papers, seminars and authored articles on numerous personal income tax planning topics.

Eric Feilden, B.Comm., C.A., is a partner in the New Westminster office of Touche Ross. He practices principally in personal and corporate income tax planning and estate planning for a wide variety of clients. He has been a lecturer for the B.C. Institute of Chartered Accountants as well as for the College of New Caledonia and the Canadian Institute of Chartered Accountants. Mr. Feilden is a frequent speaker and author on personal tax planning topics and is a member of the Estate Planning Council of Vancouver.

Preface

We have often observed when counselling our clients that a salary of $50,000 or even $100,000 a year does not necessarily prevent financial worries or difficulties. Most of our executive and professional clients needed our help because they felt uneasy about their current financial situation or their financial future. Many had incomes that, after taxes, just barely covered their expenditures. As a result, few were setting money aside for investments, even though most doubted that their pensions alone would pay for the retirement lifestyle they desired. They needed to analyze their financial objectives systematically, and didn't know exactly where to begin.

With this book, we extend to you the same help that we offer the people who attend our executive workshops and those we counsel on an individual basis. Follow the step-by-step instructions and use the forms provided and you will develop a comprehensive financial plan that will make the things you want attainable and your financial future more secure.

If you develop your own personal financial plan as outlined in this book, you could save thousands of dollars in professional fees charged by financial planners to do the same thing for you. This book should also help you minimize your income taxes, increase your investment return, improve your retirement planning and transfer your estate with less emotional and financial cost.

As you read this book, remember that it reflects applicable tax laws and regulations as of 31 January 1988 as well as the changes proposed in the February 1988 budget. We have also updated this book for the tax reform proposals originally announced in June, 1987, as well as further changes announced in December 1987. At the date of writing, these tax reform proposals have not been enacted and may be subject to further adjustments before they become law. As well, a major feature of tax reform, the reform of our existing sales tax system, may not be completed for several years. Income tax laws and other legislation relevant to personal financial management are continually changing. You should consult your professional advisors to consider the effect of any subsequent changes.

In the meantime, uncertainty about the final details of tax reform is no excuse for delaying a review of your financial situation. By taking action on your personal financial plan now, you can improve your investment strategy and make progress in retirement planning and other areas, as well as controlling your current tax expenditures as best you can under the existing tax system.

Mary Turner
Daniel Le Rossignol
Claude Rinfret
Eric Feilden

1

PERSONAL FINANCIAL PLANNING

The objective of this book is very simple—to help you get better control of your life financially. Money should not be the central concern of one's life, but the management of money is necessary in order to reach lifetime objectives—to provide funds for a home, for schooling, for travel and other leisure-time activities, for creating new employment opportunities, for retiring comfortably.

Life is exciting and challenging because it is full of opportunities and *choices*—a choice of what to study, what job to pursue, what hobby to take up, whom to marry, and on and on. Each choice has a *consequence*. A choice once made means a foregone opportunity, for a while or permanently. Your choice of university or college, career path, spouse, where to live, how to live, whether to have children and how to raise them, will affect what future alternatives will be available to you.

Financial planning also involves a series of choices and consequences. One of the countless examples that could be given here is that of a middle-aged couple who consulted us once late in April, after they had completed their tax returns. They complained that they paid too much in taxes and had decided they needed a tax shelter (their *choice*). We asked them whether they had ever owned a tax shelter. They said they had. "How did you do?" we asked. They replied, "We lost everything" (the *consequence*). We then asked them for specific and detailed information in order to get a complete picture of their needs and circumstances. From the data they gave us, it became quite clear to us and also to them after subsequent discussion that the key issue for them was an adequate retirement income. Therefore they did not need a tax shelter, which is usually risky. They needed safe investments that would give a reliable return.

The analysis of choices and consequences is the essence of decision-making. To make good financial decisions, you need good information about your financial situation and the options available to you. For example, parents wishing to fund their children's university or college education should estimate how much this will cost, plan how they will finance the expenditure, and learn about the ways available to reduce this cost through certain tax-planning strategies. In some situations, it is possible to reduce the cost by fifty percent or more. (Some ideas are discussed in Chapter 11.)

To have the financial resources you want in order to reach your goals, you also need *commitment*. You need to commit time and attention to following through on your financial choices. We have often helped clients to identify options that are financially sound. But nothing happens. They always have something else to do that seems more urgent, or they leave all financial planning and whatever actions that may entail for some vague time in the future when there may be nothing more urgent to do. Few of them realize what or how much they stand to lose, but some know it exactly. As an example, take the case of a man we advised to change his will to reduce potential income tax at death, by taking advantage of certain tax-free spousal and intergenerational rollovers. When he died before his will had been changed, his procrastination cost his widow and children approximately $250,000 in avoidable income taxes.

Failure to act does not always have such drastic consequences, but the time and attention devoted to planning one's finances and taking the requisite action will generally result in far greater returns or savings than time spent on other, seemingly more urgent, tasks.

WHY DO IT?

All of us have read or heard about some wealthy people who pay surprisingly little in taxes. In contrast, most executives and professionals who earn between $50,000 and $100,000 a year pay a third or more of their income in taxes. After that, little is left for any investments, and those investments are often made on the strength of a sales pitch, a chance conversation at a club or a cocktail party, or some newspaper article. The wealthy make use of experienced financial advisors, who plan their clients' investments carefully and often manage to double them every few years.

Maybe you can't afford the financial advisors that the more affluent can, but you can afford the time and effort to develop your plan as outlined in this book. If you do, you may be able to save between $2,000 and $3,000 in annual professional fees charged by financial planners to do the same thing for you. And if you do decide to use a financial advisor, the plan you develop by following this book will allow you to organize your financial information and communicate more effectively with your financial advisor.

People who have attended our executive seminars tell us quite often that financial planning has made a greater difference to them than a raise in salary. Whatever objectives they had—travel, cars, boats, buying or remodelling a home, a good education for their children, a comfortable retirement—they either reached or felt more confident of reaching. Once they learned the planning process and understood what was involved, they found the means to increase their net worth and their investments.

HOW TO DO IT

In our seminars, we often ask the question, "How many of you have taken a course in financial planning in university, college or high school?" Only about two percent of the participants say they have. So most people need a way to start, a structure to follow, and methods of organizing financial information, having it readily available, and keeping it up-to-date. They also need financial planning techniques and ideas for making good choices.

This book will provide both a structure for planning and managing your finances systematically and ideas and techniques to help you accumulate sufficient resources to reach your goals. The book has two basic components: its text and its forms. Between them, they will give you most of the help you need to develop a personal financial plan tailored exactly to your own particular objectives, circumstances, and obligations.

The text covers every important area of personal financial management and explains its function, showing you how to identify and evaluate alternative courses of action. It also explains and comments on each of the forms you will be asked to fill in. The forms on which you will list your financial and personal data are at the back of the book.

You may wonder whether or not to bother with the forms. If you want to make proper use of your financial resources and the financial options open to you, then fill in the forms. In that process, you will do all of the following:

- Assemble and organize all your financial data and documents.
- Calculate your present net worth.
- Analyze your present income, expenditures, and insurance coverage.
- Project your future needs, income, and expenditures.
- Identify your personal and economic objectives and their relative priorities.
- Identify the financial strategies for achieving these objectives.
- Use your projections to minimize your income tax, select your investments and plan your retirement income.

The process of financial planning we explain in this text and the forms we have included can be applied to anyone's situation. We have used the process and forms in counselling single people, married couples without children, married couples with children, divorced people, old and young people, the very wealthy and the not-so-wealthy. We may use examples in the book to clarify a point or to illustrate a form. The people in the examples may not be like you. But don't turn off at that point, because the *process* we will be explaining will be relevant to you.

You will apply the process to your situation by completing the forms with *your* data. You will be asked to make some estimates of *your* future. When you make such estimates, do not worry about precision or accuracy. Try to come up with reasonable estimates using the information available to you.

YOUR FINANCIAL PLANNER

The end result of completing the forms in this book is your "Financial Planner." It will contain all your current financial data and make them available as a reference for your future decisions, for periodic review of your goals and your progress, for updating your plan and keeping your data current, and for your survivors in the event of your death.

By preparing your Financial Planner, you may also save significant annual professional fees charged by financial planners to organize your finances for you. Once you have your Financial Planner prepared, you can use financial advisors in a much more cost-effective way and can better evaluate their advice.

Physically, your Financial Planner will be a three-ring binder holding all your filled-in forms, with dividers separating the various types of information. The top of each form specifies in which section of your Financial Planner to file the form once it has been completed. All you have to do now is to get a three-ring binder for ordinary letter-size (8½" × 11") pages and fourteen tabbed dividers for this binder.

HOW TO PROCEED

Every chapter that follows will tell you why and how specific forms should be completed and how to use the information you prepare. Many chapters will also suggest courses of action to be considered in light of your findings, circumstances, and objectives. We stress your action throughout the book. Any suggested course of action in the book that strikes you as desirable should be listed on the last of the forms, entitled *Action Steps*. From this list you will eventually choose the ten action steps you will try to implement this year. We have found that ten action steps are about all a person can implement in one year.

Now, are you ready to embark on the interesting process of shaping your finances so as to use, increase, and protect your resources to your own best advantage? In this book, you have all the information you need to get started.

2

FAMILY AND FINANCIAL RECORDS

Eventually, your Financial Planner will contain all the data necessary for the planning and management of your financial affairs. In the main, you will be the person who benefits from having all the relevant information in one place, where it is easy to access and easy to update. But you will not be the only one who benefits. Those who survive you will have to pick up where you left off, and you should make that as simple for them as you can. The sorrow that people feel about someone's death can be accompanied by irritation when the survivors have to overcome countless difficulties that could easily have been avoided by some advance planning and better record keeping.

What we kept in mind when we designed the three forms you will now be asked to complete was that those who will someday have to take over from you will need all sorts of basic information that you may carry in your head but that they may not carry in theirs.

FORM 1—PERSONAL AND FAMILY DATA

This form is an easy one—so easy we call it a warm-up. Some of the information to be listed is of the bothersome variety that you frequently look up to complete loan applications and tax returns, and to update wills. Once you have set it all down in this form, you will know where to find it and never have to go hunting for it again.

If you use advisors, information about your family situation is important. For example, knowing that you have children may trigger the advisor's recommending certain educational financing techniques with significant tax advantages. Another example: If your advisors know that your parents are self-supporting, they may be more concerned about coordinating estate planning among your parents, you, and your children.

FORM 2—FINANCIAL DOCUMENTS

In this paper-filled world we live in, we tend to keep important papers in a variety of "safe" places—in safety deposit boxes, in the desk at home, in the basement or the attic, and at the office. As a result, most of us have spent some anxious moments looking for various important papers, rifling through a mixture of documents, only to find that the one we were looking for was not where we thought it should be.

Save yourself such anxieties in the future by listing your documents and their locations here. You will be doing it at your leisure now, but the next time you need to locate one of these papers, you may well be in a hurry. While you are doing yourself and your survivors this favour, you might also check to see that the documents you have kept are up-to-date. If your last will was made out in 1940, you may want to challenge its relevance.

When you complete this form, use the *Description* column for the specifics of the various documents. Beside *Mortgage*, for instance, you might identify the property and the mortgagor. Beside *Life Insurance Policies*, you might identify the insurance company and the policy number.

FORM 3—FINANCIAL ADVISORS

At one of our executive seminars, a participant looked at this form and said, "I don't have all those advisors listed here. Does that mean there is something wrong with me?" Nothing at all was wrong with this person. And there isn't anything wrong with you if you have not used all of these advisors. If you have used some of them, though, and have found them helpful, it would be a good idea to list them here. You may be glad one day that you did—people have been known to forget other people's names and addresses—but the main purpose of compiling this list is to give your survivors some indication of the people who could be consulted and would be familiar with some aspects of your financial affairs.

Once you have completed Form 3, consider these points:

- Make sure your spouse has met all your advisors. A forty-two-year-old C.A. with complicated investment dealings died suddenly a few years ago. Because he was the "professional" in the family, he did all the financial planning. Besides, he was too "young" to die. But he did die young, and his widow spent needless hours unravelling what were now her financial affairs.
- Consider an annual financial checkup meeting with appropriate family members present, together with all or some of your advisors. It's a great way to educate family members on financial planning.
- You should have one advisor you and other family members would turn to in the event of a very important financial decision.

3

YOUR NET WORTH

The overall goal of financial planning is to have enough resources to reach your personal goals. The best overall measure of your financial resources is your net worth.

The process of determining your net worth consists of calculating your total assets and total liabilities and then subtracting your total liabilities from your total assets. It is a fundamental starting point for almost everything in financial planning.

Because it is so fundamental, most people have filled out a net worth statement at some point in their lives. If you are one of them, chances are that you did so in order to satisfy a lender's request for financial information. When you do it this time, on Form 4, it will be for your own benefit, to provide you with an essential tool for planning and managing your own finances. You will need to know your net worth for any of the following purposes:

- Finding out what your present net worth is.
  You should be more interested in your financial health than your lender is. We recommend that once a year you check on your financial health and on your progress toward the net worth goal you will be setting yourself, such as an increase of fifteen percent.

- Making "what-if" projections.
  You may, for example, want to work out what your retirement funds will be in five years' time if you presently have $100,000 to invest and can put $10,000 in an investment programme each year and get a ten percent return.

- Evaluating your assets.
  Your net worth statement gives you an overall picture of how you have used your assets. It tells you whether most of them are personal assets, such as your home, car, and furnishings, or investment assets, such as savings, stocks, bonds, and income-producing real estate. It shows you which of your assets you could quickly convert into cash. It shows whether your investments are diversified or concentrated in one or two investment categories.

- Analyzing your liabilities.
  Keeping debt under control is an integral part of good personal financial management.

- Planning or revising your life insurance.
  Generally, the more net worth you have, the less life insurance you will need.

• Estimating potential taxes at death.

Your net worth is the starting point for determining your potential tax liability at death and developing an estate plan.

Now we will briefly define total assets and total liabilities.

TOTAL ASSETS

To obtain the amount of your total assets, you add your liquid assets to the value of your investment assets and your personal assets.

Liquid Assets

Your so-called liquidity, meaning your financial ability to respond swiftly to emergencies or investment opportunities, is largely determined by the amount of your liquid assets. This amount consists of your cash accounts and short-term investments, such as Treasury bills, short-term deposits, and money market funds, and the cash surrender value of your life insurance. Your need for liquidity is influenced by the predictability of your income and expenditures, by your employment security and by your investment strategy.

It is generally held that your liquid assets should roughly equal three to six months' employment income. If you are in an unstable employment situation or about to make a large investment, the amount should probably be greater. If your employment is relatively secure and you anticipate no major cash expenditures in the near future, the amount could be smaller.

Investment Assets

These are defined as long-term investments, intended to store up value for major future needs like education costs and retirement. Canada Savings Bonds, stocks, bonds, and real estate (other than a personal residence or vacation property) are typical investment assets. Retirement funds, too, are classified as investment assets. These may include Registered Retirement Savings Plans, Deferred Profit Sharing Plans, and registered pension plans.

Personal Assets

Items you acquire for your own or your family's long-term use or enjoyment form part of your personal assets. Typically, they include your home and vacation property as well as any cars, boats, art, antiques, and furnishings that you own.

TOTAL LIABILITIES

There are two types of liabilities: short-term obligations and long-term obligations. For the average person, both should be fairly easy to compute.

Short-Term Obligations

These are defined as all sums (principal portion only) that have to be paid within the next twelve months. Thus, they also include whatever amounts are due on long-term obligations within the next twelve months. Typically, these might be consumer credit payments, installment loans, personal loans, accrued income taxes, or borrowings on life insurance.

Long-Term Obligations

Most long-term obligations are incurred for one of two purposes: to finance long-term investments like real estate or mutual funds or to finance the purchase of major personal assets like your residence, your vacation property, or a home computer. Normally, the asset purchased constitutes security for the lender in case you default on the loan. Over time, the value of the investment asset you purchased with borrowed funds may increase, while the amount of your obligation usually decreases. Thus, your equity—the difference between the current value of the asset and the current balance on the loan—usually increases.

Borrowing Costs

The rates of interest you pay on the various amounts you owe are your borrowing costs. Since you will want to minimize the overall amount you pay in interest, you should analyze your interest costs periodically and try to repay the loans with the highest rates of interest first.

FORM 4—STATEMENT OF NET WORTH

Before or while you complete Form 4, you might like to see an example of the completed form. Figure 3-1 shows you this form as it was completed for a family of five: father and mother aged forty-seven and forty-three, and their three children aged twenty, nineteen, and ten.

We might here make some generalizations about the net worth of people at various age levels. People in their twenties, thirties and forties tend to accumulate personal assets—cars, furnishings, homes—and then to trade up and buy a more luxurious car, a larger home, and vacation property. Thus, their total personal assets rise much faster than their total investments. By the time they reach their fifties, most people slow down or stop adding to their personal assets and become more concerned with their investment assets and with their financial security. Thus, the total investment assets of people who are approaching retirement will often exceed the total personal assets.

To calculate your total assets, begin by filling in the first column, *Estimated Current Value*, for each asset you own.

With regard to retirement funds, the last item listed under *Investment Assets*, enter the current value of Registered Retirement Savings Plans, employer pension or retirement plans, Deferred Profit Sharing Plans or any other retirement funds. The current value of employee retirement plans may, however, be difficult to determine because the annual information sheet employers provide will often state only what your monthly payments are likely to be when you retire. If so, omit any current value for such programmes. It is not as important to estimate the current value of your employee retirement plan for purposes of calculating net worth as it is to know, for retirement planning purposes, what the monthly benefit will be at retirement age. You will use your employee retirement information when we cover retirement planning and your sources of retirement income in Chapter 12.

When you have added up the current value of all your assets and thus obtained the dollar amount of your total assets, compute what percentage of the total each asset represents by dividing the dollar value of the asset by the dollar value of total assets and multiplying by 100, and list that percentage beside the item's current value.

In listing what you owe, any installment loans that extend beyond one year should be divided so that you list the amount due within the next twelve months under *Short-Term Obligations* and the remainder under *Long-Term Obligations*.

List the interest rate you pay for each debt beside its current value.

FIGURE 3-1

File under FINANCIAL PROFILE   Date: _February 15_

FORM 4   STATEMENT OF NET WORTH

WHAT YOU OWN	ESTIMATED CURRENT VALUE	% OF TOTAL ASSET VALUE
1 LIQUID ASSETS		
Cash (chequing, savings accounts):	$ 2,100	1%
Short-Term Investments Treasury Bills:		
Short-Term Deposits:		
Money Market Funds:	24,400	3%
Cash Surrender Value of Life Insurance	7,000	1%
TOTAL Liquid Assets	$ 33,500	5%
2 INVESTMENT ASSETS		
Canada Savings Bonds	$ 39,800	5%
Term Deposits		
Marketable Securities Stocks:	57,400	8%
Bonds:	3,200	1%
Mutual Funds:		
Real Estate (investment)	90,000	12%
Tax Incentive Investments	20,000	3%
Other Investment Assets (describe below)		
a. _XYZ Closely Held Business_	27,000	4%
b.		
c.		
d.		
Retirement Funds RRSPs	25,400	4%
Employer Pension Plan		

FIGURE 3-1 CONT'D

	ESTIMATED CURRENT VALUE	
DPSPs		
Other		
TOTAL Investment Assets	$262,800	37%

3   PERSONAL ASSETS

Residence	$275,000	39%
Vacation Property	73,500	11%
Art, Antiques		
Furnishings	56,000	8%
Vehicles		
Boats		
Other		
TOTAL Personal Assets	$404,500	58%
TOTAL ASSETS	$700,800	100%

WHAT YOU OWE	ESTIMATED CURRENT VALUE	INTEREST RATE	INTEREST DEDUCTIBLE
4 SHORT-TERM OBLIGATIONS			
Consumer Credit Obligations			
Personal Loans			
Installment Loans			
Borrowings on Life Insurance	$6,300	6%	YES
Accrued Income Taxes			
Other Obligations (describe below)			
a.			
b.			
c.			
d.			
TOTAL Short-Term Obligations	$6,300	6%	

FIGURE 3-1 CONT'D

5 LONG–TERM OBLIGATIONS	ESTIMATED CURRENT VALUE	INTEREST RATE	INTEREST DEDUCTIBLE
Mortgage on personal residences	$90,000	10.5%	NO
Loans to purchase investment assets	16,000	10%	YES
Loans to purchase personal assets	11,000	12%	NO
TOTAL Long–Term Obligations	$117,000	10.6%	
TOTAL LIABILITIES	$123,300		

TOTAL ASSETS	$700,800
− TOTAL LIABILITIES	$123,300
= NET WORTH	$577,500

When you have calculated your total liabilities by adding the current values of all your debts, subtract this sum from your total assets in order to arrive at your present net worth.

FORM 5—ANALYSIS OF NET WORTH

Use your figures from Form 4 to complete this form.

- On line 1, enter your total liquid assets.
- On line 2, enter your total short-term obligations.
- On line 3, calculate the excess or deficiency of your liquid assets by subtracting the amount on line 2 from the amount on line 1. The amount on line 3 should be positive. If it is negative, you ought to start building up liquid assets and should definitely stop borrowing short-term.
- Obtain the percentage of your liquid assets excess or deficiency by dividing the amount on line 1 by the amount on line 2 and multiplying by 100. Your target should be a positive figure between 150 and 200 percent. Your liquid assets would thus be one-and-a-half to two times greater than your short-term obligations.
- On line 4, enter your total investment assets.
- On line 5, enter your total long-term investment loans.
- On line 6, calculate the amount of equity you have in your investments by subtracting the amount on line 5 from the amount on line 4. To compute the percentage of this equity, divide the amount on line 6 by the amount on line 4 and multiply by 100. If your percentage is less than twenty, it is low, and you are significantly borrowing against your investments. If your percentage is greater than fifty, it is high, and you may want to consider getting some of your equity out by increasing your borrowings. On the other hand, you may wish to be debt-free and would therefore be aiming at an equity of 100 percent.
- On line 7, enter your total personal assets.
- On line 8, enter the amount of the loans you have taken for the purchase of personal assets, including personal residences.

- On line 9, calculate the amount of equity you have in your personal assets by subtracting the amount on line 8 from the amount on line 7. Compute the percentage of this equity by dividing the amount on line 9 by the amount on line 7 and multiplying by 100. Many people have a much higher equity in personal assets than in investment assets. If your percentage is less than twenty, it is low, and you are leveraging your personal assets. If your percentage is greater than fifty, it is high, and you may want to consider borrowing on your equity. But if your goal is to be debt-free, you should aim for an equity of 100 percent.

On line 10, check your computations by adding the amounts on lines 3, 6, and 9 and entering the total. The amount on line 10 should agree with your total net worth as shown at the bottom of Form 4.

USE OF DEBT

One way to increase your assets is to borrow funds. Borrowed funds may be used to purchase personal assets such as furnishings, automobiles, and appliances. Such loans are often called consumer loans and have short repayment periods. Managing consumer debt requires a knowledge of some basic techniques.

Know the safety limit suggested by specialists in consumer debt. They suggest that the average consumer's debt payments (excluding mortgage payments) should not exceed twenty percent of take-home income (after taxes and other payroll deductions). Specialists say a smaller percentage—say ten percent to fifteen percent—is a comfortable debt level; twenty percent gets near the debt overload position for many people.

Another use of debt is to purchase investment assets such as securities and income-producing real estate. In a financial context the use of borrowed money to acquire investment assets is sometimes called *leverage*.

Leverage is used extensively, particularly in real estate transactions. In periods of rising inflation, leverage can be very beneficial. Let us say that in the early 1970s you borrowed $50,000 at eight percent to purchase a house for rental to others. That borrowing rate was probably based on an inflation rate of four percent, giving the lender a real rate of return of four percent. Assuming that all your interest expense was tax-deductible, your after-tax cost was four percent, if you were in a fifty percent tax bracket. Although inflation went up during the 1970s, your borrowing costs would have remained steady at eight percent, but your monthly net rental income would have gone up if you, like all other landlords, increased your tenants' rents. You would therefore have had more than enough to pay back your loan, and even after paying other costs of being a landlord, such as property taxes and repairs, you might still have put some cash in your pocket. In addition, the value of your rental house would have risen as inflation went up. That shows why, during the 1970s, the real estate game was the hottest game in town—in every town.

In the meantime, what was known as creative leverage in the 1970s became creative foreclosure in the early 1980s. Why? Some people who entered the real estate game late in the inflationary spiral didn't borrow at eight percent but at much higher rates. At these rates, their rental income could not cover their high debt payments, property taxes and repairs. In addition, as inflation decreased, property values decreased.

Many financial institutions and investment promoters suggest the use of debt to implement certain investment choices. For example, some suggest reducing equity in your personal residence through refinancing and investing the proceeds elsewhere. When you are considering the use of debt, keep these questions in mind:

1. What will the borrowing cost you annually in after-tax dollars?
Assume, for example, that the bank sends you a notice saying it would be happy to refinance your home at twelve percent. If you are in a tax bracket of forty percent, your

after-tax cost would be sixty percent of twelve percent, or 7.2%, assuming that the borrowed funds were used to make an investment. Obviously, the lower your tax bracket, the higher your after-tax cost. Interest expenses that can be deducted from your taxable income are discussed in Chapter 8.

2. What is your after-tax return likely to be on the investment you make with the money obtained through borrowing?

It is a rule of thumb that any investment you make should have the potential to return you twice your after-tax cost. For example, if your after-tax cost on the borrowed money is eight percent, the investment you make should have the potential for a return of sixteen percent after taxes. In other words, since you are taking a risk with borrowed money, you should have the potential of being amply rewarded.

3. What funds will you use to pay off the debt you incur?

If you choose to invest in something that has great growth potential but little or no cash flow, you need to have other funds to make the monthly payments on the new debt you have incurred. Say you borrow $50,000 at twelve percent for twenty years to purchase a rental property; your debt repayments will be almost $6,700 a year, or $558 per month. Granted, you save taxes because of the additional interest deductions, but you still have to come up with $558 per month.

So when you are considering borrowing to make an investment, be sure you have a satisfactory answer to each of the three questions above before you take the plunge.

CHOICES AND YOUR NET WORTH

Your net worth is a snapshot of your financial condition at a particular point in time. It is the end result of choices you have made in the past. For example, if you chose to acquire an expensive home and several automobiles, you may have little in the way of investment assets. If you chose to borrow significantly to finance consumer purchases and vacations, you may not have a significant net worth because your debts will be almost as great as your assets.

Look back to understand why your present net worth is what it is but, more importantly, evaluate choices you can make at present that will have an impact on your net worth in the future. If you want your net worth to increase, here are some choices you can make:

- Make your investments grow by getting a greater rate of return on your investments. You can improve your rate of return by acquiring more knowledge of investment alternatives, by spending more time in managing your investments or by selecting an investment advisor to help you manage your investments.

- Increase your investments by putting aside more each year from your current employment income. This can be done by spending less for your current lifestyle or by decreasing your taxes through tax planning.

- Reduce your debt. If you are making monthly payments on your mortgage or other obligations you have, your debt is decreasing and your net worth is growing. Consider accelerating your debt payments; if you do, you will also save significant amounts of interest.

By making such choices, you should be able to increase your net worth by fifteen percent each year. At such an annual rate, your net worth will double in five years and quadruple in ten. For example, if your net worth is presently $500,000, it could be $1,000,000 in five years and $2,000,000 in ten years. Not bad!

4

YOUR INCOME AND EXPENDITURES

Unless you have inherited assets or married someone with substantial assets, you usually start your adult earning years with little or no net worth. In this situation, there is no magic formula for achieving financial security. What you must do is save. Save some portion of your job income on a systematic basis, invest your savings wisely and in time your investment assets will be significant. By reinvesting your investment assets so that compounding takes over, you should eventually achieve financial security.

COMPOUNDING

You can easily make calculations involving compound rates of return when you have the required compound interest tables. They let you see how much your assets will grow at various rates of return in a given number of years. The same tables can also be used to predict what income you will need in a given year if you are to stay even with whatever rate of inflation you anticipate.

With the following condensed table, you can project the future worth of an investment you make today. Assume, for instance, that you had $100,000 to invest and could get a return of ten percent on it. To what sum would a ten percent compound rate of return increase this investment in ten years?

In Table 4-1, looking at ten years from now in the ten percent column, you find the factor 2.59. Multiplying $100,000 by 2.59 will then show you that the original investment will grow to $259,000 in ten years at ten percent compound interest. Similarly, $100,000 invested at fifteen percent for ten years has a compounding factor of 4.05, and thus would grow to $405,000 in ten years.

The same table can be used to project the effect that various rates of inflation would have on your expenditures. For example, how much after-tax income will you need in some future year in order to be as well off as you are now? Assume that your present after-tax income is $24,000 and that the annual inflation rate is eight percent. In six years, you will need an income of $38,160 after taxes merely to stay at your present standard of living. Or take some specific item like university or college costs. If at present one year at university or college costs $5,000 for tuition, books, room and board and other living expenses, and costs rise at an annual rate of eight percent, how much will one year in university or college cost three years from now? As you can work out, it would cost $6,300.

If you decide that you will take some specific amount from your income each year and add it to your investment capital, Table 4-2 can show you the rewards of regular saving combined with compound interest. Suppose, for example, that you will put $2,000 in a Registered Retirement Savings Plan every year at an annual compound interest rate of twelve percent. How much do you think you would have in that account after ten years? How much after twenty years?

TABLE 4-1
COMPOUND INTEREST

Years From Now	Future Worth of One Dollar with Amount of Return Compounded Annually				
	Annual Rate of Return				
	6%	8%	10%	12%	15%
1	1.06	1.08	1.10	1.12	1.15
2	1.12	1.17	1.21	1.25	1.32
3	1.19	1.26	1.33	1.40	1.52
4	1.26	1.36	1.46	1.57	1.75
5	1.34	1.47	1.61	1.76	2.01
6	1.42	1.59	1.77	1.97	2.31
7	1.50	1.71	1.95	2.21	2.66
8	1.59	1.85	2.14	2.48	3.06
9	1.69	2.00	2.36	2.77	3.52
10	1.79	2.16	2.59	3.10	4.05
15	2.40	3.17	4.18	5.47	8.14
20	3.21	4.67	6.73	9.65	16.37
25	4.29	6.85	10.83	17.00	32.92

TABLE 4-2
GROWTH OF ASSETS FROM SETTING A CONSTANT SUM ASIDE EVERY YEAR

Years From Now	Annual Rate of Return				
	6%	8%	10%	12%	15%
1	1.00	1.00	1.00	1.00	1.00
2	2.06	2.08	2.10	2.12	2.15
3	3.18	3.25	3.31	3.37	3.47
4	4.37	4.50	4.64	4.78	4.99
5	5.64	5.87	6.10	6.35	6.74
6	6.98	7.33	7.71	8.11	8.75
7	8.39	8.92	9.49	10.09	11.07
8	9.90	10.64	11.43	12.30	13.73
9	11.49	12.49	13.58	14.77	16.78
10	13.18	14.49	15.94	17.55	20.30
15	23.27	27.15	31.77	37.28	47.58
20	36.78	45.76	57.27	72.05	102.44
25	54.86	73.10	98.35	133.33	212.79

As you can see from Table 4-2, you would have $35,100 after ten years. After twenty years, you would have a whopping $144,100.

More complete compound interest tables are included in Appendix I.

FORM 6—INCOME SOURCES

All of us are familiar with earned income, and most of us would agree that it has two somewhat unromantic characteristics. The first is that you must actually work in order to receive it. The second, and this may be worse than the first, is that it is taxed to the hilt—as much as sixty percent in some cases.

In contrast to that, look at the charms of a sound investment. It generates income for you all day and every day, even if you never get out of bed or if you spend all your waking hours playing tennis or bridge. Furthermore, the income it produces may be taxed at a much lower rate and the gain on selling your whole investment may even be tax free!

Investment income is the key to financial security and independence for many. When your investment income becomes significant, you can reduce the time you spend working for your money and turn to whatever other activities may be important to you.

To complete Form 6, use figures from the last full year for which all data are available. Your best sources of information will be your tax return, pay stubs, and monthly statements from banking and investment institutions.

To compute what percentage of your total income you derived from your investment income, divide your investment income by your total income and multiply by 100.

FORM 7—BASIC LIFESTYLE EXPENDITURES

Your basic lifestyle expenditures are those that are difficult to avoid without changing your basic standard of living. This form lists the categories that make up most people's basic lifestyle expenditures. The first four—housing, food, clothing, and transportation—account for the largest portion of basic lifestyle expenditures for many Canadians.

Your own ideas on which expenditures are basic to your lifestyle and which are discretionary may not entirely coincide with the listings you find on Forms 7 and 8. You should therefore transfer from one form to the other any item that strikes you as wrongly categorized. Contributions to church or charities, for instance, have been listed as basic here, while you may regard them as discretionary expenditures. Conversely, education costs and the support of relatives have here been listed as discretionary, though you may well regard them as basic expenditures.

To complete this form, use figures from the last full year for which all data are available. You can use either monthly or annual amounts, whichever is easier.

You might like to use Table 4-3 to compare your own expenditure patterns with the four predominant spending patterns of families in Canada.

FORM 8—DISCRETIONARY EXPENDITURES

Discretionary expenditures are those over which you can exercise a good deal of control. You decide whether you will dine at home or eat out in style and spend a small fortune. You can choose to throw either a canard à l'orange dinner for fifty or a wine and cheese party. You are not strictly obligated to take your family skiing in the Rockies or the Alps; you could take them backpacking or camping in the nearby countryside.

Even though you have quite a lot of control over the amounts you spend on entertainment, vacations, hobbies, and gifts, you will presumably be spending some

TABLE 4-3
SUMMARY OF FAMILY EXPENDITURE FOR FOUR FAMILY INCOME LEVELS—1982

	Lower Budget		Intermediate Budgets				Higher Budget	
	Amount	%	Amount	%	Amount	%	Amount	%
Family income	**$10,000-$14,999**		**$20,000-$24,999**		**$30,000-$34,999**		**$50,000 and over**	
Family expenditure								
Food	$ 2,734	21.0	$ 3,797	17.2	$ 4,760	15.5	6,562	11.5
Shelter	3,096	23.8	4,147	18.7	5,325	17.3	8,003	14.0
Household operation, furniture, and equipment	1,233	9.5	1,734	7.8	2,441	7.9	4,081	7.1
Clothing	796	6.1	1,277	5.8	1,917	6.2	3,397	5.9
Transportation	1,607	12.4	3,148	14.2	3,571	11.6	6,256	11.0
Health care	308	2.4	477	2.2	582	1.9	942	1.6
Personal care	287	2.2	434	2.0	556	1.8	843	1.5
Recreation, reading materials, and education	706	5.4	1,228	5.5	1,858	6.0	3,896	6.8
Tobacco and alcohol	560	4.3	874	3.9	1,080	3.5	1,343	2.4
Miscellaneous	352	2.7	691	3.1	1,050	3.4	1,535	2.7
Total current consumption	11,677	89.9	17,807	80.4	23,141	75.3	36,858	64.5
Personal taxes	579	4.5	2,824	12.8	5,318	17.3	15,548	27.2
Security	241	1.9	889	4.0	1,397	4.5	2,838	5.0
Gifts and contributions	497	3.8	619	2.8	859	2.8	1,872	3.3
Total expenditure	$12,994	100.0	$22,139	100.0	$30,715	100.0	$57,116	100.0

Note: Because of rounding, sums of individual items may not equal totals.
Source: Statistics Canada, "Family Expenditure in Canada." The latest year for which this comparative data is available is 1982.

amount on each of them every year. However, some discretionary expenditures are more discretionary and less regular than others. Most of us would not buy a new car or a new boat every year, nor would we subject ourselves and our budgets to home improvements with such frequency.

Form 8 lists discretionary expenditures you will likely incur every year, like hobbies and regular vacations, as well as others, like the purchase of a car, that you will only face every few years. With the latter kind of expense, you should include an annual average cost each year as if the cost were spread over several years. For example, if you expect to buy a new car for $15,000 every three years, include $5,000 each year on line 9 of Form 8.

When you complete this form, use figures from the last full year for which all data are available. You can use either monthly or annual amounts, whichever is easier.

FORM 9—INCOME TAXES AND OTHER DEDUCTIONS

After the giddy delights of discretionary expenditures, we have now arrived at the bane of modern existence. Please use your most recent tax returns to complete this form.

FORM 10—ANALYSIS OF EARNED INCOME AND EXPENDITURES

A few centuries ago, if you were anybody at all, you did not have to *make* money, you *had* money. The nobles and the gentry had it and spent it with abandon. More of this unearned income was sure to come their way soon, either in frequent tax payments from the villages they owned or in a long-awaited lump sum after the demise of their parents or their rich but childless uncle or aunt. Not only was it possible and acceptable for aristocrats to live entirely on unearned income but also it would have been downright vulgar to do anything else.

It is amazing what a difference a few centuries make, isn't it? You probably don't own a single village, let alone several; and your expectations of a huge inheritance, too, are probably dim. If that is the case, we strongly advise you to live on your earned income now if you possibly can, and to use all your unearned income as investment capital. We therefore ask you in this form to balance your expenditures only against your earned income, not your total income.

- For line 1, enter your total employment income as shown at the top of Form 6.
- For line 2, use Forms 7, 8, and 9 to obtain the necessary figures.
- For line 3, list the sum total of your three types of expenditures.
- For line 4, subtract your total expenditures from your employment income. Any positive figure that results should be used to help you reach your financial goals.

Next, calculate and list what percentage of your total employment income you have been spending on (a) basic lifestyle expenditures, (b) discretionary expenditures, and (c) taxes. To do so, divide each expenditure by your total employment income and multiply by 100. Then arrive at the percentage of excess by dividing the dollar amount on line 4 by the dollar amount on line 1, and multiplying the result by 100.

INTERPRETING THE RESULTS

Now that you have analyzed your income and expenditures, let's interpret the results and look at the choices you have.

1. How much of your earned income is left for future goals and for investment? In their employment years, people should try to set aside no less than five—preferably ten—percent of their employment income and invest it. You can increase the amount available for investment either by increasing your income or by spending less or both.

2. Can you earn more? Maybe you can make yourself more valuable in the job market by increasing your skills through continuing education courses, or by using your time more effectively, or by focusing on job results rather than the details of the job. The best investment you will ever make is in yourself.

   Can someone else in your family earn more? Perhaps your spouse can work part-time. If your spouse is already working, perhaps he or she can expand the scope of the job. Maybe the answer is career counselling and a new job that will let you use your skills more effectively.

3. Does the amount of income tax paid seem unacceptably high? If so, perhaps something can be done to reduce that tax drain. Chapters 6, 7, and 8 will offer you various suggestions.

4. Do the combined percentages of your basic lifestyle expenditures and your discretionary expenditures come to more than sixty to sixty-five percent? If they do and your earned income is more than $50,000 a year, then it is likely that you could reduce your expenditures without seriously reducing the quality of your life; and then you could use the difference for making investments.

Maybe it would make sense to start to simplify your life; to emphasize quality versus quantity; to evaluate your needs versus your wants; and to examine the "instant gratification" lifestyle that usually leads to significant consumer debt, resulting in the need to earn more and more with less and less time to use what we thought we couldn't live without.

If you need a system to monitor and control your expenditures, here are some useful techniques:

- Segregate your income and expenditures to assist in record-keeping and control. Deposit all your employment income in an interest-bearing savings account. We call this your "income account."
- Deposit all your investment income in another interest-bearing savings account, which we will call your "investment account." By doing so, you ensure that all your investment income is reinvested and is compounding.
- Monthly or semimonthly, transfer from your "income account" to a chequing account sufficient funds to handle all planned basic lifestyle expenditures, taxes, and discretionary expenditures for the period.
- Through the use of this chequing account, you have a running total of your expenditures for each period and an indication of what is left to cover the period's remaining expenditures. Make a commitment that the balance can never go below zero in this account before the next transfer from the "income account."
- Pay for most of your expenditures by cheque. The use of a chequebook provides a written record of your expenditures for later analysis for tax purposes and an indication of the current balance for control purposes. If you make some payments in cash, save your receipts or write the amount in a pocket diary to collect information for summarizing your expenditures.

5. If you are contemplating major expenditures like university or college, extended travel, or home improvements over the next few years, your figures on Form 10 will show you how feasible such plans are under your present circumstances.

6. If you are toying with the idea of taking a cut in employment income in order to gain greater independence or a more stimulating professional environment, these figures will give you some guide to the impact that such a career move might have on your lifestyle.

So analyze your income and expenditure patterns periodically because it helps you to be in control of your finances and highlights the areas in which action ought to be taken.

5

ANALYZING YOUR TAX SITUATION

For many of us, taxes are the fastest rising category of expenditures, and the largest. Taxes influence every phase of personal financial management, from producing and investing your income, to your retirement and your estate planning. Much of financial planning is therefore centered on maximizing your after-tax income—the dollars from your earned income and investments that are left after paying taxes and that can actually be spent by you. Most people want to reduce their personal taxes but have not taken the time to obtain the necessary knowledge. Knowing how the tax system works and what tax-planning techniques you can legally use to reduce your taxes will allow you to salvage a great many dollars to spend or invest that would otherwise be swallowed by taxes.

THE CRAZY APRIL GAME

For many Canadians, the game commences on April 15, builds to a frenzied rush on April 28, and comes to an abrupt finish at about 11:45 P.M. on April 30, when the tax return is hand-carried to the local post office. There is much yelling and screaming and frothing at the mouth during the latter stages of the game; even some mad dashes to the local bank to arrange financing to pay for the taxes due.

We're not making this up. It's the normal pattern of behaviour for too many taxpayers. What makes it worse is that once the tax return is completed, nothing is done to look ahead at the current year's tax situation and to see what tax-saving ideas can be implemented. That is, not until about December 15, when time is again running out and there's all too often a frenetic scramble to save taxes by making quick decisions.

There is a better way, a much better way. Start right after you have completed last year's return, with projections of your estimated total income, deductions, and taxable income for the current year. Next set yourself a taxable income target—in other words, what you would like your taxable income to be. Your target should not be zero but some realistic level that can be achieved through implementing legitimate tax-saving ideas without undue risk on your part.

By starting with an estimate of your current year's taxable income and targeting a desired taxable income, you will be active in your tax-saving research and have the time to seek out good tax-saving investments. You will be managing your taxes rather than letting your taxes manage you. Again, it's your choice. Do you want to control your tax expenditures or do you prefer to watch your taxes increase year after year, always constituting one of your largest annual expenditures?

FORM 11—TAX-PLANNING WORKSHEET

Before or while you complete this form, it might be helpful to look at Figure 5-1, which is an example of the completed form.

Last Year

The starting point will be your last tax return, form T1 and form TP1 for Quebec residents. Use the information to complete the *Last Year* column of this form. You will notice that this form follows the format of your 1987 tax return fairly closely, though it combines some of the items and gives some of them different captions in order to help you with your analysis and estimates.

When you have transferred all the relevant figures to the *Last Year* column and have entered last year's taxable income on line 6a, look that amount up in the appropriate tax schedule in Appendix II and find out the percentage at which your top dollars were taxed. This percentage is called your *marginal tax rate*. Then list that percentage on line 6b.

Many of the deductions and exemptions which were available in 1987 have been eliminated in 1988 or replaced with tax credits, as a result of the tax reform proposals announced on 18 June 1987. Most Canadians will have higher taxable income amounts in 1988 compared to 1987. As an offset to this increase, tax rates will generally be lower after 1987 and a new system of tax credits, discussed in Chapter 6, will be introduced.

The most positive result of tax reform for the majority of Canadians will be a reduction in their personal tax rates. In 1987, there were ten federal marginal tax rates ranging from six percent on the first $1,320 of taxable income to a top rate of thirty-four percent payable on taxable income over $63,347. As well, there was a three percent federal surtax.

Provincial taxes add approximately fifty percent of the federal rate before surtax, so that the top combined federal and provincial rate was in the range of fifty-two percent. (The maximum combined federal and provincial rate including provincial surtax actually ranged from 52.5% in Ontario and British Columbia to 58.1% in Manitoba in 1987.)

Starting in 1988, there will be only three tax brackets for individuals. The existing three percent surtax will remain until sales tax reform is implemented.

Taxable Income	Federal Tax Rate	Combined Federal and Provincial* Tax Rates, including Federal Surtax
$27,500 or less	17%	26.0%
27,501 to 55,000	26	39.8
55,001 and over	29	44.4

*Assumes a fifty percent provincial tax rate.

The following table compares combined rates in 1987 with the rates in 1988 after tax reform:

	Combined Federal and Provincial*	
	Tax Rates, including Federal Surtax	
	Before Reform	After Reform
Taxable Income	1987	1988
$1,320 or less	9.2%	26.0%
1,321 to $2,639	24.5	26.0
2,640 to 5,279	26.0	26.0
5,280 to 7,918	27.5	26.0
7,919 to 13,197	29.1	26.0
13,198 to 18,476	30.6	26.0
18,477 to 23,755	35.2	26.0
23,756 to 27,500	38.3	26.0
27,501 to 36,952	38.3	39.8
36,953 to 55,000	45.9	39.8
55,001 to 63,347	45.9	44.4
63,348 and over	52.0	44.4

*Assumes a fifty percent provincial tax rate.

Although the tax rate of most Canadians will fall under tax reform, note that the marginal tax rate on taxable income from $27,501 to $36,952 is actually higher after tax reform than before.

As well, the tax rate of Canadians with very low incomes will rise after tax reform. But with the increase in tax credits discussed in Chapter 6, the overall tax bill for lower income Canadians should remain the same or be reduced, and many will pay no tax at all.

Because of the conversion of many existing exemptions and deductions to credits, and the reduction or elimination of other deductions, taxable income after tax reform will not compare directly with taxable income under the pre-1988 system. You can't determine how much tax reform has saved or cost you by simply comparing your 1988 tax rate to your 1987 rate. A worksheet is included in Appendix III to help you calculate taxes payale after tax reform on the taxable income you will determine on Form 11 later in this chapter.

Estimate For Current Year

The next step in analyzing your tax situation is to estimate your taxable income for the current year by performing the following steps.

1. **Estimate total income**
   - On line 1(a)(i) estimate income from employment including commissions and taxable benefits for this year. In our example, we assumed an increase of 6.2% over last year in estimating employment income. You may have a different assumption on which to base your estimate. Subtract any allowable deductions, like expenses to earn commission income, to determine net employment earnings on line 1(a)(iv). The general employment expense deduction (maximum $500) is not available after 1987 as a result of tax reform.
   - On line 1(b)(i) and (ii) respectively, estimate Old Age Security and Canada or Quebec Pension Plan benefits, and any other pension income expected for the year.
   - Section 1(c) contains income from other sources, including Family Allowance payments, line 1(c)(i), and Unemployment Insurance benefits, line 1(c)(ii). Beginning in 1988, Family Allowance payments must be reported by the spouse with the higher income.
   - On lines 1(c)(iii) and (iv), estimate your taxable dividends, interest and other investment income for this year. As outlined in Chapter 6, you must include 1.25 (1.33 in 1987) times the amount of dividends actually received from Canadian

companies in taxable income. Refer to your net worth statement (Form 4) for your present dividend and interest-paying investments and make some assumptions about the amount they will produce. In our example, we have assumed an increase in dividends and interest based on the assumption that interest rates will rise during the next year.

- On line (1)(c)(v), estimate your net rental income or loss. Such income or loss will come from rental assets you presently own or plan to own during the next year. The amount is your total rental income less expenses paid on the properties and capital cost allowance. Capital cost allowance is the deduction permitted by *The Income Tax Act* over time for the capital cost of a rental building. Note that capital cost allowance cannot be claimed to create a rental loss, except for a special class of rental properties commonly called "MURBs" which are discussed in Chapter 7. In our example, we have included rental income. Our assumption is that net rental income will increase by approximately ten percent during the next year.

- On line 1(c)(vi), estimate taxable capital gains or allowable capital losses. These estimates should be based on your assumptions about sales of capital assets (such as shares, bonds, real estate, etc.) during the next year.

  For 1987, only one-half of any capital gain (known as a "taxable capital gain") is included in income. One-half of any capital loss (known as an "allowable capital loss") in 1987 can be deducted from taxable capital gains. You cannot deduct allowable capital losses realized in years after 1985 from income other than taxable capital gains. The portion of a capital gain included in your taxable income will increase from one-half to two-thirds after 1987 and to three-quarters after 1989 as a result of tax reform. The calculation of allowable capital losses will be changed in the same way as taxable capital gains, and will continue to be deductible only against taxable capital gains.

- On line 1(d)(i), estimate your net business income. Most people who work for a company do not have business income. In our example, we have shown no business income.

- On lines 1(d)(ii), (iii), and (iv) respectively, estimate net self-employment income from a profession, from commissions and from farming or fishing. In our example, we have not included any such income.

- On line 1(e), determine the estimated total income for the year. In our example, the estimated total income is $93,600.

2. Estimate net income

- On lines 2(a) through 2(i), estimate any deductions from total income and record the sum of these deductions on line 2(j). If you are unsure whether a deduction qualifies, refer to the discussion of deductions in Chapter 6. Some deductions available in 1987 will be converted into tax credits in 1988. These are discussed in more detail in Chapter 6.

- On line 3, enter the result of subtracting your total estimated deductions for next year, line 2(j), from your estimated total income, line 1(e). This is your net income. In our example, the net income estimate is $86,100.

3. Estimate claim for personal exemptions

- A central feature of tax reform is the conversion of personal exemptions into personal tax credits in 1988 and future years. The new credit system will be described in Chapter 6.

- Accordingly, you need only enter the personal exemptions you claimed in your 1987 tax return on lines 4(a) to (e) in the column for last year. The total personal exemptions claimed can then be entered on line 4(f).

4. Estimate other deductions from net income

- If you received eligible Canadian investment income in 1987, you were entitled to claim an annual deduction of up to $1,000. This deduction has been eliminated after 1987, as a result of tax reform.

- As is the case for personal exemptions after 1987, many of the other deductions available in 1987 have been converted to tax credits. The deductions affected include the deduction for eligible pension income, certain medical expenses, charitable donations, and tuition fees as well as the deduction for disabled persons and persons age 65 years or older. The credits which replace these deductions are outlined in Chapter 6.
- Non-capital and net capital losses of other years not previously deducted are claimed on line 5(h) and (i) respectively. Net capital losses can only be claimed to the extent of $2,000 (where the loss arose before 23 May 1985) plus the excess of any taxable capital gains over any allowable capital losses in the current year.
- Enter the amount of taxable capital gains exemption claimed for the year on line 5(j). See Chapter 6 for a discussion of this exemption.
- On line 5(k), enter the total of the amounts from lines 5(a) to (j).

5. Estimate taxable income
- On line 6(a), enter the result of subtracting lines 4(f) and 5(k) from line 3.
- Determine the top tax bracket (marginal tax rate) for your estimated taxable income from the appropriate tax rate schedule in Appendix II. In our example, the estimated taxable income is $81,100; the tax bracket is 44.8%, assuming our taxpayer is an Ontario resident.

Target Taxable Income

You have now estimated your taxable income for the next year. For those of you still in your working years, your estimated taxable income is probably higher than it was last year. This is because your employment earnings probably will increase.

Now you are ready to start tax planning. It begins with your setting a *target* taxable income. If you have never set a target for taxable income, don't worry. It is like setting any other target. The target should be realistic. You should feel good when you achieve the target (remember, you are saving taxes and that's a good feeling). You should keep the following points in mind as you set the target.

- *Feasibility*   Set a target that you are able to reach. To reduce your taxable income to a substantially lower target level will require you to find good tax-saving ideas and *cash* to implement them.
- *Risk*   Substantial reductions of taxable income usually require tax-shelter investments, and such investments are usually risky.
- *Tax bracket*   To target your taxable income at a level substantially below the maximum tax bracket is often self-defeating, since many tax-saving strategies are tax-deferral programmes. Reducing taxable income now in order to be taxed at lower rates usually results in your being taxed at higher rates in later years. Substantial reduction of taxable income involves risk. It is not a good idea to deal in risky investments in order to save taxes at marginal rates much below the top tax rates.
- *Income deferral*   Defer income to years when your tax bracket may be low. You may be planning to take a sabbatical, for example, that would mean a substantial decrease of your employment income for that year. By deferring income, such as sale of property, to a year when your taxable income will be low, you may not only defer taxes but actually reduce them.

With these various observations in mind, enter your targeted taxable income and tax bracket on lines 7a and 7b of Form 11. You will, of course, need to take action if you are to reduce your taxable income to the targeted amount. The means you can use to achieve this will be discussed in the next chapters.

FIGURE 5-1

File under TAX PLANNING   Date: *April 19*

FORM 11   INCOME TAX PLANNING WORKSHEET

	LAST YEAR	CURRENT YEAR
1. TOTAL INCOME		
(a) (i) Income from employment	$72,500	$77,000
(ii) Less employment expense deduction (1987 only)	(500)	N/A
(iii) Less other allowable expenses		
(iv) Net employment earnings	$72,000	$77,000
(b) Pension Income		
(i) Old Age Security and Canada or Quebec Pension Plan benefits		
(ii) Other pension income		
(c) Income from other sources		
(i) Family Allowance payments		
(ii) Unemployment Insurance benefits		
(iii) Taxable amount of dividends from Canadian companies	3,800	3,900
(iv) Interest and other investment income	1,900	2,200
(v) Rental income (loss)	5,000	5,500
(vi) Taxable capital gains	5,000	5,000
(d) Self-employed income		
(i) Business income		
(ii) Professional income		
(iii) Commission income		
(iv) Farming or fishing income		
(e) Total income	$87,700	$93,600

FIGURE 5-1 CONT'D

		LAST YEAR	CURRENT YEAR
2.	DEDUCTIONS FROM TOTAL INCOME		
	(a) Canada or Quebec Pension Plan payments (1987 only)	$ 445	N/A
	(b) Unemployment Insurance payments (1987 only)	650	N/A
	(c) Registered pension plan contributions		
	(d) Registered Retirement Savings Plan contributions	7,500	7,500
	(e) Union and professional dues		
	(f) Tuition fees (1987 only)		
	(g) Child care expenses		
	(h) Allowable business investment losses		
	(i) Other deductions		
	(j) Total deductions	8,595	7,500
3.	NET INCOME	$79,105	$86,100
4.	PERSONAL EXEMPTIONS		
	(a) Basic personal exemption (1987 only)	4,220	N/A
	(b) Age exemption (1987 only)		N/A
	(c) Married exemption (1987 only)	3,700	N/A
	(d) Exemption for dependent children (1987 only)	560	N/A
	(e) Additional personal exemptions (1987 only)		N/A
	(f) Total personal exemptions	8,480	N/A
5.	OTHER DEDUCTIONS FROM NET INCOME		
	(a) Interest and dividend deduction (1987 only)	1,000	N/A
	(b) Pension income deduction (1987 only)		N/A

FIGURE 5-1 CONT'D

		LAST YEAR	CURRENT YEAR
(c)	Medical expenses (1987 only)		N/A
(d)	Charitable donations (1987 only)	500	N/A
(e)	Disability deduction (1987 only)		N/A
(f)	Education deduction (1987 only)		N/A
(g)	Deductions transferred from spouse (1987 only)	400	N/A
(h)	Non-capital losses of other years		
(i)	Net Capital losses of other years (1972-1985)		
(j)	Taxable capital gains exemption	5,000	5,000
(k)	Total other deductions	6,900	5,000
6. (a)	TAXABLE INCOME	63,725	81,100
(b)	Tax bracket	52.5	44.8
7. (a)	TARGETED TAXABLE INCOME		72,000
(b)	Targeted Tax Bracket		44.8

6

WHERE AND HOW TAXES ARE SAVED

The question that people ask us most frequently is, "How can I save on my income taxes?" The answer to that is, "You can save on your taxes by knowing how various types of income are taxed and what tax-planning techniques you can use to reduce your taxes, and then by taking the appropriate action."

Governments provide certain economic incentives by taxing different types of income at different rates. Some income is tax-free; some income is given tax-favoured treatment; some income gets tax-deferred treatment, meaning that it is not taxed until several years later. Some investments, called tax shelters, enable investors to make deductions that require no additional cash outlay, such as capital cost allowance on real estate. If you want to lower your taxes, you should know which types of income are taxed at low rates or not taxed at all.

This chapter will give you a lot of tax ideas in a general sense, but bear in mind that the tax laws are complex. *The Income Tax Act* and its *Regulations* consist of hundreds of closely printed pages. A good tax practice has knowledgeable professionals and a library of case law books and loose-leaf tax services to support their research. In this one chapter, the best thing we can do is to sketch an outline of tax-saving ideas for you, with some brief explanations of these ideas. Applied to your own situation, with some additional research on your part or on the part of a tax professional, these ideas should help you to cut your taxes. Needless to say, the ideas by themselves will not do it. When you have found an idea that fits your situation, you'll have to put it into practice. All too often, taxes are not saved because people procrastinate and don't follow through on their tax-saving ideas.

TAX-SAVING IDEAS

Generally speaking, the following six means can be used to effect long-term tax savings:

1. Tax-free income.
2. Tax-favoured income.

3. Tax-deferred income.

4. Shifting income to a family member whose tax bracket is lower than yours in order to achieve such family goals as education.

5. Expenditures that result in tax deductions or in credits against your tax liability.

6. Tax-sheltered investments, which combine some tax-saving aspects of the means mentioned above with certain non-cash deductions (discussed in Chapter 7).

TAX-FREE INCOME

For tax purposes, your tax-free income is entirely excluded from your income. Tax-free income falls into one or more of the following categories:

- gain on the sale of your principal residence. Note that a married couple can only have one principal residence for tax purposes in any given year, and thus it is no longer possible to realize completely tax-free gains on both the family home and the family vacation property, except by using up your capital gains exemption.

- most amounts you receive through gifts or inheritances. That's why it is said that the simplest way to become financially independent is to choose your parents wisely!

- in many circumstances, proceeds you receive in the form of a lump sum from a life insurance policy of which you are the beneficiary will be tax-free. Exceptions to this are discussed in Chapter 13.

- significant changes in the tax treatment of capital gains and losses were outlined in the 1985 federal budget. These initial proposals were later amended as part of the tax reform proposals. Individual taxpayers will now be entitled to a cumulative lifetime exemption of $100,000 for capital gains realized after 1984. In certain circumstances, individual taxpayers may qualify for an exemption of up to $500,000 for gains on the sale of farm property or shares of a small business corporation. The present exemption for gains realized on the sale of principal residences will be in addition to, and will not affect, this lifetime entitlement.

Because of the importance of the capital gains exemption, it is discussed separately in more detail below.

Capital Gains Exemption

When the capital gains exemption was introduced in 1985, it was to be phased in over several years, reaching a $500,000 maximum limit in 1990. No phase-in period existed for the $500,000 limit for a gain on the sale of a qualified farm property—it became available in 1985.

Under tax reform, the basic capital gains exemption will be capped at its 1987 level of $100,000. Exceptions are provided for qualified farm property which continues to be eligible for the full $500,000 exemption, and for shares of a small business corporation, which will be eligible for the maximum $500,000 exemption starting in 1988—two years earlier than under the original phase-in rules.

A small business corporation is generally defined as a Canadian-controlled private corporation with substantially all of its assets used in an active business in Canada or invested in shares of operating companies that qualify as small business corporations. As well, the business cannot have been owned by anyone but the individual or a related person throughout the two years before the sale in order to qualify for the exemption.

Note that this increased exemption is available only on shares of a small business corporation and not on other small business assets. Gains on these assets would be sheltered by the $100,000 exemption. If you are currently operating a business in Canada as a sole proprietor or in a partnership and you intend to sell your business, you can gain access to the $500,000 capital gains exemption by incorporating your business before the sale.

Despite the term *small business corporation*, shares of any Canadian controlled private corporation, regardless of its size, will qualify for the $500,000 capital gains exemption provided they meet the tests described above.

Qualified farm property includes farm land and buildings, shares of a family farm corporation and an interest in a family farm partnership where you, your spouse or your child were actively engaged in the farming business either in the year the farm was sold, or within at least five years during which it was owned by the family. Qualified farm property acquired after 17 June 1987 will not include farm land and buildings unless they are owned by you, your spouse or your children for at least two years immediately before their resale and:

- in at least two years, gross revenue from the farming business exceeds your net income from all other sources; or
- throughout any two year period, the property was used by a family farm partnership or family corporation to carry on a farming business in Canada.

Contrary to some predictions, tax reform did not limit the types of property eligible for the $100,000 capital gains exemption. You should note, however, that this exemption is not in addition to the $500,000 exemption available on qualified farm property and small business corporation shares. Your total exemption cannot exceed $500,000. If the maximum $100,000 exemption is claimed on sales of other capital assets, only $400,000 is left to shelter qualified farm property or gains realized on the sale of small business corporation shares. Conversely, if the $500,000 exemption is used for farm property or small business shares, the $100,000 exemption is not available for other capital property.

To the extent that a taxpayer has unabsorbed capital losses available to be carried forward from prior years, these may continue to be offset against capital gains realized in subsequent years, eliminating the need to claim part of the cumulative exemption for this purpose.

If you are holding capital property that has increased significantly in value since you acquired it, the new rules may provide a windfall tax saving. In other cases, your investment strategy should be reviewed to assess the opportunities offered by the changes. It may be more advantageous to invest in equities that have a high potential for growth. Remember, however, that the exemption does not have to be claimed in a particular year even though it is available. If you have realized a capital gain and it will not significantly increase your taxes payable (for example, in a year when your other income is lower than usual), you may decide not to claim part of your exemption, to save it to offset gains likely to be realized in later years.

The availability of the capital gains exemption will be restricted in some circumstances by the new net investment rules introduced under tax reform. These rules are discussed in Chapter 7.

The above discussion of tax-free capital gains assumes that the alternative minimum tax will not increase your total taxes in the year such gains are realized. If this is *not* the case, the tax on these otherwise exempt gains can be increased from nil up to approximately 17% to 20%, depending on the province in which you live. The minimum tax rules are discussed more fully in Chapter 7.

TAX-FAVOURED INCOME

The two most common types of income that are taxed in a favoured manner are capital gains and dividends paid by Canadian companies.

Capital Gains

As discussed in the previous section, capital gains can be realized entirely tax-free (subject to the application of the minimum tax) under the lifetime capital gains exemption. But even capital gains which are not eligible for this exemption (for example, because the taxpayer has already used up his existing exemption limit, or chooses not to use it to exempt a gain in a particular year) are still taxed in a favoured way, because only two-thirds of a capital gain need be included in taxable income (again, subject to the application of the alternative minimum tax and the new investment loss rules which are discussed more fully in Chapter 7).

Tax reform has reduced the tax-favoured status of capital gains not eligible for the capital gains exemption. The portion of a capital gain included in your taxable income has been increased from one-half in 1987 and prior years to two-thirds in 1988 and 1989 and to three-quarters after 1989. Despite the reduction of personal tax rates which start in 1988, the increased rate of inclusion of capital gains in income will result in a higher tax bite on capital gains for all taxpayers after 1989, although the rate will decrease slightly for some people in 1988 and 1989. This is illustrated in the following table, which assumes a provincial tax rate equal to fifty percent of the basic federal tax rate.

	Combined Federal and Provincial Marginal Tax Rates On Capital Gains including 3% Federal Surtax		
Taxable Income	*1987*	*1988 & 1989*	*1990 & Beyond*
$23,775 or less	4.6% to 17.6%	17.3%	19.5%
23,756 to $27,500	19.1	17.3	19.5
27,501 to 36,952	19.1	26.5	29.8
36,953 to 55,000	23.0	26.5	29.8
55,001 to 63,347	23.0	29.6	33.3
63,348 and over	26.0	29.6	33.3

Loss carryovers will be adjusted to reflect the new inclusion rates. For example, an allowable loss of $50 realized in 1987 or prior years becomes a loss of $67 when applied in 1988 or 1989 and $75 when applied in 1990. Similarly, a 1990 allowable capital loss of $75 will only offset $67 of taxable capital gains in 1988 or 1989 and $50 of such gains in 1987. The rules governing the timing of loss carryovers do not change; they may be carried back three years and forward indefinitely.

Capital gain treatment will normally be given to any gain realized from the sale of capital assets like shares, bonds and real estate that you hold as an investment. A gain is realized to the extent that the selling price exceeds the sum of your adjusted cost base (ACB) plus any costs of disposition. Your ACB is generally your cost of acquiring the asset plus the cost of any capital additions or improvements in the case of real estate. There are numerous other rules which may affect the determination of the ACB, plus special rules for property owned on 31 December 1971, when tax on capital gains was first introduced. Taxation of capital gains can be quite complex in certain circumstances; if you might realize a large capital gain in the near future, you should consider consulting a tax advisor.

To illustrate how capital gains are calculated, consider the following simple example. Assume you purchased 100 shares of a company for $1,000 three years ago. They are now worth $2,500. You decide to sell them, and net $2,430 after brokerage fees. In this case, your capital gain will be $1,430 ($2,500-$1,000-$70) and the taxable capital gain you include in taxable income will be two-thirds of $1,430 or $953.

Dividends

Dividends received by individual taxpayers from Canadian companies are also taxed on a favoured basis as a result of the dividend tax credit system. (Dividends received from foreign companies are treated as ordinary taxable income with no special tax treatment.) The dividend tax credit system is designed to give credit to shareholders for all or part of the tax already paid by the corporation on its earnings distributed as dividends. There is no similar credit for interest paid by a corporation because the corporation does not pay tax on earnings paid out as interest.

Because tax reform reduces corporate as well as individual tax rates, the dividend tax credit for corporate taxes assumed to have been paid is lower in 1988 and later years compared to the 1987 credit. The taxable amount of the dividend will also be reduced for dividends received after 1987 compared to those received in 1987, to reflect reduced corporate tax rates.

The system operates as follows in 1988 and subsequent years. You include in income 1.25 times the amount of the dividend actually received, but you can then claim a tax credit equal to $13\frac{1}{3}\%$ of the grossed-up (taxable) dividend against your federal tax for the year. Because this reduces the base on which your provincial income tax is calculated (except in Quebec which has its own dividend tax credit provisions), the combined result is a tax reduction approximately equal to a twenty percent tax paid by the corporation.

The attractiveness of this treatment can be illustrated by the following comparative example (assuming a taxpayer in the top federal tax rate bracket and subject to a fifty percent provincial tax rate).

Although the tax rate on Canadian dividends is substantially lower than that for interest income, this does not mean that dividends are always preferable to interest income. It may be better to pay more tax if the after-tax yield is improved as a result. To illustrate, if you were in the top tax bracket and had a choice of investing at nine percent interest or in shares paying a six percent dividend, you would realize a net after-tax return of approximately 5.0% for interest, compared to approximately 4.2% for dividend income. Therefore, even though the tax cost is higher, you would be better off receiving the nine percent interest rather than the six percent dividend.

	Dividends	Interest
Amount received	$1,000	$1,000
Gross-up (dividend only)	250	nil
	$1,250	$1,000
Federal tax at 29%	$ 363	$ 290
Dividend tax credit	(167)	nil
	196	290
Federal surtax (3%)	6	9
Provincial tax	98	145
Total tax	$ 300	$ 444
Net after-tax dollars	$ 700	$ 556

It is always important to compare the after-tax yield on potential investments in order to make an appropriate investment decision. In the lowest bracket (taxable income under $27,500), dividends are taxed much more favourably than interest (approximately seven percent vs. twenty-six percent). If your taxable income is higher than $27,500, you will achieve the same after-tax income from the receipt of approximately $80 in Canadian dividends as from $100 in interest income. Accordingly, for middle- and upper-income Canadians, an interest-bearing investment should yield about twenty-five percent more than a comparable investment in dividend-paying Canadian shares, assuming all other factors such as risk, liquidity and so on are equal.

It is interesting to note than an interest-bearing investment had to yield approximately thirty-three percent more than a comparable dividend-paying investment in 1987 and fifty percent more than in 1986, to provide the same after-tax income for higher income Canadians. Even though the tax rate on Canadian dividend income is lowered by tax reform, it has not been reduced to as great a degree as the tax rate on interest. The tax changes introduced in the 1986 federal budget and in tax reform have significantly reduced the tax incentive for individuals receiving dividend income. As well, since companies can deduct interest from their taxable income, but cannot deduct dividends, financing through debt rather than preferred shares will almost certainly be more tax effective for corporations and their investors in future.

TAX-DEFERRED INCOME

The income from certain investments is tax-free for a specified time and is therefore known as tax-deferred income. Since there is a period in which compounding income on the investment is not reduced by taxation, tax-deferred income can increase at an accelerated rate.

Deferred Income Plans

Generally, the most important method of tax deferral for the majority of taxpayers is the use of one or more of the deferred income plans described below. The main purpose of these plans is to shelter income from immediate taxation. Unlike the ideas about tax shelters discussed in Chapter 7, the deferred income plans described here not only permit an income deduction for the amounts you invest but also provide for the tax-free accumulation of income while the funds remain in the plan.

In late 1986, details of a significantly revised system for tax-assisted retirement savings were released. The objective of the new system is to provide equitable tax treatment for retirement savings. It is intended that the amount of tax assistance available should be comparable for individuals with the same income, whether they save for retirement through an employer-sponsored pension plan or through a registered retirement savings plan. As well, individuals will have greater flexibility in timing their retirement savings contributions, so that the opportunity to build a reasonable pension need not be permanently lost because more immediate financial pressures prevent maximum contributions in a year.

The rules introduced to implement this new system are complex. As a result, the new system will be introduced in stages. Under the original proposals, many changes were to be introduced in 1988 with the remainder phased in by 1990. As part of tax reform, the government now proposes to slow down the phase-in of the new registered retirement savings plan contribution limits until 1995 and to delay the implementation of many other changes from 1988 to 1989. The rules introduced in 1986 to limit additional voluntary contributions to registered pension plans will, however, come into force as originally scheduled.

Registered Pension Plans

Registered pension plans (RPPs) generally include requirements for minimum employee contributions (except where the plan is only funded by employer contributions) and restrictions on the maximum contributions an employee can make. Annual employee contributions can only be made within this range, even where *The Income Tax Act* would permit the deduction of larger contributions.

Your ability to deduct pension contributions depends on whether you belong to a money purchase plan or a defined benefit plan. These plans differ in the way pension benefits received after retirement are determined. Money purchase plan benefits are dependent on the amount of funds accumulated in the plan for the employee, while benefits under a defined benefit plan are determined by formula, usually based on salary levels and years of service. These terms are described in more detail in Chapter 12.

Employees who are members of a defined benefit RPP can deduct the full amount of the current service contribution required under the plan, even if it exceeds the former deduction limit of $3,500. A limitation on contributions is not necessary because Revenue Canada limits the amount of benefit that can be paid from a defined benefit RPP. The current maximum benefit is $1,715 per year of service to a maximum of 35 years. This represents a maximum annual pension of approximately $60,000.

Employee past service contributions which are required under a defined benefit plan are also deductible, but only to a maximum of $3,500 per year. Additional voluntary contributions (AVCs) made after 1987 for the current year's service will not be deductible. AVCs for past years' service made before October 9, 1986 and not deducted before 1987 will not be deductible in future years and must be withdrawn before 1989 to avoid being included in income upon eventual withdrawal. AVCs for past service can no longer be made after October 8, 1986.

The maximum combined employer/employee contributions to money purchase plans, taking into account the delayed phase-in of the higher contribution limits under tax reform, are outlined below:

1987	$7,000
1988	7,000
1989	10,500
1990	11,500
1991	12,500
1992	13,500
1993	14,500
1994	15,500
1995	indexed

Beginning in 1989, money purchase plans will also be required to limit combined employer and employee contributions to the lesser of the above amount and eighteen percent of that year's pensionable earnings (generally equal to T4 earnings).

Deferred Profit Sharing Plans

In the past, Deferred Profit Sharing Plans (DPSPs) provided essentially the same tax benefits as money purchase RPPs, and were often used by small businesses because they are generally simpler to set up and administer than RPPs and have a broader range of allowed investments. Since 1981, the use of DPSPs to provide retirement income for a company's controlling shareholders has been restricted and the use of these plans has declined as a result.

Employees will not be allowed to contribute to a DPSP after 1988. Employee contributions of up to $5,500 per year can be made in 1987 and 1988. Although these contributions are not tax deductible, the contributions are not taxed when withdrawn from the DPSP and will earn income tax-free while they remain in the plan. The amount of deductible employer contributions is limited to one-half of the amount outlined above as deductible contributions to money purchase RPPs.

Registered Retirement Savings Plan

The most advertised and perhaps the best-known type of tax deferral investment is the Registered Retirement Savings Plan (RRSP).

Up to specified limits, amounts contributed to an RRSP are deductible for tax purposes, and income earned on these funds accumulates free of tax as long as the funds remain in the plan. When funds are withdrawn from the plan, the amounts received (both capital and income) are fully taxable at that time.

The limit on contributions to an RRSP depends on several factors. First, let's consider the limits in 1987 and 1988. If you are not a member of an RPP and are not a beneficiary under a DPSP, your maximum allowable contribution to an RRSP for 1987 and 1988 is the lesser of $7,500 or twenty percent of your earned income. Therefore, the maximum contribution is available only if your earned income (essentially, income excluding investment income) is at least $37,500 in 1987 and 1988.

If you are a member of an RPP, or if either you or your employer made a contribution to a DPSP on your behalf in the year, your RRSP contribution in 1987 and 1988 is limited to the lesser of $3,500 or twenty percent of your earned income minus the amount of any contribution that you have made for the year to a registered pension plan. RPP members who do not have any benefits accruing by reason of their employment in the current year are not limited by this $3,500 maximum deduction.

The rules for determining maximum RRSP contributions change significantly in 1989. The overall contribution limit will be the lesser of eighteen percent of earned income and the following amounts:

1989	$8,500
1990	10,500
1991	11,500
1992	12,500
1993	13,500
1994	14,500
1995	15,500

These amounts reflect the more gradual phase-in of higher contribution limits included as part of tax reform. Earned income will be based on the previous year's income and after 1990 will no longer include pension benefits, retiring allowances, death benefits and amounts received out of an RRSP or a DPSP.

If you save for retirement through an RRSP and have not earned any retirement benefits under a DPSP or RPP in the previous year, you will be able to make RRSP contributions equal to the above limits, provided you have sufficient earned income in the preceding year ($47,222 earned income in 1988 for 1989 contributions, $58,333 in 1989 for 1990, $63,889 in 1990 for 1991, etc.). If your earned income is lower than these amounts, your maximum available contribution is reduced by eighteen percent of the difference. If you do not make all your maximum available contribution, you can "save" the unused portion to increase your allowed contribution in any of the next seven years.

If you are earning benefits for retirement through your membership in a DPSP or an RPP, in addition to your RRSP, your maximum RRSP limit will be reduced from that otherwise available to reflect these retirement benefits. If you are a member of a DPSP or a money purchase RPP, this reduction or "pension adjustment" will equal the total of your and your employer's contributions made in the year. If you are a member of a defined benefit RPP, the calculation of your pension adjustment is much more complicated, as it is based on the value of retirement benefits you earned in the preceding year. The information necessary to calculate this pension adjustment will not be available to most taxpayers. Accordingly, Revenue Canada will notify taxpayers by the end of each year of their RRSP contribution limit for that year, based on RPP information provided by their employers.

Both before 1989 and after, RRSP contributions can be deducted if they are made in the year or within sixty days after the end of the year. Therefore, if you over-contributed in 1987, all or part of the excess may be claimed in 1988, if the payment was made in the first sixty days of 1988.

Excess RRSP contributions made which are not deductible from taxable income may be subject to a special penalty tax of one percent per month until withdrawn. This excess will be taxable when it is withdrawn, even though no deduction was allowed for the contribution. In 1987, contributions in excess of your annual limit, but not exceeding $5,500, are not subject to the penalty tax, although they too will be taxed when ultimately withdrawn, unless they are withdrawn in the year you receive your assessment or the following year.

As an alternative to contributing to your own RRSP, you may wish to consider contributions to an RRSP for your spouse (see discussion under *Shifting Income to Someone in a Lower Tax Bracket* later in this chapter) provided the combined contributions to your and your spouse's RRSPs do not exceed the limits described above. (Note that if your spouse has earned income, contributions that he or she makes to an RRSP do not affect your contribution limits.)

To appreciate how much an investment of pre-tax dollars can grow while the interest it earns is not taxed, take a look at table 6-1. Also note the large differences that result from different rates of return. Investing $2,000 a year for thirty years at eight percent will give you $226,570, while at twelve percent it will give you $482,670. That is a difference of $256,100 or about 115 percent, though the difference in rates of return is only fifty percent.

Self-administered RRSPs

If you like to make your own investment decisions, you can establish an RRSP and administer it yourself. You might contribute cash and direct the investment of these funds. Alternatively, you might transfer eligible securities to the plan (up to your

TABLE 6-1
INVESTMENT GROWTH IN RRSPs WITH ANNUAL COMPOUNDING

Annual contributions of $2,000

Years in Plan	Your Deposits	Principal with interest 8%	10%	12%
10	$20,000	$28,970	$31,870	$35,100
20	$40,000	$91,520	$114,550	$144,100
30	$60,000	$226,570	$328,990	$482,670

Annual contributions of $7,500

Years in Plan	Your Deposits	Principal with interest 8%	10%	12%
10	$75,000	$108,640	$119,510	$131,630
20	$150,000	$343,200	$429,560	$540,380
30	$225,000	$849,640	$1,233,710	$1,810,010

contribution limit). Remember, however, that security transfers to such a plan must be made at fair market value and could trigger immediate capital gains to you. (No deduction is allowed for capital losses on such transfers, and therefore transfers of securities in a loss position should be avoided.)

Qualified investments for an RRSP include a wide range of marketable securities. (If the funds in the plan are used to acquire non-qualified investments, you may be required to take an equivalent amount into income). In some cases, mortgages qualify as eligible investments for an RRSP, but care should be taken if you wish to have your RRSP hold a mortgage on your own home or other property:

- The mortgage must be administered by an approved lender under the *National Housing Act* or by a corporation offering its services to the public as an issuer of mortgages, and
- the mortgage interest rate, repayment terms, etc., must reflect normal commercial practice (i.e. it must be administered as if the property were owned by a stranger).

If it fails these tests, a mortgage held by your RRSP on your home could be considered a non-qualifying investment.

For some types of investments, the advantage of tax-free accumulation of income in an RRSP must be weighed against the loss of other tax benefits available if the income were taxed outside the plan. If, for example, shares of taxable Canadian companies are held personally, any dividends received are eligible for a dividend tax credit, and capital gains may qualify for the capital gains exemption. In contrast to this, such income earned in an RRSP will be taxed in full when the funds are eventually withdrawn from the plan. On the other hand, you should probably hold deep discount bonds, stripped bonds and bearer coupons in an RRSP, rather than directly, because no special tax advantages apply to such income and tax on amounts earned in the RRSP can effectively be deferred until payments are later made out of the plan. One final point to note is that most self-administered RRSPs have an administration cost which usually exceeds similar costs for an ordinary RRSP.

Other Types of Tax-Deferred Income

In addition to deferred income plans, there are other less commonly encountered methods of deferring income, some examples of which follow.

Capital gains reserves

Capital gains reserves, primarily used in the sale of real estate, provide a way of deferring taxes on capital asset sales. By claiming this reserve, a taxpayer can defer recognition of the capital gain until payments are received from the purchaser.

A taxpayer can claim a reasonable reserve for sale proceeds not receivable until after the year of the sale. For example, if you sold a rental property for a twenty-five percent cash down payment, with the remaining seventy-five percent due the following year, you could reduce the capital gain that would otherwise be reported in the year of sale by seventy-five percent. Note that a reserve cannot be used to defer taxation of a capital gain for longer than four years after the year of sale and that at least twenty percent of the capital gain must be reported each year, regardless of the actual amount of cash received. (Special rules provide a ten-year limit, with similar terms, for sales of family farms and shares of family farm corporations.)

With the introduction of the capital gains exemption, these reserve provisions will no longer be as beneficial where the gain does not exceed the available exemption. The reserve provisions will still present an opportunity for deferral of income and tax reduction when the capital gains exemption has been used up and a large gain would trigger a high rate of tax if it were all included in one year's income.

Replacement property

In certain circumstances, taxable income realized on the sale or involuntary conversion (for example, expropriation or loss through fire) of certain capital assets, such as land, buildings and equipment used in a business, can be deferred when the former capital property is replaced with similar property of the same or greater value. The income deferral will last until the ultimate sale of the replacement assets.

A similar deferral is available when rental properties are replaced after an involuntary conversion. This deferral is not available if a rental property is sold, and the proceeds are reinvested in another rental property.

SHIFTING INCOME TO SOMEONE IN A LOWER TAX BRACKET

The basis of several tax-planning techniques is the fact that the tax bracket of children or parents whom you support may be lower than your own tax bracket. Therefore, any given source of income will yield them more spendable after-tax dollars than it would yield you.

Opportunities for income splitting were significantly reduced by the May 1985 federal budget. However, there are still several effective ways to split income with other family members. The examples which follow use income transfers from parents to children but the same method will generally work for shifting income to elderly parents.

Gifts

Gifts to your spouse, or to children, grandchildren, nieces, nephews, etc. under eighteen years of age are not particularly effective for income-splitting purposes. Income from the gifted property or from the reinvestment of the gift will normally be attributed back to you and taxed as part of your income. These attribution rules continue to apply, in the case of gifts to your spouse, as long as you remain married and resident in Canada. On the other hand, the attribution of income back to you in the case of gifts to minors ceases to apply in the year in which the child reaches eighteen years of age. As well, the attribution rules do not apply to future capital gains (where the property has increased in value since the time of the gift) realized on property given to a child, regardless of age, although they do apply to gains realized by a spouse on gifted property.

For income tax purposes, gifts of capital property (such as shares or real estate) are generally considered to have been made at fair market value, resulting in an immediate capital gain for the person making the gift. The exception to this is that, in the case of a gift to your spouse, you may choose either to treat the transfer as having been made at the property's adjusted cost base, thereby deferring any resulting capital gain until your spouse later disposes of the property, or to transfer it at fair market value.

If you transfer the property to your spouse at its adjusted cost base, the eventual gain will be attributed back to you, as will any income your spouse earns on the property in the meantime. But the reinvestment of the income or the gain from the property by your spouse will generate income taxable in his or her hands, thereby accomplishing some income splitting.

Transfers at Fair Market Value

Where property is sold to your spouse or children and fair market value consideration is received, neither the income nor capital gains attribution rules will apply. If you take back a loan, interest must be charged at commercial rates (and must be paid within 30 days after the end of the year). For this rule to apply to transfers to your spouse, you must transfer the property at fair market value and recognize any resulting gain. You cannot elect to treat the transfer as having been made at adjusted cost base for tax purposes.

The fair market value transfer to your spouse is particularly advantageous where the transfer does not result in a capital gain or results in a gain which is offset by the capital gains exemption or unused capital losses. Your spouse will be taxed on any future additional gain which can be sheltered by his or her capital gains exemption. As a result, you will have effectively doubled-up on the capital gains exemption. If your spouse is indebted to you because of the transfer, you will have to report the interest earned until the debt is paid off, but you will no longer have to report the income from the transferred property.

Loans

Before the 1985 federal budget, it was possible to loan funds interest-free to your spouse or children and have the income earned on the property acquired with the borrowed funds taxed in the hands of the borrower.

The existing income attribution rules were amended in 1985 to apply to loans between spouses—except for loans made before 23 May 1985 if repaid before 1988. The benefits of loans to your spouse for income splitting purposes are now limited. Income attribution will only be avoided on future loans if interest is paid on the loan at a market rate prescribed in *The Income Tax Act*. This limits income splitting to income earned with the borrowed funds in excess of this prescribed rate.

On the other hand, although the amended income attribution provisions also apply to loans to other family members under age eighteen, bona fide loans to children eighteen years of age or older will not be affected by the changes. Income splitting can also be accomplished with children over fourteen by lending them money through a trust to purchase interest-bearing investments, which will not pay interest before the year the children turn eighteen. A deferral of interest income greater than three years is not possible because of the investment income deferral rules described in Chapter 8.

A loan to a child attending university or college, for example, is still an effective way to reduce the cost of putting the child through school. Instead of subsidizing the student's costs of tuition, room and board, etc. out of your after-tax income, the loan proceeds should be invested by the student, with the resulting income being used for those purposes. Typically, the student will pay little or no tax on such income after claiming his or her basic tax credit, credit for tuition fees etc.

RRSP for spouse

A better alternative to making contributions to a Registered Retirement Savings Plan in your own name may be to contribute to an RRSP for your spouse. Such contributions are deductible by you up to the same limits as those applicable to your own plan (see *Deferred Income Plans*) but when your spouse later withdraws the funds, or starts to receive an annuity out of the plan, he or she will in most cases be taxed on the amounts received.

There are, however, rules to discourage the immediate collapse of a spousal RRSP. If your spouse withdraws funds from a plan to which you contributed, the withdrawal will be added to your income to the extent of any contributions to the spousal RRSP in that year and in the two immediately preceding taxation years. This means that if you contribute to your spouse's RRSP early in 1988 (for 1987) the funds should not be withdrawn before 1991. (This assumes, of course, that you will not have made further contributions to an RRSP for your spouse in the meantime; if you have, any withdrawal should be delayed to a later year if you wish to avoid tax.)

This income attribution rule does not apply if you and your spouse are legally separated and living apart when funds are withdrawn. This rule also does not apply where the particular plan "matures" and annuity payments start to be received by your spouse. Moreover, if the funds are left to accumulate in the plan until your spouse reaches age sixty-five, he or she will then qualify for the pension income credit that might not otherwise be available.

An RRSP may mature (be converted into an annuity or a Registered Retirement Income Fund) at any time but, in any event, must either be converted or the funds withdrawn by the end of the year in which the owner reaches age seventy-one. If a taxpayer is prevented from making further contributions to his own RRSP because he has reached age seventy-one, he can still contribute to an RRSP for his spouse until she also reaches age seventy-one.

There is no longer a minimum age limit of sixty for maturing an RRSP. This change is intended to assist taxpayers who retire before age sixty and who may require the additional retirement income before that time.

Registered Education Savings Plan

Registered Education Savings Plans can be a very effective way of shifting income to school age children. Because these plans are intended only to provide financing for your children's (or grandchildren's) post-secondary education, they will be discussed in Chapter 11 which deals with education financing.

TAX DEDUCTIONS AND CREDITS

So far, we have discussed how you can minimize your taxable income by making use of all available exclusions from income, by shifting income, and by making tax-favoured and tax-deferred investments. These are the methods used to pare down the amount that must be included in total income in the first place. Another means by which you can reduce your taxable income is to make expenditures that result in tax deductions or credits. There are numerous opportunities for reducing taxes payable, if you know what deductions and credits Revenue Canada will accept and what you must do to obtain them. A brief description of the more common sources of deductions and credits follows.

Employment Expense Deductions

The general employment expense deduction of twenty percent of employment income to a maximum of $500 is no longer available after 1987, under tax reform.

An employee earning commissions can still deduct expenses paid and not reimbursed in the year (except membership fees for a dining, recreational or sporting facility) to earn employment income, up to the amount of commission income received, if *all* the following conditions are met:

1. the employee is employed in connection with the selling of property or negotiating of contracts for his employer;
2. the employee is required by his employment contract to pay his own expenses;
3. the employee is ordinarily required to carry on his duties away from his employer's place of business;
4. the employee is paid in whole or in part by commissions; and
5. the employee does not receive a tax-free travelling allowance (a reasonable non-accountable advance, calculated by reference to time actually spent travelling away from the city where the employer is located).

Where the commission remunerated employee receives an unreasonably low travelling allowance, he may choose to add this allowance to his income and deduct the eligible portion of his actual travelling and automobile expenses, as discussed below. (This option is not available for Quebec tax purposes.)

Automobile Expenses

If you are a self-employed person who uses your car for business purposes, you will be able to deduct the business portion of your automobile expenses, subject to new restrictions added by tax reform. Expenses include gas, oil, insurance, repairs, interest costs to finance the purchase of the car, lease payments and capital cost allowance. An employee can similarly deduct a portion of his automobile expenses, but only if the following conditions apply:

a. the employee is ordinarily required to carry on his employment duties away from his employer's place of business or in different places;

b. the employee is required to pay his own travelling expenses; and

c. the employee does not receive a non-taxable travelling allowance.

Form T2200, signed by your employer, must be filed with your tax return to verify that these criteria are met.

Tax reform introduced significant new restrictions on the deductibility of automobile expenses. (These new rules actually apply to all passenger vehicles, including automobiles, station wagons and passenger vans designed to carry less than ten people and intended for use primarily on highways and streets. The rules to not apply to taxis, rental cars and certain other special purpose vehicles).

Only the first $20,000 of the cost of an automobile will be eligible for deduction over time as capital cost allowance (CCA). The maximum deduction for car lease payments will be the least of three amounts: the actual monthly lease payment, $600 per month, or the ratio of $20,000 to eighty-five percent of the manufacturer's list price times the actual monthly lease payment. Interest expenses to finance the purchase of a car will be limited to a maximum of $250 per month.

These restrictions apply to all passenger vehicles purchased or leased after 17 June 1987, for taxation years starting after 17 June 1987 and ending after 1987.

Tax reform also introduced a new restriction on the deductibility of certain automobile expenses. Operating expenses (including gasoline, oil, maintenance and repair costs) will continue to be deductible to the extent of the proportion of business miles to total miles, as was the case prior to tax reform.

Starting in 1988, the fixed costs of operating a car (CCA, interest, lease payments, insurance and licence fees) will also be deductible to the extent of the proportion of business miles to total miles, but the deductible portion will be reduced where business use is less than 24,000 kilometers per year. The deductible amount of your fixed costs is determined by multiplying the business portion of these expenses by the number of kilometers you travel on business in a year divided by the lesser of 24,000 and the total number of kilometers driven in the year.

This additional restriction is perhaps best illustrated by an example. Assume the fixed costs of your car total $5,000 and you drive 20,000 kilometers for business out of a total of 40,000 kilometers in a year. Your allowable deduction for these fixed costs would be $5,000 times fifty percent (your business portion of total kilometers driven) times 20,000 divided by 24,000. Thus your deduction would only be $2,083, rather than the $2,500 deduction you would have been allowed before tax reform.

These changes apply for taxation periods starting after 17 June 1987 and ending after 1987.

Reasonable travel allowances or reimbursement of travel expense by your employer for business trips continue to be tax-free after tax reform. However, travel allowances in excess of twenty-one cents per kilometer (twenty-five cents in the Yukon and Northwest Territories) will not be deductible by your employer after 1987. As a result, most employers in future will be reluctant to pay allowances in excess of these amounts.

Deductions from Total Income

These deductions include:

- Contributions to a registered pension plan. The annual contribution limits are discussed in an earlier section of this chapter.
- Contributions to Registered Retirement Savings Plans. Again the annual contribution limits are discussed in an earlier section of this chapter.
- Annual union and professional dues, but not including initiation fees, special assessments or amounts charged for any purpose other than the organization's ordinary operating costs.
- Child care expenses in 1987 of up to $2,000 per child under fourteen at any time during the year (unless the child is mentally or physically infirm) can be claimed by the parent with the lower net income in the year, provided the child care services are required to allow this parent to earn income from employment, self-employment, training courses or research. The deduction cannot exceed two-thirds of the earned income, and the maximum $2,000 deduction cannot be claimed for more than four children. In 1988, the deduction for child care expenses will be doubled to $4,000 for children aged six and under and for older children with special needs. The deduction remains at $2,000 for children aged seven to fourteen but the total limit of $8,000 per family is being removed to ensure fair treatment for larger families.
- There are substantially different rules governing the deduction of child care expenses for Quebec tax purposes. In 1987, the maximum claim is $3,640 ($3,770 in 1988) for a child under six and $1,820 ($1,885 in 1988) for other eligible children.
- Allowable business investment losses. These are two-thirds of the losses on the disposition of
  - shares or certain debt of a Canadian-controlled private company (CCPC) carrying on an active business in Canada sold to a person with whom you deal at "arm's length", or
  - certain debts of a CCPC carrying on an active business in Canada established to be bad debts and certain shares of a bankrupt or wound-up CCPC.

This loss is generally calculated in the same way as other allowable capital losses, in that only two-thirds of the loss can be claimed for tax purposes. Unlike other capital losses, however, the allowable portion of a business investment loss may be deducted without limit against income from all sources.

Allowable business investment losses claimed after 1984 will reduce the amount of available capital gains exemption. Starting in 1986, these losses will be treated as ordinary capital losses (not deductible against other sources of income) to the extent that a capital gains exemption has been claimed in previous years.

- Other deductions from total income include:
  - periodic alimony or maintenance payments pursuant to a decree, order, judgement or written agreement.
  - expenses to move within Canada to a new home at least 40 kilometres closer than your previous home to your new work location (applicable to both

employees and self-employed persons), but only to the extent of earnings from your new work location.

- Students may also claim expenses to move to a job (including a summer job) or to start a business, but only to the extent of earnings from the job or business. Students who incur moving expenses to attend full-time courses at a post-secondary school may also claim these expenses, but only to the extent of any scholarship, research grant or similar award income from the school.

- Interest paid on money borrowed to earn investment or business income is generally deductible. Contrary to many people's predictions, tax reform did not contain any proposals to directly limit interest deductibility. However, the new investment loss rules described in Chapter 7 may reduce the capital gains exemption you can claim on capital gains you realize after 1987, if you are deducting interest expense that is higher than your investment income.

If you have outstanding debts on which the interest is non-deductible, it may be possible to convert the non-deductible interest into deductible interest in respect of investments. If, for example, you have an outstanding mortgage of $50,000 on your home and you hold $20,000 of Canada Savings Bonds, you should consider cashing the bonds, reducing your mortgage and then, if you wish, borrowing the necessary funds (interest deductible) to reinvest in some form of income-producing securities. Even if you decide not to borrow for reinvestment, you will be ahead of the game because the rate of non-deductible interest payable on your mortgage is almost certain to be higher than the after-tax rate of return on your investments.

If you are paying a substantial amount of tax-deductible interest, you can apply to your local district taxation office to reduce the amount of tax withheld from your paycheque. You will have to demonstrate that the taxes being withheld by your employer will significantly exceed your total tax liability for the year, when your interest deduction is taken into account. Revenue Canada will then provide your employer with permission to reduce your tax deductions accordingly. As a result, you will have extra money each month to pay your interest charges or to use for other investments, instead of waiting until after you file your tax return the following spring to receive your tax refund. You can also apply for permission to reduce tax deducted from employment earnings where you have other large tax deductions like alimony or deductions resulting from tax shelter investments.

- Other carrying charges or costs of holding investments which can be deducted include safety deposit box charges, investment counsel fees, accounting fees for recording investment income, and fees for the management or safe custody of investments.

Quebec Stock Savings Plan

The *Quebec Taxation Act* permits Quebec residents to claim a deduction from income of the cost of eligible shares contributed to a Quebec Stock Savings Plan (QSSP). A QSSP is established and administered by a registered broker or other financial institution that retains custody of share certificates contributed to the plan. Only newly-issued shares of public corporations are eligible for inclusion in a QSSP—either common shares, or non-redeemable preferred shares that are convertible into common shares.

In 1987, a Quebec taxpayer will be entitled to deduct the lesser of $5,500 or 10% of his total income, less 150% of the cost of Fonds de Solidarité des Travailleurs du Québec (FTQ) shares, without reduction for any contributions to an RRSP or registered pension plan.

If the taxpayer does not hold the shares (or other eligible investments substituted for them) in the QSSP for at least two complete years following the year of contribution, an amount equal to the cost of the shares withdrawn from the plan will be included in income in the year of withdrawal.

The deduction to be claimed by the taxpayer varies, depending on the nature of the corporation whose shares are being contributed to the QSSP and the type of share issued. For example, in 1987 if the corporation is a developing one—one with assets between $2 million and $25 million, or net shareholders' equity between $750,000 and $10 million—its common shares with full voting rights contributed to a QSSP qualify for a deduction equal to 100 percent of their purchase price. In contrast, shares issued by large corporations (assets of $250 million or more) qualify for only a 50 percent deduction in 1987 with a maximum annual deduction of $1,000; shares of other corporations entitle the investor to a deduction ranging from 50 to 100 percent of their cost.

Contributions to a QSSP are deductible from income for Quebec tax purposes only, and dividend income received on shares included in a QSSP is taxable to the investor. By comparison, contributions to a registered pension plan or RRSP are deductible from income for both federal and Quebec purposes, and income earned in these plans accumulates tax-free until termination of the plan. Accordingly, although shares held in a QSSP can be withdrawn without tax consequences after the required two-year period (achieving a permanent savings), Quebec taxpayers should consider the alternative of obtaining a greater immediate tax deferral (both federal and provincial) by contributing the maximum allowable amount to their registered pension plan or RRSP, as the case may be, before applying any available excess to the purchase of an investment in a QSSP.

Other Provincial Stock Savings Plans

Several provinces have introduced or are considering the introduction of stock savings plans to provide incentives for direct equity investment in a broad range of corporations. Many of the basic features of the Quebec Stock Savings Plan, in effect since 1979, have been adopted in these new plans.

The plans provide for a tax credit to be allowed against provincial taxes payable, equal to a specified percentage of the taxpayer's cost of eligible shares. The shares must be newly-issued common voting shares (or in some cases, non-redeemable preferred shares convertible to common at the holder's option) of corporations that operate through a permanent establishment in the province and pay a specified portion (at least twenty-five percent, under the Alberta, Saskatchewan and Ontario plans) of their total wage and salary expense in the province.

The shares must be contributed to a special plan, administered by an approved trustee. The shares (or eligible substitutes) must be held for at least two years following the year of purchase, or the credit must be repaid. Shares qualifying for any other provincial or federal tax deduction or credit are not eligible under these programmes.

The Alberta Stock Savings Plan and the Saskatchewan Stock Savings Plan, which came into force in 1986, offer tax credits of up to thirty percent for emerging companies, decreasing to fifteen or ten percent for companies with larger revenue or asset bases. The yearly maximum tax credit is $3,000, but excess or unused credits may be carried forward.

Nova Scotia has a stock savings plan similar to that in Alberta and Saskatchewan, that should be under way in 1988.

Venture Capital Programmes

To stimulate the supply of venture capital for small businesses, several provinces have enacted special incentive legislation, which apply to new corporations created to provide equity capital and management expertise to small businesses.

At present, such programmes exist in British Columbia, Alberta, Saskatchewan, Quebec and Ontario. Although the specifics of the programmes vary from province to province, generally the venture capital corporation may acquire up to fifty percent of the equity shares of a small business engaged in an approved activity, such as manufacturing and processing, research and development, tourism or various service industries. To qualify, the small business must carry on all or most of its operations in the particular province. The incentive to the person investing in a venture capital corporation is that purchasing newly issued shares in the corporation results in a grant from the province (in Ontario and Alberta), a credit against provincial income taxes (in Saskatchewan and British Columbia), or a deduction from income (Quebec). The grant or credit is equal to thirty percent of the taxpayer's cost of the investment, for the programmes in British Columbia, Alberta, Saskatchewan and certain regions of northern and eastern Ontario. For other areas in Ontario, the former thirty percent rate was reduced to twenty-five percent for shares issued after October 24, 1985. The deduction available to Quebec investors is 100 percent of the cost of the shares purchased, but not exceeding twenty percent of total income.

For tax purposes, the grants or tax credits received by the investor are not taxable and will not reduce the cost base of the shares in calculating any capital gain realized on subsequent resale (but will restrict the deduction for any capital loss incurred).

The incentive for investing in a venture capital corporation is obvious, but it must be recognized that some investment risk is involved because the corporation is required to use most of its capital to invest in equity shares of small developing businesses.

Tax Credits

By subtracting the deductions outlined above from total income, you establish the amount of your taxable income. Then you use the appropriate tax rate schedule to establish the gross tax payable on your taxable income. Once the gross tax payable has been computed, tax credits are subtracted to determine net tax payable. A schedule is included in Appendix III to help you calculate your net tax payable after deducting tax credits.

In the past, the number of tax credits available under the Canadian income tax system has been quite limited. This is not the case after tax reform.

Personal Tax Credits

A central feature of tax reform was the conversion of personal exemptions into personal tax credits in 1988 and future years. Exemptions are deducted in calculating taxable income and are more valuable as your income and tax rate rises. Tax credits, in contrast, reduce taxes payable to the same extent for all taxpayers, regardless of their income level. With the move to tax credits, the tax value of personal exemptions will be reduced for middle- and higher-income Canadians and increased for lower-income Canadians.

Following is a table of the new personal tax credit system:

	1988 Federal Tax Credit	Approximate Federal and Provincial Value of Tax Credit, *Including Federal Surtax
	($)	($)
Basic	1,020	1,561
Married and equivalent to married	850	1,301
Dependants under 19 (1st and 2nd child)	65	100
(3rd and each subsequent child)	130	200
Dependants 19 and over		
—infirm	250	383
—other	NIL	NIL
Age 65 and over (transferable)	550	842
Disability (transferable)	550	842

*Assumes average provincial tax rate of fifty percent of basic federal tax.

These new tax credits will be indexed to the annual increases in the Consumer Price Index over three percent starting in 1989.

If you claim the married or equivalent to married federal credit, the credit will be reduced by seventeen percent of your spouse's or dependant's net income over $500. Any other credit claimed for a dependant will be reduced by the dependant's net income over $2,500.

The unused portion of any of these new credits will not be refunded if you otherwise have no tax to pay. The unused portion of the age credit can be transferred to your spouse, and the disability credit to your spouse or a supporting parent or grandparent. The amount of the federal tax credits that can be transferred will be reduced by seventeen percent of your net income over $6,000.

After 1987, there will no longer be a deduction for dependent children over eighteen, unless they are infirm. Along the same lines, the availability of the equivalent to married credit will be tightened to exclude dependent children unless they are under nineteen or are infirm.

To be eligible for the equivalent to married credit, you must be single, divorced, separated or widowed and must, by yourself or jointly with another, maintain a self-contained domestic establishment in which you live and support a person resident in Canada who, during the year, is wholly dependent on you for support and who is connected by blood relationship, marriage or adoption. In the case of a child, however, it is not necessary that the child reside in Canada.

Other New Credits After Tax Reform

Other tax deductions that were available in 1987 and earlier years were also converted in 1988 to federal tax credits at a rate of seventeen percent, as outlined in the table below. Taxpayers at all income levels receive the same tax relief from these deductions after 1987.

If your taxable income is below $27,500, the credit will equal the tax reduction you would have realized from the exemption under the old system, because your federal tax rate in 1988 will be seventeen percent. However, if your taxable income is higher than $27,500, the new credit system will reduce your tax savings from these deductions.

	1988 Federal Tax Credit
Pension Income	Seventeen percent of eligible pension income, maximum $170. Unused credit transferable to spouse.
Tuition Fees	Seventeen percent for post-secondary fees; up to $600 transferable to spouse or supporting parent or grandparent.
Education	$10 credit for each month in full-time attendance; transferable as part of the $600 limit for tuition fees.
Medical Expenses	Credit of seventeen percent for uninsured medical expenses in excess of three percent of net income.
CPP/QPP and UI Premiums (employee share)	Credit at seventeen percent.

The definition of eligible pension income has not changed. For taxpayers sixty-five and over, eligible pension income includes annuity payments from a pension plan (except amounts transferred into an RRSP or registered pension plan), as well as annuity payments out of an RRSP or a deferred profit sharing plan, payments under a registered retirement income fund, and amounts included in income for certain other annuities.

For individuals under sixty-five, eligible pension income includes annuity payments from a pension plan and certain other payments received as a result of the death of a spouse.

For persons under sixty, the sixty to sixty-five rules apply with one further restriction: no credit may be claimed if, for the same year, you deduct any amount for a rollover contribution of pension benefits to another pension plan or RRSP.

The tuition credit will apply to tuition fees (but not books or other expenses) greater than $100 paid to a post-secondary educational institution in Canada (or outside Canada, in limited circumstances). Tuition fees can be claimed for any twelve month period starting in the year, and can be claimed on a calendar or academic year basis. Students will be able to claim a seventeen percent credit on eligible tuition fees without limit plus the $10 credit for each month of full-time attendance.

Where a student does not owe enough tax to make full use of these credits, the unused portion is not refundable, but can be transferred to a spouse or supporting parent or grandparent to a maximum of $600 less the amount used by the student to offset taxes owing.

The seventeen percent federal credit can be claimed for medical expenses (excluding non-prescription drugs and provincial health care premiums) paid for yourself, your spouse or any dependants claimed in your tax return, to the extent they exceed three percent of your net income.

Political Contributions

A credit of up to $500 (seventy-five percent of first $100, fifty percent of next $450, and 33⅓% of any excess) is available for contributions to registered federal political parties or candidates for election to the House of Commons. Depending on your province of residence, you may be eligible for a similar credit or a deduction for contributions to provincial parties or candidates in provincial elections. There is no credit or deduction available for contributions to candidates in civic elections.

Child Tax Credit

Child tax credits of up to $489 in 1987 ($559 in 1988) per child under eighteen are available to lower income Canadian families. The child tax credit available for children aged six and under or seven to fourteen with special needs will be increased by $100 in 1988 and $200 in 1989 and subsequent years for parents who care for their children at home or who do not claim a deduction for child care expenses. This credit is reduced by $5 for every $100 of net income of the supporting parents over a threshold amount of approximately $24,000. Both the child tax credit and the federal sales tax credit described below are fully refundable to the extent they are not required to reduce taxes payable. Contrast this with the new credits introduced under tax reform which are not refundable and are only transferable in limited circumstances to other family members.

Business Investment Tax Credit

Both corporate and individual taxpayers are eligible for investment tax credits in 1988 of between three and sixty percent of the cost of new buildings or machinery used in Canada in qualifying activities such as manufacturing, farming, fishing, logging, construction and scientific research. The amount of the credit depends on the location of the equipment. Higher rates generally apply for assets used in scientific research compared to other qualifying activities, and for assets used in designated areas such as the Atlantic region. The credit reduces the amount of federal tax otherwise payable, but also reduces the cost of the asset which can be deducted over time as capital cost allowance.

Foreign Tax Credit

You may claim a credit for income taxes paid to foreign countries. The credit is limited to the amount of Canadian tax due on income from the foreign country. For foreign taxes paid on investment income, you can also deduct any excess foreign taxes which do not qualify as a credit.

Federal Sales Tax Credit

This credit was introduced in 1986 to assist lower-income families. In 1988, the credit provides up to $70 for each adult and $35 for each child. It is paid in full to individuals whose family net income is less than $16,000 and is refundable to families who pay no federal income tax. The credit is reduced by $5 for every $100 of family net income in excess of $16,000.

Dividend Tax Credit

A commonly encountered credit is the dividend tax credit. As explained earlier in this chapter, a grossed-up amount (133⅓ percent in 1987, 125 percent in 1988) of dividends received from Canadian companies is included in taxable income, but a credit is then allowed against the resulting taxes payable. As a result, the net tax rate on Canadian dividend income is lower than that on many other types of investment income.

7

WHERE AND HOW TAXES ARE SAVED: Tax-Sheltered Investments

Another traditionally important tax-saving technique involves investing in tax-sheltered investments. Simply put, a good tax shelter enables you to use dollars that you would otherwise pay in taxes (along with some of your own investment dollars) to acquire investments that will increase your net worth.

Investment in tax shelters was a very popular way of reducing tax in the 1970s. But many of these tax shelter deals turned out to be poor investments and sometimes the promised tax savings were not accepted by Revenue Canada. As a consequence, tax shelters generally have a tarnished image in Canada and are usually approached warily by investors in the 1980s. In addition, the *Income Tax Act* has restricted the deductibility of costs related to tax shelter investments, and has actually eliminated certain types of tax shelters. Therefore, tax-sheltered investments are not as important in personal tax planning as they once were.

Most tax shelters are a means of deferring, not eliminating, taxes. Most, if not all, tax shelters are characterized by leverage and the availability of deductions that require no investor cash to obtain.

LEVERAGE

Leverage is a term used to describe a situation in which you control a large investment with a relatively small amount of your own money. The rest is financed with somebody else's money, and this will give you interest deductions. But leverage increases risk.

To illustrate, assume you invest in a $100,000 two-bedroom condominium for rental purposes. You make a $20,000 down payment and get a five-year loan from the seller at 10.5% a year for the remaining $80,000. The seller allows you to make payments on the loan using an amortization schedule of thirty years, but expects you to pay off the remaining balance on the loan at the end of five years. After three years, you resell this condo for $120,000 (net of selling expenses). Your annual payments on the $80,000 loan are about $8,800. After three years, you've paid off about $1,000 on the loan. Assuming that the rental income you received on the condo has covered your interest payments on the loan, then your total outlay has been $21,000 (the down payment plus the principal payments), but your gain before taxes would be about $20,000. That's a profit of almost 95 percent in only three years. If you had paid $100,000 cash down, your gain would still have been $20,000 or twenty percent. Note, however, that instead of using your rental income for interest payments, you would have received significant cash amounts each year, and these would increase your rate of return.

However, leverage also increases risk, as some real estate speculators found out when real estate prices softened in recent years. Using the same condo example, let's assume that you can't sell your condo after three years for as much as you paid for it, so to pay off the loan balance of $79,000 you have to sell it for $90,000. Now you have lost $10,000. Since you invested $21,000 that is a loss of about forty-eight percent. If you had paid the $100,000 in cash, your loss would have been a mere ten percent.

DEDUCTIONS

One attractive feature of tax shelters is that they provide you with deductions without requiring any cash contributions on your part (because assets are being purchased with borrowed funds). Tax shelters normally provide one of the following deductions:

Capital Cost Allowance

This is the deduction of the capital cost of equipment or a building over a period which may be shorter than its estimated useful life. In the case of manufacturing equipment purchased before 1988, the deduction period is three years; for other equipment the deduction period is much longer, and buildings are generally depreciated on a five percent declining basis (2½% in the first year).

Tax reform included changes to the CCA rates for various classes of assets acquired after 1987. For example, manufacturing equipment acquired after 1987 can only be depreciated for tax purposes on a twenty-five percent declining balance basis (12½% in the first year). This reduction will be phased in gradually between 1988 and 1991. Buildings acquired after 1987 can only be depreciated on a four percent declining balance basis (two percent in the first year).

These rate reductions are intended to make CCA rates more comparable with actual depreciation in the value of assets, to remove the tax incentive which can affect investment decisions. A comparison of the present value of manufacturing equipment CCA under the pre-1988 and the current system shows a ten percent reduction in the value of the CCA claim. A $1,000 expenditure under the pre-1988 system provides benefits of approximately $400 which reduce to about $300 after tax reform.

Natural Resources Exploration and Development Deductions

Investors in natural resources (mining and energy) exploration and development pro-grammes are allowed various write-offs for expenditures incurred. The timing of the write-offs depends on the nature of the expenditures, which range from Canadian exploration expenses (100 percent write-off available in the first year) to Canadian development expenses (written off on a thirty percent declining balance basis) to

Canadian oil and gas property expenses and foreign exploration and development expenses (ten percent declining balance basis). These deductions are not changed under tax reform.

Depletion

Investors may also be entitled to an additional depletion allowance over and above the deductions described above, for certain qualified activities (for example, mining exploration). For federal and provincial purposes, this earned depletion allowance has been $33\frac{1}{3}\%$ of the cost of qualified activities. Under tax reform, earned depletion allowances are to be phased out by reducing the rate from $33\frac{1}{3}\%$ to $16\frac{2}{3}\%$ for eligible expenditures incurred after 30 June 1988 and by eliminating it completely for expenditures made after 31 December 1989, except for certain expenditures made in the first sixty days of 1990.

Scientific Research and Development Deductions

Direct investors in scientific research programmes and partnerships can deduct current or capital expenditures on qualified research undertaken in the year, except for most expenditures on building acquisitions and rental payments for buildings after 1987.

In addition, interest paid on the money borrowed to finance all of the above expenditures will be deductible.

INVESTMENT TAX CREDIT

This is a dollar-for-dollar reduction of taxes due. The investment tax credit can amount to as much as sixty percent of the cost of new equipment or scientific research expenditures used in qualifying activities (see Chapter 6) to produce income. Tax credits are more valuable than tax deductions. A deductible dollar reduces your taxable income by one dollar. A dollar of tax credit reduces your taxes by one dollar. Say you have taxable income of $60,000 and are considering a tax-sheltered investment. You are considering one investment that provides current year deductions of $5,000 and another investment that provides current year deductions of $3,000 and tax credits of $2,000. Which investment is best from a tax standpoint in the current year? The analysis below will help answer the question.

	Investment #1	Investment #2
Taxable income before tax-sheltered investment	$60,000	$60,000
Deductions	(5,000)	(3,000)
Taxable income after investment	55,000	57,000
Tax on taxable income (using 1987 rates for an Ontario resident)	20,247	21,175
Credit against tax	—	(2,000)
Net Tax Due	$20,247	$19,175

But as a result of changes introduced in the 1986 budget, investment tax credits will be a less important feature of tax shelters in the future. Beginning in 1987, the existing rates for many types of investment tax credits will be phased out over three years.

DEFERRAL OF TAXES

Most tax shelters do not eliminate taxes; they simply defer them to a later period. The tax deferral created by claiming tax losses in earlier years and recognizing the income in later years may have varying results:

- It may be a simple deferral of tax that gives the investor the benefit of using the tax dollars for a period of years before repaying them without interest.
- The deductions may be taken when your tax rate is high (or low), and when the income is recognized your tax rate may be low (or high). Depending on your circumstances, this could be either to your advantage or to your disadvantage. You should therefore know what your tax bracket is at the time you invest in a tax shelter and what it will be at the time you plan to dispose of the investment.
- In some limited instances, the losses claimed by the investor may later have to be included in income, but at the favourable capital gain rates.

UNFAVOURABLE TAX CONSEQUENCES

Tax-sheltered investments have "tax goodies." They also have some "tax gotchas." The "tax gotchas" include the at-risk rules, the alternative minimum tax, and the new net investment loss rules. These are discussed in the following paragraphs.

The At-Risk Rules

In the past, many tax shelters were structured as highly leveraged limited partnerships. In some cases, a substantial portion of the investment was financed with funds for which the borrower had no personal liability (non-recourse debt), and investors claimed deductions for expenses that they might never be called on to pay.

In response to such situations, new "at-risk" rules were introduced in the 1986 budget to strengthen Revenue Canada's ability to deny such deductions. Under these rules, an investor in a limited partnership tax shelter can only deduct business losses or claim investment tax credits that exceed the amount of his at-risk investment in the partnership. Generally speaking, the at-risk amount is calculated as the adjusted base cost of the partnership interest, plus the current year's income, less certain amounts owing by the investor to the partnership. As well, the at-risk amount is reduced by investment tax credits allocated to the investor.

Minimum Tax

The alternative minimum tax (AMT) was introduced in 1986. The government was concerned that some taxpayers with large incomes were able to avoid paying part or all of their income tax. Part of this avoidance was being accomplished legally through tax-favoured or tax-sheltered investments. The government felt that this was unfair and that no one should be permitted to avoid his or her fair share of the tax burden.

All higher-income Canadians are potentially subject to this tax, although it actually only affects a relatively small group of taxpayers. The minimum tax is most likely to affect taxpayers who have contributed large amounts (for example, a retiring allowance) to an RRSP, those who have made substantial tax-sheltered investments or those who have realized significant capital gains in the year.

In order to determine whether you must pay a minimum tax over and above the taxes you would otherwise pay, you must recalculate your net income (line 3 on Form 11) for the year to include or exclude certain items which the government feels can be used to unfairly reduce taxes. Accordingly, net income is recalculated to deny tax-shelter deductions such as losses arising from Canadian exploration expenses, Canadian development expenses and depletion deductions, and capital cost allowance claims on multiple-unit residential buildings or Canadian films. Deductions for contributions to an RRSP or a registered pension plan must be added back to net income as well. Adjustments are also necessary for tax-favoured income. The untaxed portion of net capital gains for the year, less the amount of capital gains exemption claimed, is included in adjusted net income.

This adjusted net income amount is then reduced by any non-capital or capital losses of other years deducted from ordinary net income. Adjusted net income can also be reduced to delete the grossed-up portion (i.e. $33\frac{1}{3}\%$ in 1987, 25% in 1988) of any dividends received from Canadian companies, so that only the actual amount of dividends received are potentially subject to the minimum tax. (Your net income may also be adjusted for less common items than the ones just described.)

This amount is then further reduced by $40,000; the remaining amount, if any, will be subject to a federal minimum tax of seventeen percent plus a provincial tax of about nine percent. The actual provincial tax rate varies depending on the province in which you live. This minimum tax amount is then reduced by the personal tax credits you are entitled to (as described in Chapter 6) plus other tax credits for charitable donations, tuition fees, and so on. You are required to pay the higher of the two taxes, so that you either pay on your unadjusted taxable income or you pay the minimum tax, calculated as above.

Where the minimum tax does apply, the extra tax paid can be carried forward for up to seven years to reduce future income taxes, to the extent that regular tax in that year exceeds the minimum tax.

The above is a simplified (believe it or not!) version of the minimum tax rules. It is not possible to briefly deal with all the circumstances in which this tax may apply. This potential additional tax cost should certainly be considered by anyone thinking of investing in a tax shelter or anyone who has already made substantial tax-sheltered investments. It will also be an important consideration for anyone with significant realized or expected capital gains, whether or not exempt under the lifetime capital gains exemption. But for the average taxpayer, whose major income source is salary or business earnings, and who does not have any large deductions, the minimum tax should not apply.

The Quebec government also imposes a minimum on provincial tax paid by Quebec residents. The Quebec minimum tax rules are substantially the same as those introduced by the federal government.

Net Investment Loss Rules

Tax reform introduced the concept of a cumulative *net investment loss*. These new rules will restrict your ability to claim the capital gains exemption in 1988 and future years to the extent you have claimed a cumulative net investment loss.

Your cumulative net investment loss account will be investment expenses deducted after 1987 minus investment income earned in the same period. Investment income includes interest, taxable dividends, rental income from real property and other income from property or a business in which you are not actively involved. Investment expenses include one-half of resource deductions other than earned depletion from flow-through shares or a limited partnership, rental losses from real property, business losses, including interest expense, where you are not actively involved in the business, and carrying charges of investments, including interest expense.

These rules do not match the investment expenses of a particular investment with the gain on the investment. If you realize a gain on an investment for which you have not incurred any expenses, you will not be able to claim an exemption on this gain, to the extent your cumulative investment expenses exceed your cumulative investment income. For example, if you realize a capital gain in January 1988, your capital gains exemption will be reduced by any carrying charges incurred in 1988 even if these are incurred after the sale on other investments.

ECONOMIC SUBSTANCE

An investor needs to analyze any prospective tax shelter from an economic viewpoint. The potential profit should be commensurate with the risk involved. If an investment fails economically, you are probably going to lose money in real dollars, and consequently it does not make much sense to go into it only for tax reasons.

Unfortunately, many individuals are lured into "investments" by tax shelter promoters who promise large tax savings. Upon analysis, many shelters with promises of large tax savings may turn out to have very little economic potential and a very aggressive interpretation of tax laws. The promised deductions may be challenged and disallowed by Revenue Canada, or the tax shelter itself may even be considered a fraud, which will cause you more problems. Take care, therefore, to evaluate the economic substance of any tax shelter. Get a prospectus, read it, have your questions and concerns answered to your satisfaction. Check on the reliability, reputation, and track record of the promoter, and apply the following tests, adapted from an article in *Medical Economics.**

1. Why is the tax shelter promoter contacting you? Is it based on a long-standing business relationship, or is it an unknown phone call promotion for an out-of-country orange-growing project? Perhaps the promoter has run out of close contacts who trust his projects.
2. What's the track record of the tax shelter manager? Has he or she compiled a successful track record in substantially similar projects? Tax shelters have some common characteristics, but they are worlds apart in most business aspects. A specialist in rental properties may know very little about oil-drilling ventures.
3. Can you read the prospectus without raising your eyebrows? See what the general partner in the deal is taking out. How much of your money will actually go to the proposed project rather than into the promoter's pocket through commissions and management and acquisition fees? If much less than eighty-five cents of every investment dollar is going to the project, be skeptical. The more money the promoters skim off the top in fees, commissions, and promotion costs, the smaller the part of your investment that will actually be working for you.
4. Is there a clear profit motive in the deal? Revenue Canada policy toward tax shelters can be summed up in two words: economic reality. This means that a shelter should be structured as parliament intended—to encourage investment in a risky but potentially profitable business venture. If a venture has little chance of making a profit, Revenue Canada may say that its true purpose is only to avoid taxes.
5. What do tax advisors think? After you have done the initial research on a tax-sheltered investment possibility, get backup advice from a lawyer or tax expert whom you trust—and one whose specialty is the field you're interested in. Get advice on the economic substance of the investment and the credibility of the tax benefits. This advice may cost you several hundred dollars in fees paid to the expert, but may save you a bundle later on.
6. Is there a better way? After you have checked out the risks and rewards, and if

---

* "Tax Shelters—Seven Tests Any Deal Should Pass." *Medical Economics*, March 31, 1980.

the tax shelter still looks like a good bet, ask yourself whether there isn't some other way to shave your tax bill just as much without the risk of a tax shelter— with an RRSP, or by investing in Canadian equities to receive tax-favoured dividends or tax-free gains.

TYPES OF TAX SHELTERS

As you study the tax shelters described below, keep in mind that each type of investment has its own range of economic risk. The following comments relate solely to the tax issues and do not deal with investment potential or provide a risk analysis.

Rental Real Estate

In the past, rental real estate, particularly multiple-unit residential buildings (MURBs) were a popular form of tax shelter. MURBs (certified as such by Canada Mortgage and Housing Corporation) were more attractive from an income tax standpoint than other rental real estate because the maximum available capital cost allowance (generally five percent of the declining balance cost of the building) could be deducted even if it created a rental loss. Capital cost allowance on other rental real estate is generally limited to an amount that will reduce net rental income to nil after first claiming all other deductible expenses such as interest, property taxes, insurance, repairs. Tax reform contained several changes that will reduce the tax incentives for rental real estate after 1987. The ability to deduct rental losses created by claiming capital cost allowance on MURBs will be eliminated. If you are the owner of a MURB bought before 18 June 1987, it will be treated in the same manner as any other rental property after 1993—that is, you will no longer be able to deduct a rental loss created by claiming capital cost allowance. If you buy an existing MURB after 18 June 1987, you will not be able to claim a loss from capital cost allowance in any year.

Tax reform will also reduce the capital cost allowance rate on buildings bought after 1987 to four percent from five percent.

The deduction of so-called soft costs, including interest during the construction period, financing fees, landscaping, and rental guarantees, has also attracted investors in the past who are looking for tax shelter. The deduction of these costs have been significantly restricted in recent years. For example, most soft costs (particularly interest expense) incurred before or during the construction, renovation or alteration of a building are no longer deductible. Instead, these expenses must be added to the cost either of the land or the building, with the cost of the building then being eligible for capital cost allowance. As a result, what was once an immediate deduction has now been limited to a deduction of five percent (or four percent, for buildings bought after 1987) a year on a declining balance basis.

In addition, the maximum capital cost allowance claim permitted in the year of purchase of any assets, including rental buildings, is limited to one-half of the normal annual rate.

Hotels, motels, retirement homes, recreational vehicles, etc.

Investments in these properties may seem to be unlikely ways to shelter income from tax, but these investments have been a popular form of tax shelter in recent years for high-income taxpayers, even though the investors may have little knowledge of the particular industry.

Typically, a group of investors would buy the property with the down payment largely financed by a bank loan and the balance of the purchase price represented by a longer-term mortgage. A professional manager and staff would usually be hired to operate the business.

Until recently, these investments offered good tax shelter advantages. Capital cost allowance could be claimed at relatively high rates on the various classes of assets (even with the rule that now permits only one-half the normal allowance in the year of acquisition) so that business losses for tax purposes often resulted in the early years of operation. Each partner could then deduct his share of these losses and the resulting tax savings were often sufficient to repay the initial borrowings in a few years.

The government considered such arrangements to be abusive, with overly generous tax treatment. As a result, the *Income Tax Act* has been amended to limit the ability to shelter other income with losses created by capital cost allowance on property used in businesses that offer services combined with the use of that property. In effect, income from such property is to be treated as rental income and capital cost allowance claims will be limited to an amount that reduces net income to nil. These rules apply, unless the investors are personally active in the daily business operations.

Where available capital cost allowance is a key factor in the decision to make a tax shelter investment, investigate thoroughly to ensure that these restrictions do not apply. Such investments should be evaluated as normal business investments rather than as conventional tax shelters, as no shelter is generally provided against other income except to the extent of any actual operating losses excluding capital cost allowance. As well, existing shelters of this type will be affected indirectly by tax reform: the lower tax rates after 1987 will reduce the value of any write-off (thereby increasing the after-tax cost of the investment) and any tax write-offs in excess of income earned will be included in the net investment loss calculation.

Natural Resource Investments

There always seems to be interest in oil, gas or mining investments that offer tax shelter opportunities. One of the most common forms of such investments has been the limited partnership, where the general partner is the operator of the project and the investors are limited partners (with limited legal responsibility for partnership debts). At the end of each year, the limited partners are provided with a statement showing their share of the year's income, the amounts of exploration and development expenses incurred by the partnership during the year and any special deductions such as the amount of oil and gas property expense. This information is then included in the investor's tax return for the year.

Before tax reform, the at-risk rules did not apply directly to deductions for resource expenses or certain losses flowed out to partners. However, these expenses did reduce the adjusted cost base of the partnership interest, which could limit claims for investment tax credits and business losses. The at-risk rules have been extended to most resource expenditures incurred by partnerships after 17 June 1987.

Another popular form of tax-sheltered natural resources investment is the so-called "flow-through" share. The investors purchase newly issued shares of a company which uses the funds for exploration. Instead of the company claiming the tax deduction that it would otherwise be entitled to for the exploration costs, these deductions "flow through" to the investor, who may also be entitled to an additional depletion allowance in the case of qualified exploration. The investor recoups a substantial part of his investment in the short term through current tax savings, and thus has purchased an investment in the natural resources company at a reduced cost. When he eventually sells these shares, the entire proceeds will normally be taxed as a capital gain, which may be tax-free to the extent that the investor has not used his lifetime capital gains exemption. The new net investment loss rules will significantly reduce the attractions of flow-through shares for many investors. If you invest in flow-through shares and claim the resource deductions after 1987, you will not be able to realize a completely tax-free gain after 1987 on their sale by claiming the capital gains exemption, unless you have other investment income to offset one-half of the resource deductions (other than depletion) claimed.

Scientific Research and Development Funds

Investments in qualified scientific research and development projects can provide significant tax benefits—a 100 percent write-off for qualifying current and capital expenditures and investment tax credits ranging from twenty to thirty-five percent. As a result, these projects have often been financed as tax shelter vehicles.

A common form of financing is the limited partnership, as already described in *Natural Resource Investments*. At the end of each year, the limited partners are entitled to their share of the income, deductions and tax credits associated with the operations of the partnership for the year, subject to the at-risk rules described earlier.

An extremely popular form of tax shelter financing for research and development projects in recent years was the scientific research tax credit. Because of abuses by some issuers of these credits, this form of investment is no longer available.

Films

Before tax reform, one of the main tax incentives for investing in a certified Canadian feature film or videotape was that the entire cost of the investment could be deducted as capital cost allowance over two years. The capital cost allowance could be deducted against any other income thus providing significant tax deferral opportunities. As well, as little as five percent of the purchase price could be paid in cash at the time of purchase with the balance paid within four years. For example, you could buy a $100,000 Canadian film interest for a $5,000 cash payment resulting in tax savings of approximately $50,000 over a two year period.

Under tax reform, the ability to shelter non-film income through capital cost allowance claims on certified productions is significantly curtailed. The capital cost allowance on such films is reduced from a two-year write-off to an annual deduction of thirty percent on a declining balance basis. Any film loss resulting from the claim of this reduced level of depreciation will continue to be available as a tax shelter for income from all other sources. An additional capital cost allowance claim for the unclaimed cost of the film will be available to the extent you have any film income in the year.

FORM 12—YOUR TAX-SAVING IDEAS

Now that you know how taxes can be saved and you have a targeted taxable income on Form 11, which you completed before, fill in Form 12. Then take *action*. You may want to discuss your tax-saving ideas with a tax advisor. You will probably make best use of your advisor's time by first doing your homework on Forms 11 and 12. Figure 7-1 shows you a sample of a filled-in form related to the sample shown in Form 11 in Chapter 5.

- Many tax-saving ideas, once implemented, have a multi-year impact. For example, when you purchase real estate for rental purposes, capital cost allowance and interest deductions are predictable for many years according to a capital cost allowance schedule and a loan repayment schedule.
- You may need significant resources to implement some tax-saving ideas. For example, to purchase rental real estate you may need a substantial down payment. Other tax-saving ideas may require the sale of existing investment assets or borrowing against these assets.
- Prepayment of planned multi-year tax-deductible expenditures such as large charitable contributions is a very good idea when your top tax rate will decrease over the next few years.
- The earlier you implement your tax-saving ideas, the better. The later it is in the year, the harder it is to reduce your taxable income without making riskier investments.

FIGURE 7-1

File under TAX PLANNING   Date: _April 28_

FORM 12   TAX-SAVING IDEAS

TAX-SAVING IDEA

Tax-Free Income: _Shift $10,000 into equities (growth oriented mutual fund) to take advantage of capital gains exemption._

Tax-Favoured Income: _Borrow $10,000 to invest in dividend paying Canadian stock_

Tax-Deferred Income: _Continue maximum contribution to RRSP_

Tax-Sheltered Income: _Borrow $5000 to invest in flow-through shares_

Shifting Income to Dependants: _Set up a registered education savings plan for my son ($10,000)_

Tax-Deductible Expenditures: _Increase amount of interest paid which is tax-deductible (ie. investment loans) while decreasing personal loan interest_

Action	Action Date	Funds Needed	Reduction of Taxable Income	
Tax-Free Income	_June 30_	_None - use existing assets_	_($1,000)_	
Tax-Favoured Income	_June 30_	_$10,000_	_—_	_gross amount of dividends will approx. equal interest expense but will generate tax credit of approx $350_
Tax-Deferred Income	_Feb. 28_ _(or earlier if possible)_	_$7,500_	_Already in Schedule 11_	
Tax-Sheltered Investments	_June 30_	_$5,000_	_($5,500)_	_including interest deduction_

FIGURE 7-1 CONT'D

Shift Income to Dependents	*May 15*	*none - use existing funds*	*(800)*
Tax Deductible Expenditures	*June 30*	*none - rearrange existing debt*	*(1500)*
TOTALS		*22,500*	*(8,800)*

8

YEAR-END PLANNING

The last steps in the tax-planning process as the end of the year approaches are the computation of your current year's actual taxable income; the comparison of your actual taxable income with the targeted taxable income for the current year that you established some months ago; and the implementation of some year-end action steps to make sure you achieve your targeted taxable income.

Thus, year-end action is merely the last phase of a process that began with your formulation of your tax plan and the implementation of some tax-saving ideas some months or even years ago. Although these are the last steps in the process, they are very important, for after December 31 there is little you can do to save taxes other than contribute to an RRSP in the first sixty days of the next year. For those of you who have procrastinated, despite our discussions in Chapters 5, 6, and 7 about the importance of tax planning long before year end, year end is the only time you have to do any tax planning.

The best time to do year-end tax planning is the fall, no later than November. Fall is the proper time of year for finalizing your tax plan, for by then you have most of your financial data for the year, but there is still time to take action before the end of the financial year.

If you have capital gains or losses for the year, probably the best place to begin year-end planning is with Forms 13A and 13B. If you have no capital assets, skip Forms 13A and 13B, and begin your final tax-saving thrust by completing Form 14, *Year-End Tax Plan*.

FORMS 13A and 13B—CAPITAL GAINS AND LOSSES

Once completed, Form 13A will provide you with an estimate of the amount of taxable capital gains you must include in taxable income for the current year. Form 13B will indicate the taxable capital gains or allowable capital losses that could be triggered before the year end to adjust the amount determined in Form 13A.

FIGURE 8-1

File under TAX PLANNING   Date: *November 5*

FORM 13A   CAPITAL GAINS AND LOSSES REALIZED TO DATE

Number of Units	Investment Type	Date Acquired	Adjusted Cost Base	Date Sold	Net Proceeds	Gain (Loss)
100	Acme Stock	5/30/85	$2,400	4/10/88	$4,000	$1,600
10	Best Bonds	7/1/86	7,800	10/30/88	8,900	1,100
300	Chance Stock	6/30/86	3,200	11/1/88	1,400	(1,800)
200	Dandy Stock	2/28/82	3,000	5/1/88	7,000	4,000
5	Early Bonds	11/30/84	4,000	7/1/88	3,200	(800)
200	Grinch Stock	6/24/86	1,200	10/30/88	1,900	700

Capital Gains Dividends
    (received from mutual funds)   1100

Capital Loss Carry-overs*
    (full amount of loss--not two-thirds)   (—)

Total   5,900

Taxable Capital Gains (Allowable
    Capital Losses)--two-thirds X Total   3,933

Cumulative <u>Taxable</u> Capital Gains
    exemption available (two-thirds of Cumulative
    Capital Gains exemption available)   66,667

Taxable Capital Gains (Allowable Capital
    Losses) to be included in Taxable income   ∅

* Up to $2,000.00 of allowable capital losses realized before
  May 23, 1985 can be claimed to reduce taxable income from any
  source. Capital losses realized after May 22, 1985 cannot be used
  to reduce taxable income other than capital gains.

FIGURE 8-2

File under TAX PLANNING

Date: _November 5_

FORM 13B   UNREALIZED GAINS OR LOSSES IN CURRENT INVESTMENTS

Number of Units	Investment Type	Date Acquired	Adjusted Cost Base	Current Market Value	Unrealized Gain (Loss)
400	Dandy Stock	2/28/82	$6,000	$12,000	$6,000
5	Early Bonds	11/30/84	4,000	3,500	(500)
100	Hotshot Stock	6/24/86	2,000	1,200	(800)

Total Unrealized
Capital
Gains and Losses $4,700

The discussion of the tax treatment of capital gains and losses and of the lifetime capital gains exemption (included in Chapter 6) can be consulted to help you complete these forms. As well, a completed sample of each form is shown in Figure 8-1 and 8-2.

The appropriate year-end action plan for you depends on your specific circumstances. The following comments can, however, provide you with some general guidelines.

The introduction of the capital gains exemption has been a somewhat controversial move by the government and there are some who suggest it will not be a lasting part of the Canadian tax system. As a result, it may be prudent to sell sufficient investments to use up the available capital gains exemption in the current year.

To the extent that you are currently paying tax at a lower rate than you expect to in the future, you may also wish to trigger some additional taxable capital gains to increase your current taxable income, thereby reducing future years' income. But make sure you take into account the cost of paying tax now rather than deferring it for a year or more.

On the other hand, if you are currently paying tax at a high rate and you have realized taxable capital gains in excess of your available capital gains exemption limit, you may wish to sell some investments with unrealized losses to offset these taxable gains.

Before any of these strategies are undertaken, however, you should also consider the investment implications; it makes little sense to sell a promising investment just to create a tax loss or gain.

If you do decide to sell, don't forget that Revenue Canada treats the settlement date, not the trade date, as the effective selling date. Therefore, your sales should be done in time to permit settlement by December 31 (usually five business days before December 31 are needed). Also remember that, under the so-called superficial loss rules, Revenue Canada will not allow the deduction of any loss triggered on the sale of an investment if you (or your spouse or a company you control) repurchase the same investment within thirty days.

In analyzing our example situation we might recommend selling the 400 shares of Dandy Stock before year end to use up more of your available capital gains exemption, thereby receiving the proceeds tax-free. But remember, in selecting year-end strategies, do not be guided solely by tax considerations. For example, do not sell a stock to trigger a gain (or a loss, for that matter), if you believe it is ready to take off.

FORM 14—YEAR-END TAX PLAN

To help you analyze your tax situation for the current year and determine what year-end action is required, we have provided Form 14. The listed items on the form are similar to those on Form 11 and follow the structure of your 1988 tax return. Form 11 has been modified to remove items which only apply in 1987, before the effects of tax reform applied. In the first column, *Actual to Date*, you record your actual taxable transactions for the current year up to the date you complete Form 14. In the second column, *Estimates to Year End*, you record your estimates of taxable transactions from now until the end of the year. In the third column, *Estimates for Total Year*, you place the total of the amounts in the first two columns.

To help you complete the form, refer to the instructions in Chapter 5 for completing Form 11 and to Figure 8-3 that shows you a filled-in sample of Form 14.

Here are some observations on the sample that may be of help to you in completing Form 14:

- The amounts shown under *Actual to Date* come from your records—pay records, information from financial institutions on dividends and interest and securities transactions, chequebook information on deductible expenditures, etc. You need to summarize this information to record it on Form 14. To summarize the data, you probably should have a lined pad and a calculator or home computer handy.
- The amounts shown under *Estimates to Year End* are your best estimates of transactions that are likely to occur, if you do not take any other action between the time you prepare Form 14 and the end of the year. In our example, the form was completed on November 7, and $13,000 is the estimate for additional salary during the remaining two months of the year. These estimates should be based on what you believe is likely to happen for each line on the form. For example, based on what you have received to date in compensation, you probably have a good idea of what you are likely to receive in compensation for the rest of the year. You may not have made your RRSP payment yet, but if you plan to, as our example family does, then put the estimated amount of the RRSP contribution under the "estimates" column.
- The amount of targeted taxable income comes from Form 11, *Tax-Planning Worksheet*, on which you targeted your taxable income for the current year. In our example, the targeted taxable income is $72,000. This amount is compared to the estimated taxable income for the year on line 6a of Form 14—$72,300 in our example. If you have implemented all your tax-saving ideas on Form 12, your estimated taxable income for the year should be pretty close to your

targeted taxable income. If you have procrastinated, you may be way off your target. Again, let us emphasize the need to start tax planning long before year end, so that you are on or near your target by the time the end of the year rolls around. In our example, the difference between estimated and targeted taxable income is $300. If no action is taken in the remainder of the current year, the example taxpayer, who is in a 44.8% tax bracket, will have to pay an additional $134 in taxes over the targeted amount—$300 multiplied by 44.8%.

- This brings us to the point of this whole year-end exercise—to highlight year-end action required. If you want to get closer to your targeted taxable income, you have to take some additional tax-saving steps between the time you prepare *Your Year-End Tax Plan* and December 31. The rest of this chapter will focus on year-end action.

As you read the rest of the chapter, list your action steps on Form 15, *Year End Tax Action*. It would now be useful to complete the top of Form 15 using data from Form 14.

- At the top of Form 15 fill in your estimated taxable income from line 6a of your Form 14.
- On the next line of Form 15 fill in your targeted taxable income from line 7a of your Form 14.
- Then determine the required year-end reduction in taxable income. At the end of this chapter, we shall see if you have listed enough year-end actions steps to reach the required reduction.

SHIFTING INCOME AND DEDUCTIONS

Effective year-end tax planning will generally involve the following:

- The implementation of tax-saving ideas you listed in Form 12 but have not yet carried out.
- The postponement of income to next year.
- The acceleration of deductions and credits into the current year.

You may be able to save taxes either by postponing income or by accelerating deductions and credits this year in the expectation that your tax rate next year will be lower. Even if your tax rate is the same next year, a deferral of taxable income to next year is the equivalent of an interest-free loan because it enables you to use funds that you would otherwise pay out in taxes. With a significant rate of inflation, any tax deferred to a later year will be paid with cheaper dollars.

Bear in mind that in some situations shifting taxable income into the *current year* may result in greater tax savings. For example, if you anticipate that your income next year will be substantially higher, or if you think you will have unusually large invest-ment losses or other deductions this year, then you may want to accelerate income this year and defer deductions until next year to minimize your tax liability over this year and next.

Tax professionals who use computers to make "what-if" analyses can be very helpful at year end. For example, at Touche Ross we provide such year-end analyses for many clients.

DEFERRING INCOME

There are ways of deferring income to next year, although there is little room for such manoeuvres as far as your income from salaries or wages is concerned. You are, of course, taxed on salaries or wages received in cash. But as well, you are considered by

FIGURE 8-3

File under TAX PLANNING   Date: _November 7_

FORM 14   YEAR-END TAX PLAN

	ACTUAL TO DATE	ESTIMATES TO YEAR END	ESTIMATES TOTAL
1. TOTAL INCOME			
(a) (i) Income from employment	$64,000	$13,000	$77,000
(ii) Less other allowable expenses			
(iii) Net employment earnings	64,000	13,000	77,000
(b) Pension income			
(i) Old Age Security and Canada or Quebec Pension plan benefits			
(ii) Other pension income			
(c) Income from other sources			
(i) Family Allowance payments			
(ii) Unemployment Insurance benefits			
(iii) Taxable amount of dividends from Canadian companies	3,500	400	3,900
(iv) Interest and other investment income	1,500	500	2,000
(v) Rental income (loss)	3,500	1,400	4,900
(vi) Taxable capital gains	3,900	4,000	7,900
(d) Self-employed income			
(i) Business income			
(ii) Professional income			
(iii) Commission income			
(iv) Farming or fishing income			
(e) Total income	76,400	19,300	95,700

FIGURE 8-3 CONT'D

	ACTUAL TO DATE	ESTIMATES TO YEAR END	ESTIMATES TOTAL YEAR
2. DEDUCTIONS FROM TOTAL INCOME			
(a) Registered pension plan contributions			
(b) Registered Retirement Savings Plan contributions	–	7,500	7,500
(c) Union and professional dues			
(d) Child care expenses			
(e) Allowable business investment losses			
(f) Other deductions (deductible interest and flow-through shares)	7,200	800	8,000
(g) Total deductions	7,200	8,300	15,500
3. NET INCOME	69,200	11,000	80,200
4. OTHER DEDUCTIONS FROM NET INCOME			
(a) Non-capital losses of other years			
(b) Net capital losses of other years (1972-1985)			
(c) Taxable capital gains exemption	3,900	4,000	7,900
(d) Total other deductions	3,900	4,000	7,900
5. (a) TAXABLE INCOME	65,300	7,000	72,300
(b) Tax bracket			44.8
6. (a) TARGETED TAXABLE INCOME			72,000
(b) Targeted Tax bracket			44.8

Revenue Canada to have received your salary when you have control of it or when it is set aside for you. Therefore, you cannot defer taxation of your salary to next year by not cashing year-end paycheques or by arranging with your employer to postpone issuing your regularly scheduled pay cheque until after December 31. And the 1986 budget eliminated the tax advantage of many more sophisticated salary deferral methods, such as employee benefit plans.

Distributions from Pension or Profit Sharing Plans

If you are about to retire and expect a lump-sum distribution from a registered pension or Deferred Profit Sharing Plan in the near future, you may wish to defer the distribution to a lower-income year. Part or all of the distribution can generally be rolled over into an RRSP. This will be discussed in more detail in Chapter 12.

Investment Income

A person has more opportunity to defer investment income, such as interest. An individual may choose to report interest income on the cash, receivable or accrued basis. On the cash basis, interest income is only reported when received. On the receivable basis, interest is included in income when you have a clear legal right to receive it. To illustrate, assume that you bought a $1,000 bond on its issue date of 1 April 1985, bearing interest of nine percent payable by semi-annual coupon on April 1 and October 1. On 1 October 1985, interest of $45 would be receivable, and would be included in your 1985 income, even if you did not cash the $45 coupon until 1986 or even later. In 1986 and subsequent years, until the year the bond becomes due, you will report $90 income on the receivable basis, if you still hold the bond. If the bond matures on 1 April 1995, income for that year would be $45.

Under the accrual method, interest is considered to be earned on a daily basis, regardless of when the interest actually becomes receivable or is received. Using the example above, under the accrual method you would report interest of $67.80 in 1985 for the 275 days in the year during which you owned the bond (275/365 x 9% x $1,000 = $67.80). The same interest income of $90 would be reported in each subsequent year up to the year of maturity. But in 1995, income of only $22.20 (90/365 x 9% x $1,000) would be reported.

Under all three methods, the same total amount of interest is reported over the bond ownership period. The only difference is the timing of inclusion in income during the period. Which method is best for you? It depends on your estimated tax position throughout the expected ownership period, although the cash method will generally be preferable if you are expecting your tax rate to stay about the same or decrease during the ownership period.

Revenue Canada will allow you some flexibility in choosing how to report interest income. Interest income from different sources can be reported using different methods, although all interest from the same source (i.e. same payor, on the same type of interest-yielding property) must be reported using one method. As well, Revenue Canada will generally allow a taxpayer to switch either from the cash to the receivable or accrual basis or from the receivable to the accrual basis. Revenue Canada will not, however, approve a change of method to one which delays the recognition of interest income (i.e. from accrual to receivable or cash basis).

There are additional rules in the *Income Tax Act* designed to limit the opportunity to defer interest income. Before these rules were introduced in 1981, an individual could purchase, for example, a five-year compound-interest term deposit and report no income until the fifth year when all the interest was received (assuming he could choose the cash method for his investment). This is no longer possible. There are comprehensive (and complicated!) rules which essentially prevent you from delaying recognition of interest earned but not yet received for more than three years. These rules are important to consider before buying any investment which does not pay interest at least every three years (long-term deposits, deferred annuities, long-term stripped bonds, and compound interest Canada Savings Bonds). If you're not careful, you could end up paying tax currently on income you aren't entitled to receive until a future year.

Note that these income accrual rules will apply for the first time in 1988 to any compound-interest or other deferred-income investments you acquired before 1982.

Now that you have ideas about how to defer income to next year, note them on Form 15, *Year-End Tax Action*.

USING DEDUCTIONS

Deferring income can be an important strategy for year-end tax planning. Another is to increase or accelerate your deductions and credits. We will now describe some possible deductions. As you read of deductions you may be able to make but have not yet included in your tax plan, note them on Form 15, *Year-End Tax Action*.

Expenses of The Office In The Home

Most taxpayers cannot deduct expenses for the business use of space in their homes. However, in certain circumstances, deductions for the cost of maintaining a home office can be allowed to employees or self-employed persons earning business, professional or commission income. As a result of tax reform, fewer self-employed people will be able to claim home office expenses after 1987.

If you are an employee, you must meet all of the following requirements in order to claim a deduction for home office expenses:

1. you must be required by your employment contract to pay these expenses, and will not be reimbursed by your employer;
2. the expenses are incurred solely for the purpose of earning employment income;
3. the home office is used exclusively for business purposes—it cannot double as a part-time spare bedroom or den; and
4. your employer can not have an office within a reasonable distance from your home.

If you are a self-employed person, you can deduct expenses of a home office used to earn business, professional or commission income provided certain tests are met. Again the office must be used exclusively for business purposes and should be separate from the family living quarters. It should be necessary for the operation of your business, profession or sales activities and not merely a convenience. It should be used regularly and not just occasionally. As well, for fiscal periods starting after 1987, home office expenses will only be allowed if your home office is either your principal place of business, or is used on a regular basis for meeting clients, customers of patients.

After 1987, home office expenses are deductible only up to your income for the year from the business; therefore, you cannot create a deductible loss from a part-time business run out of your home by claiming home office expenses. You can, however, carry forward expenses, disallowed because of this limitation, and deduct them against business income of a subsequent year.

Revenue Canada will be more likely to accept the deduction of your home office expenses if there are indications of business activities such as a separate business telephone line, or a sign on your home indicating the presence of a business office.

If you qualify to deduct home office expenses, add up all the allowed costs of maintaining your home discussed below, and deduct a reasonable portion related to your office. For example, let's say you live in a home with 2,500 square feet of space and you devote 250 square feet to a home office. Ten percent (250 of a total of 2,500 square feet) of the allowed costs could be deducted from your income.

An employee who rents his home may claim a portion of the rent paid. Where an employee owns his own home, a reasonable portion of the costs of maintaining the home (such as fuel, electricity and other utilities, minor repairs, etc.) can be deducted. A commission remunerated employee will also be able to deduct a portion of property taxes and insurance paid on the home.

In addition to the home office expenses that can be deducted by an employee, a self-employed person can also claim capital cost allowance on the business portion of the home, and on any furniture or equipment used for business purposes. A self-employed person may also be able to deduct a portion of the mortgage interest paid to finance the purchase of the home.

Note that if you claim any expenses for a home office, Revenue Canada will treat that part of your home as being converted to a business property, unless you make a special election available under Section 45 of the *Income Tax Act*. If you do not make this election, a portion of any gain ultimately realized on the sale of your home could be taxable. If you do make this election, you will not be able to claim capital cost allowance on the portion of your home used for your home office. It is almost certainly better to make this election if you claim home office expenses, assuming the value of your home will increase over time.

Other Business Expenses

Taking some action now to avoid trouble later should be part of your tax planning. So be sure to document all your travel, entertainment and other business expenses carefully. Court decisions have continually supported Revenue Canada in disallowing numerous types of expenses because they were not adequately substantiated. All these cases showed the importance of maintaining a current record of expenses. Spending a little time now could save a lot of dollars later.

Receipts for your expenses do not need to be filed with your tax return, but should be retained in an orderly fashion for presentation to Revenue Canada on a subsequent review of your return.

Touche Ross has prepared a Business Expense Log to assist taxpayers in recording and organizing their business expenses, particularly automobile expenses. This log can also be used by employees who are eligible to deduct automobile expenses (see Chapter 6) or who wish to reduce their taxable benefit from an employer-provided car by demonstrating business use. Contact the nearest Touche Ross office if you are interested in obtaining the Business Expense Log.

Registered Retirement Savings Plans

You can deduct contributions to an RRSP each year up to certain limits which have been discussed in Chapter 6. These contributions can be made at any time in the year or during the first sixty days of the following year. Although you can delay your contribution, consider contributing to your RRSP in the early part of each year, so that you may maximize the deferral on the income earned by the RRSP. Generally, it is not worthwhile to borrow to make early contributions because interest paid on the borrowed money is not deductible.

Interest Expense

In general, interest paid on money borrowed to earn business or investment income is deductible. Interest paid on money borrowed for personal use (such as buying your home) is not deductible.

Interest on business or investment loans can be deducted even if the business or investment does not immediately generate profits in excess of the interest paid. However, there must be a reasonable expectation of such a profit in the long term. For example, Revenue Canada would not let you deduct all of your interest expense if you borrowed at eleven percent to invest in a term deposit which had a fixed yield of nine percent, since it would never be possible for you to make a profit on this transaction.

Because Canada's personal tax rates reach a fairly high level even for middle income earners (See Appendix II—not just the rich pay high rates of tax, as I'm sure you're already well aware), structuring your borrowings to maximize your interest deduction can result in very significant tax savings. If at all possible, borrow to finance your investments and use your excess cash to pay off personal debt or contribute to an RRSP. If you have substantial equity in your investments yet still have a mortgage on your home, consider selling your investments, using the proceeds to reduce your mortgage, and borrowing to repurchase the same or similar investments.

But before you do this, consider the tax and other effects of this transaction. If you buy the same investments within thirty days of selling them, any loss triggered by the sale will not be deductible under the superficial loss rules. If, on the other hand, the investments have significant accrued gains, their sale may trigger capital gains tax to the extent they exceed your available capital gains exemption. You may have to pay brokerage or other fees to sell and repurchase your investments. There may also be a risk that you cannot repurchase investments of the same quality as those you sell.

But the rewards of converting non-deductible interest to deductible are potentially so significant that you should always look for opportunities to do so. This is one of the most effective tax-planning strategies available.

OTHER DEDUCTIONS, EXEMPTIONS AND CREDITS

Charitable Donations

The deduction available in 1987 and prior years for charitable donations has been converted to a two-tier non-refundable tax credit in 1988. A seventeen percent federal tax credit will be available for the first $250 of charitable donations paid in the year, with a twenty-nine percent credit for any additional gifts.

Only charitable donations up to twenty percent of net income can be claimed in a year, except for gifts to the Crown or gifts of cultural property, for which there is no limit. Unclaimed gifts can be carried forward for credit for up to five years.

Apart from the first $250 of donations, the new credit system provides all taxpayers with the tax relief calculated at the maximum federal rate (an approximate combined federal and provincial tax rate of 44.4%). This provides a greater tax incentive to lower and middle-income Canadians for charitable giving compared to the existing system.

You may also wish to donate investments or other property to a charity. You will generally be able to claim a credit calculated on the current value of the donated property (subject to the twenty percent net income limit), but will be considered to have sold the property for the same amount. This may trigger a taxable capital gain for property that has increased in value since you acquired it. You may be able to shelter this gain with your available capital gains exemption, but will only pay tax on two-thirds of any unsheltered gain, while being able to claim a credit on all of the value of the gift.

If this does not produce desirable tax results, you may choose to contribute your property by transferring it at your adjusted cost base. Your credit will be calculated on this lower amount, but no gain will be triggered by your donation.

Review the other deductions, exemptions and credits described in Chapters 5 and 6 for any other opportunities to reduce your taxable income or taxes payable.

OTHER YEAR-END TAX-PLANNING STRATEGIES

Tax Shelters

Late autumn is traditionally the most active time for marketing tax shelters—the largest range of products is available at this time. Tax shelters can allow you to reduce your current taxable income, as discussed in Chapter 7. But always remember to examine the investment quality of any tax shelter deal—don't just buy in for the tax savings.

Electing Capital Gains Treatment

If you frequently buy and sell investments, there is some concern that Revenue Canada will treat you as a trader (i.e. tax you on the full amount of your net gains) rather than as an investor realizing capital gains and losses. This can be a particularly harsh treatment if it prevents you from using your available capital gains exemption.

If your investment activities are sufficiently frequent that this is a concern, consider making an election to ensure your future transactions in Canadian securities will be given capital gain or loss treatment. This election will only apply, however, to Canadian shares, trust units and certain debt instruments. It has no effect on the tax treatment of real estate transactions or the sale of foreign securities. As well, once made, the election cannot be revoked and therefore should not be made without carefully considering the potential consequences, preferably with the help of a qualified tax advisor.

Salary and Dividend Mix

If you own an incorporated business, there is considerable opportunity for tax savings by choosing the right mix of salaries and dividends for your total compensation package. This can be a complicated calculation, influenced by many factors, and is best done with the help of your tax advisor.

FORM 15—YEAR-END TAX ACTION

Year end is the last time you have available to do anything about this year's tax situation. You should already have completed the top of Form 15 to determine the required reduction of taxable income by year end. Also, we hope you have listed action steps on Form 15 as you read this chapter. If not, spend some time now listing those steps you want to take between now and year end to reduce your taxable income.

Some of the action steps on your list may require no cash expenditures on your part, but others will. Work out and list how much cash is required for each of the tax-reducing steps you have proposed. Eliminate the steps for which the necessary funds are not available either from your capital or from borrowing. Then work out and list how much each of the remaining steps will reduce your taxable income. Total the reductions. Compare that figure with the required reduction you computed at the top of the form to see whether your year-end action steps result in the reduction in taxable income you require. Then put the feasible, desirable tax-saving steps into action as soon as you can. After all the work and thought involved in analyzing your tax situation and targeting the taxable income you desire, you don't want to end up with a lot of splendid ideas but no results.

9

SETTING FINANCIAL OBJECTIVES

The setting of objectives may be the single most important part of financial planning. We tend to live from day to day—"muddling through" or "operating in mediocrity"—with only the haziest notion of where we are going or what we really want out of life. Living in this way, we may never have the sense of fulfillment or the variety of experiences we vaguely hoped for, and we may never be in control of our lives or achieve financial security. The effort to focus on what we really want to achieve and do with our lives propels us toward those goals and we also gain a sense of purpose and direction.

As you set your financial objectives, you will evaluate the trade-offs between your short-term and your long-term goals, you will investigate the various alternatives you have for using your financial resources, and then you will decide which alternatives are best for you.

Keep in mind that researchers who have studied peak performance in individuals —executives, professionals, athletes, teachers—have observed that the successful ones have one common characteristic: They set goals for themselves. So give these next four forms on your objectives—Forms 16, 17, 18 and 19—some careful thought and set goals you can live by, goals you can achieve with knowledge, effort, commitment and persistence.

FORM 16—FINANCIAL SECURITY

Item 1 asks you to define financial security, which has different meanings to different people. Some might say, "It is not having to depend on a salary," or "Financial security is $60,000 a year before taxes." Some express it in terms of debt: "I'll feel financially secure when I have no more debts." To others, financial security is a way of life: "Being able to do what I want when I want," or "Not having to worry about meeting income needs."

First, write your own definition of financial security. Then try to express it in quantitative, measurable terms that will give you specific targets to reach for.

- What specific annual income would give you financial security? Would you feel financially secure with *earned income* of $50,000 or $75,000 or more than $100,000? Maybe you would rather express financial security in terms of annual *investment income*—having your money work for you so you would be free to pursue your avocational interests more frequently or for longer periods of time. As you will see below, you can determine the amount of investment assets required to provide your desired investment income level.

- What specific net worth are you seeking in order to gain financial security? If your goal is $60,000 of annual investment income, then you will need a certain level of investment assets. For example, if you believe you can realize an eight percent before-tax return on your investments, you will need investment assets of $750,000 to achieve financial security.

- What specific debt level do you want to accept in order to achieve financial security? Most people we counsel still believe in having relatively little debt when discussing financial security. They may have relatively high debt levels at some stage of their lives in order to finance investments and personal assets but when they get around to financial security, they are really worried about keeping debt at high levels. For most people, high debt levels mean anxiety and stress that they would rather do without at some point.

Item 2 on Form 16 asks you to determine when you want to achieve financial security, based on your present financial position, earning power, expenditure patterns, and investment strategy. This question may be less difficult to answer than most people initially believe if you use the information you prepared in the first part of this book. For example, if you believe you need $750,000 of investment assets to achieve financial security and your net worth statement, Form 4, currently shows investments of $500,000, you may be able to achieve that goal in the next few years. If, on the other hand, you currently have investment assets of $1.23 and a pack of chewing gum, you may take a long time to achieve your goal without marrying for money or becoming the favourite niece or nephew of that aging, rich uncle.

Item 3, asking what you perceive as the chief obstacles to your financial security, commonly receives one of the following answers: *taxes, inflation, my boss, lack of knowledge, lack of time.* Most of the obstacles people perceive, though, are self-imposed and therefore can usually be removed by self-management. There is something you can do about your taxes, your inflation rate, your lack of knowledge. You can choose to spend time on financial planning instead of some other activity.

To determine whether your timetable for achieving financial security is realistic or a pipe dream, do some overall analysis.

- Use the Rule of Seventy-two to determine how many years it will take to double your money. Merely divide seventy-two by the expected annual after-tax rate of return on your investments. For example, if your expected annual after-tax rate of return is six percent, your investments will double in twelve years ($72 \div 6 = 12$). For your investments to double in five years, you will need an annual after-tax rate of return of 14.4% ($72 \div 5 = 14.4$).

- Use compound tables such as Tables 9-1, 9-2, 9-3, and 9-4, and the more complete tables in Appendix I.

Table 9-1 lets you see how much a lump-sum investment will grow in various years at varying rates of return. Merely multiply the amount listed for the rate of return and number of years involved by your investment assets divided by 10,000. For example, if you have $100,000 to invest and you want to know what such a lump sum will grow to in fifteen years at twelve percent, you find the amount $54,735 in Table 9-1 and multiply it by ten ($100,000 ÷ $10,000) to get your answer — $547,350.

Table 9-2 lets you determine what lump-sum investment you need in order to accumulate a targeted investment amount by the end of a specified period. Let's say you want to have $500,000 of investment assets in ten years and believe you could invest your present assets to return fifteen percent per year. You would need to invest $123,590 today ($24,718 × $500,000/100,000).

Tables 9-3 and 9-4 show you how much an invested amount will grow at varying rates for varying periods. For example, if you have $1,200 per year to invest (approximately $100 per month), such an investment programme will produce $160,000 in twenty-five years if your investment funds return twelve percent per year. If you were able to invest $2,400 per year ($200 per month) at fifteen percent, your investments would grow to $245,864 at the end of twenty years, according to Table 9-3.

Table 9-4 shows how much you have to invest each year for how many years and at what rate in order to get $100,000. For example, if you wanted $100,000 in five years and thought you could get a ten percent return each year, you would need to invest $14,890 per year.

Obviously, these tables can also be used to see what your investments might be at the end of an expected number of years with an expected rate of return, assuming you either invested a lump sum (your present investment assets) or an annual amount or both. For example, if you have $50,000 of investment assets today and can invest another $5,000 per year, your investment assets would be approximately $842,600 at the end of twenty years at a rate of twelve percent. The computation is shown below:

- From Table 9-1 (Investment of $50,000 @ 12% for 20 years):
  $50,000/10,000 × 96,462 = $482,310
- From Table 9-3 (Investment of $5,000 per year @ 12% for 20 years):
  $5,000/1,200 × 86,463 = $360,263
  $482,310 + $360,263 = $842,573

As well as the Rule of Seventy-two and compound tables, you can use an inexpensive financial analysis calculator to do the calculations. For less than $40 you can buy some makes of hand-held calculators programmed to do financial analysis. Such calculators have keys for each of the five financial variables we have used in the calculations with the compound tables. These five keys are:

1. **PV**, or the present value or amount of your investment assets
2. **PMT**, or the annual amount or payment you can make in your investment programme
3. **N**, or the number of periods (years, months) you expect to invest your money
4. **i**, or the rate of interest or return you expect to get on your investments
5. **FV**, or the future value or amount of your investment assets (ie. *the value to which your assets will grow* over a specified number of years at a specified rate of interest)

Using a calculator with these five function keys, you can determine, in a matter of seconds, the answer to investment questions such as:

- If I have $20,000 (PV) in my present investment fund and can put aside $2,400 (PMT) per year to invest, what rate of return (i) do I need to have $500,000 (FV) in ten years (N)? Answer: 32.88%.
- If financial security for me is $1,000,000 (FV), how long will it take to reach that objective if my present assets are $300,000 and I can set aside $15,000 a year for investment and can get a fifteen percent return on my investment? Answer: a little more than seven years.

TABLE 9-1
$10,000 LUMP-SUM INVESTMENT COMPOUNDED ANNUALLY END OF YEAR VALUES

End of Year	6%	8%	10%	12%	15%
5	13,382	14,693	16,105	17,623	20,113
6	14,185	15,868	17,715	19,738	23,130
7	15,036	17,138	19,478	22,016	26,600
8	15,938	18,509	21,435	24,759	30,590
9	16,894	19,990	23,579	27,730	35,178
10	17,908	21,589	25,937	31,058	40,455
15	23,965	31,721	41,772	54,735	81,370
20	32,071	46,609	67,274	96,462	163,665
25	42,918	68,484	108,347	170,000	329,189

TABLE 9-2
RATES OF RETURN AND THE INVESTMENT AMOUNTS REQUIRED TO HAVE $100,000 AVAILABLE AT END OF SPECIFIED PERIOD

Rate of Return	End of Year				
	5	10	15	20	25
6%	74,726	55,839	41,727	31,180	23,300
8%	68,058	46,319	31,524	21,455	14,602
10%	62,092	38,554	23,940	14,864	9,230
12%	56,743	32,197	18,270	10,367	5,882
15%	49,718	24,718	12,289	6,110	3,040

TABLE 9-3
FUTURE WORTH OF $1,200 INVESTED EACH YEAR AT VARYING RATES COMPOUNDED EACH YEAR

Rate of Return	End of Year				
	5	10	15	20	25
6%	6,764	15,817	27,931	44,143	65,837
8%	7,040	17,384	32,583	54,914	87,727
10%	7,326	19,125	38,127	68,730	118,016
12%	7,623	21,058	44,736	86,463	160,001
15%	8,091	24,364	57,096	122,932	255,352

TABLE 9-4
APPROXIMATE ANNUAL INVESTMENT REQUIRED TO EQUAL $100,000 AT VARYING RATES

Rate of Return	End of Year				
	5	10	15	20	25
6%	16,736	7,157	4,053	2,565	1,720
8%	15,783	6,392	3,410	2,024	1,267
10%	14,890	5,704	2,861	1,587	924
12%	14,055	5,088	2,395	1,239	670
15%	12,898	4,283	1,828	849	409

FORM 17—INCOME AND EXPENDITURE OBJECTIVES

For most people, what is left of their employment income after paying current expenses is the primary means of accumulating net worth and achieving financial security. Therefore, any increase in employment income without a similar increase in expenditures, or any reduction in expenditures without a similar reduction in employment income, will provide you with that much more money to invest—money that could be working for you to help you reach future goals.

When answering the questions in this form, refer to Form 10, *Analysis of Earned Income and Expenditures*, for your current total employment income and expenditures.

To answer item 2, refer to Form 7, *Basic Lifestyle Expenditures.*
To answer item 3, refer to Form 8, *Discretionary Expenditures.*

- When estimating your and your spouse's employment income for the next three years, start with an estimate of an annual percentage increase. For example, maybe you think employment income will increase by ten percent per year for each of the next three years. Maybe you think next year your income will be the same as last year, but will increase by ten percent per year for years two and three. Once you have estimated a rate of increase, estimate the amount of employment income for each of the next three years.

- Questions 2 and 3 ask you to evaluate how much you could reduce your present expenditure levels. Such evaluation is important in order to do the following:
  - Determine whether your expenditures are resulting in the quality of life you expect
  - Determine whether your present lifestyle expenditures are using up dollars that are important for future goals
  - Remind you that the best way, from a tax standpoint, to increase amounts available for investment is to reduce your expenditures.

    Every expenditure dollar saved means one whole dollar available for investment. Every additional dollar of employment earnings produces only 50¢ for investing if you are in a fifty percent tax bracket, or 67¢ if you are in a thirty-three percent tax bracket.

- Question 4 gets at your "wish" list. Everybody has one. The items on the list are your dreams—the sleek sports car, the sailboat cutting sharply through the dashing waves, the cobblestone streets of a European village, the entertainment room in your home. If you are married, sit down with your family and discuss a family wish list. Determine what you would like. If you are single, talk to a close friend or advisor about your dreams and get some feedback on your list.

    In developing your list, determine not only what you want but by when. Keep in mind that some goals can be achieved in the near future, while others can only be achieved in the long term.

You will use your estimates of income and expenditures in building a summary financial plan in Chapter 15.

FORM 18—EDUCATION AND OTHER SUPPORT OF CHILDREN

Inflation has had a noticeable impact on family expenditures, especially on education costs and living expenses of young adults after leaving high school. As a result, most of them now require assistance from their parents to pay for their university or college tuition and living expenses. Some families also incur, or plan to incur, considerable expenses by sending their children to private elementary or secondary schools.

- If you are planning to send your children to private elementary and secondary schools, be aware that it is expensive and that financial plans should be made well in advance. Good private elementary day schools may cost anywhere from $1,000 to $5,000 or more per year. Secondary schools run higher. Of course, boarding schools are even more expensive because they also cover room and board.

    Question 1 asks you to estimate for each child the total cost of private education in today's dollars. For example, if your children are aged nine and seven and you plan to send them to private secondary schools in six and eight years, respectively, and you estimate the cost for each year to be $5,000 (in today's dollars), the total estimated cost for each child will be $20,000; the total for both children will be $40,000.

- If you are planning to send your children to a college or university, you should begin well in advance to evaluate the potential costs. University or college education may cost anywhere between $2,000 and $10,000 per year, including room and board, books, and incidentals. Question 2 asks you to estimate the amount you will provide for each child in today's dollars. For example, if you have two children and plan to help each of them with eighty percent of their university or college costs for each of the four years, you will have to pay $16,000 for each child if each year of university costs $5,000 in today's dollars ($5,000 × 80% × four years); a total of $32,000. Depending on the rate of inflation, the amounts required for university costs could, and probably will, be significantly higher in future years.

- Obviously, with many families facing the possibility of significant educational expenditures, plans should be made to set aside funds before the schooling begins. A good idea may be to start an educational fund for your children when they are very young. Let the power of compounding work over a period of years so that significant funds are available when your children go off to college or university.

    Question 3 asks you to indicate what funds have been set aside for your children's education. Some families start a savings programme for their children; some make annual money gifts to the children and invest the money in high-yielding securities; others set up a trust with a lump-sum fund and let the earnings on the fund accumulate in the trust until the children's education begins. In Chapter 11 we will discuss educational financing techniques and how to get the most after-tax dollars for your children's education.

- Question 4 asks you to estimate what support your children may need apart from education. Some families have a disabled child who needs support. Others are supporting unemployed children or helping their children finance the purchase of a home.

Again, you will use the information on your objectives for the education and support of your children to build your summary plan in Chapter 15.

FORM 19—RETIREMENT PLANNING

The retirement years are generally referred to as "the golden years"—a time for leisure activities and relaxation after many years of work. They are not likely to be golden, however, unless you have planned how you will use your time, where you will live, and how you will finance your expenses.

Information gathered by Statistics Canada indicates that few people prepare adequately for retirement, particularly from the financial point of view. Over a quarter of the men and about one-tenth of the women aged sixty-five to sixty-nine were still in the labour force when the 1981 Census (latest figures available) was taken. Certainly, not all of these people were working purely for job satisfaction, but rather needed to supplement their retirement income. As well, the major source of income reported by Canada's elderly in 1980 was government transfer payments, such as Old Age Security and Canada or Quebec Pension Plan. Given the amount of these payments, it seems safe to assume that many of Canada's elderly cannot look forward to a financially secure future.

We strongly believe a retirement programme should be started early in your life—at least ten to fifteen years before you plan to retire. This form asks you some questions about the financial aspects of retirement, such as the age at which you plan to retire, your financial requirements at retirement, and the financial sources available to meet your needs.

You will use the information on Form 19 in Chapter 12, when we ask you to analyze the feasibility of your retirement objectives.

SUMMARY

In this chapter, we have discussed the importance of financial objectives and have asked you to determine your objectives for financial security, income and expenditures, education and support of your children, and retirement.

In setting objectives, you have to weigh the trade-offs between short-term and long-term goals (Do I take an expensive vacation this year or set aside some funds for my child's university or college education five years from now?) and identify the steps involved in reaching your goals. (To reach my financial security goal, I need to set aside more each year for investment and get a higher return on my assets. I should probably reduce my tax expenditures, get more knowledge about investment alternatives, and monitor my investments more closely.)

Once your objectives have been established, you need to take some action. In the chapters that follow, we will discuss investments, educational financing, and retirement, and you will identify what action you can take.

10

INVESTMENTS

As you must surely realize by now, the road to financial independence is paved with good investments. You, too, should be able to obtain investment results that are above the average, once you know your investment objectives and take the time to evaluate and monitor your investments.

Broadly speaking, your investments consist of all the means by which you store up assets for the future. These would include your home and your retirement programme, which should form a part of your overall investment programme and should relate to such other investments as your stocks, bonds, and income-producing real estate.

This chapter will guide you to formulate an investment programme of your own that is specifically geared to your age, responsibilities, and objectives, as well as your expendable income and your taxes.

INVESTMENT OBJECTIVES

What are the important factors in making an investment decision? Most people answer this very quickly by saying, "I want my investments to give me a good return." Then we say, "Okay, but what kind of return are you looking for?" Some reply, "A steady return." Some say, "The kind I don't have to watch and worry about." Others say, "The highest return I can get for the risk I am willing to take."

When you analyze these and other answers, you find the following concerns:

- Safety of principal
- Hedge against inflation
- Future income
- Current income
- Tax consequences
- Liquidity of the investment
- Ease of management

We will now investigate these objectives and, in as much as some are contrary to others, we will consider them in pairs.

Safety of Principal Versus Hedge Against Inflation

If your overriding concern is to keep a sum of money intact for a specific purpose, such as a down payment on a house, you might invest in a regular savings account, Treasury bills, Canada Savings Bonds, or a money market fund, since these will pretty much guarantee that you can get your principal back when you need it. Liquidity and safety of principal are usually the main considerations when you invest in such funds. You should be aware, however, that in inflationary periods the longer you hold an investment that provides the safety of principal you get with something like a savings account, the more you will lose in purchasing power. As the inflation rate goes up, so the purchasing power of your funds goes down. Thus, investments that are safe with regard to return of principal are not always a good hedge against inflation.

For those who want a return that will keep up with inflation, the primary objective should be safety of purchasing power, not safety of principal. In years of high inflation, safety of purchasing power has usually been achieved by investment alternatives that are not commonly chosen by Canadians. Traditionally, Canadians have invested in five areas: savings accounts and Canada Savings Bonds, Treasury bills and money market instruments, common stocks, corporate and government bonds, and real estate. In the five-year period from 1980 to 1985, money market instruments, bonds, real estate, and stocks were the traditional types of investment that brought a rate of return greater than the rate of inflation as measured by the Consumer Price Index. In Table 10-1, you can see how stocks, bonds, money market instruments (Treasury bills), and real estate performed in relation to the Consumer Price Index and to some other, less traditional, investment categories.

It should be noted that 1980 to 1985 covers a period which is historically unusual in that it featured a significant decline in inflation and interest rates. This pattern naturally favours the fixed-income type investments like bonds, where returns were locked in at very high interest rates at the beginning of the period. Traditionally, over longer periods, the riskier investments like stocks have yielded a better return.

Investment Performance

The following data show the *annual* returns for investment categories for the five years ended 30 November, 1985, as well as the rise in the Consumer Price Index. For example, the Consumer Price Index (the inflation rate) increased by an average of 6.9% *per year* during this five-year period. Stocks increased in value 7.8% per year during the five-year period.

TABLE 10-1
INVESTMENT PERFORMANCE

Investment Category	Annual Return
Bonds	18.5%
Treasury Bills	13.2
European Art	12.5
Pearls	10.0
Stocks	7.8
Housing	7.3
Consumer Price Index	6.9
Diamonds	−2.0
Canadian Art	−2.5
Gold	−12.2
Silver	−19.7

Current Income Versus Future Appreciation and Tax Consequences

Some people, particularly those who have retired or are widowed, may regard current income as their primary investment objective. Such current income could take the form of interest on savings accounts or Canada Savings Bonds, or dividends from common or preferred stock, or rent from income-producing real estate. In assessing current income from investments, the two terms commonly used are *current return* and *current yield*. Current return is usually expressed in dollars; yield is expressed as a percentage. Thus, the current return on a $1,000 savings account with a yield of five percent is $50. With common stock, the current return is the dollar amount of your dividend per share, while the current yield shows the dividend received as a percentage of the current price of the stock. So with a dividend of $1 per share and a stock price of $15, the current yield would be one divided by fifteen, or 6.67%.

Some investors have both safety of principal and current income as their investment objectives. They are the investors who need this investment income to cover their living expenses and cannot risk the loss of their principal. As a rule, this would apply to people who are unemployed or fear unemployment in the future, those about to take a substantial reduction in employment income, and those in or near retirement.

For people whose employment income covers their lifestyle expenditures and people of substantial net worth, the *future return* or *appreciation* of their investments will be their main concern. Though they may not need further current income, they may want to add to their capital base through appreciation in order to meet future expenditures such as the costs of education or retirement. Known as *growth investments* or *capital gain investments*, these investments with a potential for appreciation will usually provide little or no current income.

When considering your return on investment, there are three points to keep in mind. The first is *total return*. Investments—stocks and income-producing real estate, for instance—may result in appreciation as well as current income. Their total return is the sum you get from adding their current yield to their appreciation yield. Thus, a stock that had a six percent dividend yield and an appreciation of five percent in the last year had a total return of eleven percent for the year.

The second point to bear in mind is the investment's *after-tax return*. Capital gains eligible for the life-time capital gains exemption are exempt from tax. Furthermore, only two-thirds of other capital gains (not eligible for the exemption or in excess of the exemption limit) realized from the sale of investments is subject to tax. Dividends from Canadian companies are subject to tax at approximately two-thirds of the marginal tax rate otherwise applicable, as a result of the dividend tax credit system. Other investment income, such as dividends from foreign companies, royalties, etc., are taxed like ordinary earned income. Therefore, different types of investment income can be taxed very differently. Thus, total after-tax return is an important measure of investments.

The third point to consider is the *certainty of return* on your investment. With investments that solely or primarily provide current income, you can usually be quite certain of receiving this current income. Bonds, for instance, carry contractual agreements to pay their interest when due. Dividends are not contractually fixed, but are decided upon by the company's board of directors, who increase or decrease them according to the company's financial situation. The future capital appreciation of an investment is not a certainty. For that type of investment, the potential total return should therefore be much higher than for investments made to generate current income. The higher the potential of losing all or some portion of your invested capital, the higher should be the potential return.

LIQUIDITY

Liquidity refers to the ease with which you can convert an investment into cash. If you might need the money you invested to take care of emergencies or to take advantage of some other investment opportunities, liquidity can be very important.

Regular savings accounts, Canada Savings Bonds, and money market investments provide great liquidity, and so do most common stocks and the bonds of large companies. When you invest in smaller companies, you have less liquidity or marketability, because there are fewer shares of such stocks or bonds and fewer people interested in such investments.

Real estate is another example of a non-liquid investment. You may have to wait for months before you find a buyer who is willing to buy the property at your asking price, and then it will take additional time to close the transaction and get your cash out. Furthermore, your purchaser may not be able to give you the entire amount in a lump-sum payment, but only in installments payable over several years.

Typically, a higher liquidity is tied to a lower return. If you want high returns, be prepared to accept low liquidity.

EASE OF MANAGEMENT

There are a lot of people who say, "Investments and financial matters are not the most important things in my life, and I don't want to spend much time watching or worrying over them." For such people, ease of management is an important investment objective. If they don't want to spend much time managing their investments, they should either pay someone like an investment advisor or a trust company to manage their investments, or they should choose the kind of investments that demand little involvement or judgement: savings accounts, Canada Savings Bonds, term deposits, mutual funds and bonds held to maturity. What they need to avoid are investments that are subject to large and rapid price fluctuations.

Table 10-2 summarizes the general investment characteristics we have been discussing.

RISK AND RETURN

Risk and *return* occur in tandem. In Table 10-2, you can see how expected risk increases with investments which offer a higher expected return. Risk can be defined as the probability of loss in the future. Loss usually means partial loss of your invested capital, not total loss, although some investments may result in total loss. For example, if you are investing in an exploratory oil well deal and the drillers do not find oil, your investment is a total loss except for the value of any tax write-offs. A totally new company with unproven products has a much higher probability of going bankrupt in the near future than a company with a proven record of profitability in a stable industry.

With most investments, the probability of losing all of your investment capital in the foreseeable future is relatively low. However, the probability of losing some portion of your investment—say twenty percent—may be very high with such investments as common stock in a company in a volatile industry, or with real estate in a depressed market.

If you are prepared to accept greater risks, you have the chance of getting higher returns. The only way to attract investors to an enterprise with a high probability of loss is to offer them the possibility of a high return. Conversely, a low-risk enterprise attracts investors readily and therefore does not have to offer investors a chance of high return. Figure 10-1 is an Investment Vehicle Pyramid that shows many types of investments and the relative risk and return. Figure 10-2 shows the expected risk/reward for selected investments as measured by the incremental return above what most would call a risk-free investment—treasury bills. Note that as you go up the risk/return line, you have a higher probability (known as the standard deviation) that you will earn more or less than the expected return.

TABLE 10-2
INVESTMENT OBJECTIVES

Type of Investment	Safety of Principal in Constant Dollars	Hedge Against Inflation	Current Income	Future Appreciation	Liquidity	Ease of Management
Regular savings accounts/ Canada Savings Bonds	Excellent	Not very good	Fixed; very steady but low rate	None	Excellent	Very easy
Money market investments (Treasury bills, money market funds)	Good to excellent	Not very good	Fixed; very steady; rate near inflation	Generally none	Very good	Easy
Common stocks						
Income stocks	Fair	Fair	Relatively fixed; rate near inflation rate	Some	Good	Easy
Growth stocks	Moderate to poor	Generally good	Variable; low rate	Moderate to great	Good	Difficult
Bonds (high-quality corporate and government issues)	Good to excellent	Not very good	Fixed; very steady; rate near inflation rate	Generally none except discounted bonds	Good	Fairly easy
Mutual funds (common stocks)	Fair to poor	Variable but generally good	Variable	Moderate to great	Good	Easy
Real estate (income producing, other than residence)	Generally good	Generally good	Variable	Moderate to great	Relatively poor	Moderate to difficult
Precious metals (gold, silver)	Fair to poor	Generally good	None	Moderate to great	Good	Difficult

Risk of Purchasing Power

As you know to your sorrow, high inflation results in the reduced purchasing power of your dollar. In consequence, if you buy a four-year term deposit and inflation increases significantly, the principal and interest that are returned to you will have less purchasing power than the dollars you paid for it four years ago. Even though such investments are good with regard to safety of principal, they are not good with regard to maintaining your purchasing power.

During the early 1980s and late 1970s, years of high inflation, fixed-return investments that were tied up early in the inflationary cycle in savings accounts, term deposits, insurance policies, and bonds resulted in a substantial loss of purchasing power for those who invested in them.

Investments with growth potential will usually offer better protection in periods of inflation. If you refer to Table 10-2 once again, you will see that real estate and growth stocks generally do relatively well in periods of inflation. During periods of

FIGURE 10-1
INVESTMENT VEHICLE PYRAMID

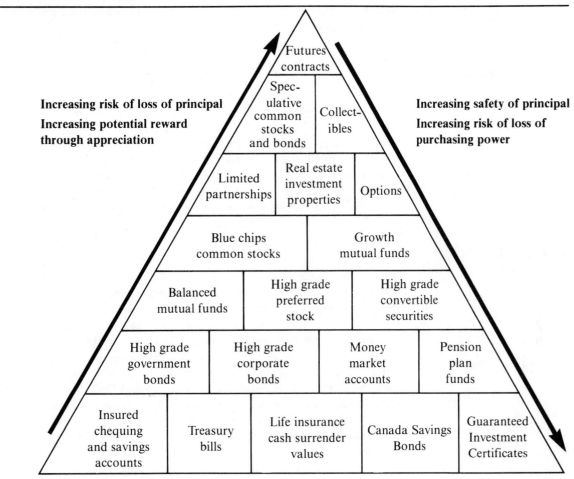

Increasing risk of loss of principal

Increasing potential reward through appreciation

Increasing safety of principal

Increasing risk of loss of purchasing power

FIGURE 10-2
RISK AND RETURN TRADE-OFF

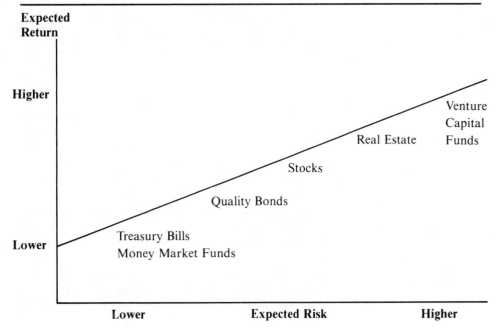

declining prices and severe recession, fixed-return investments become profitable, while variable-return investments lose in value. During the 1930s, a period of economic depression, people who owned real estate and common stocks watched the value of their investments decline steeply as rents, corporate profits, and dividends declined.

Financial Risks

Financial risk, also called business risk, is the possibility that unfavourable business conditions may reduce the expected returns from an investment. This might happen if the company you have invested in has a competitor who starts to produce a better product or finds a cheaper method of producing the same product, thereby reducing the earning potential of the company in which you have invested. It could happen if new rent control legislation applies to an apartment building you own, making it less attractive for potential purchasers. It could also be brought about by environmental protection laws that increase the operating costs of a company whose shares you hold.

Interest Rate Risk

This risk is usually associated with fixed-return investments such as bonds. What you risk here is a decline in the market value of your investment due to a higher rate of return on comparable new investments.

As an example, take some Government of Canada bonds that were issued in October 1968 at 6.50% annual interest or $65 per $1,000 bond. In October 1987 these bonds, which mature in the year 1995, were selling for about $795. The Canadian government is financially sound, so why did the price of these high-quality bonds go down by 20.5%? The reason is that between 1968 and 1987 the interest rates for bonds of similar quality and maturity had risen from 6.5% to more than ten percent.

If you had purchased those Government of Canada bonds in 1968 and sold them in October 1987, you would have suffered a capital loss of $205 for every $1,000 bond you held. You would have suffered the adverse effects of interest rate risk, because investors will not pay $1,000 for a bond that earns $65 a year when they can buy another bond of comparable quality and maturity date that pays them over $100 a year. By the same token, when interest rates have fallen, the bonds you bought before the fall will have risen in market value.

Real estate, too, is affected by interest levels. For example, when interest rates rose dramatically in the early 1980s, it became much more difficult for buyers to obtain financing at a rate they could afford. As a result, the housing market declined, and many a seller had to offer his house on contract at a lower interest rate or had to reduce the price of the house in order to make a sale.

Market Risk

Volatility in investment prices that is due to changes in "market psychology" or investors' attitudes is known as market risk. Such price fluctuations may affect the whole securities market—as was the case in the Depression, again in 1974, and in late 1987, when stock prices, as measured by widely used indexes, dropped by one-third to fifty percent. Price fluctuations may affect a particular industry or a particular security regardless of the financial ability of a particular company to pay the promised or expected investment returns. As an example, several smaller Canadian financial institutions experienced a drop in their share prices as a result of the failure of two regional banks in western Canada in 1985, although their own financial situation had not changed.

Price fluctuations give rise to buying and selling opportunities. For example, when the stock market is depressed because investors' attitudes are sour, buying opportunities in general for stocks may be very good. Also, when an individual stock is depressed but its fundamentals are still strong, the buying opportunity may be very good. On the other hand, when the market in general has experienced a significant increase in prices and investor attitudes are favourable, look around, evaluate the price increases in the securities you hold, and contemplate selling.

Leverage and Risk

Leverage denotes the borrowed money you invest together with your own funds in order to get a higher return on your money. When leverage works in your favour, it is great; but when leverage works against you, it can be disastrous.

To illustrate how leverage works, let's use a common leverage investment like real estate. Assume you buy a condominium for $60,000 and finance it with a $15,000 down payment and a $45,000 mortgage. After three years, you decide to sell the condominium and get $65,000 for it. You now have a gain of roughly thirty-three percent—a $5,000 gain on your $15,000 investment. If the $60,000 you invested had all been your own money, your gain on the sale would only be about eight percent—$5,000 on your investment of $60,000.

Conversely, with leverage you can lose money faster than without it when prices decline. Assume, for example, that after three years your leveraged $60,000 had dropped in price to $55,000. By selling it now, you would suffer a loss of thirty-three percent—a $5,000 loss on your $15,000 investment. Without leverage, your loss would be only eight percent—a $5,000 loss on your $60,000 investment.

Using leverage in buying stocks or bonds is called "buying on margin." When you buy on margin, you pay only a portion of the total cost, and your broker extends credit to you on the balance—and charges a monthly interest rate. The word margin refers to the difference between the market value of the stock bought and the loan which the broker will make against it.

The reason for buying on margin is capital appreciation. If you choose a stock that you think will increase in price fairly rapidly, you may make more profit by buying a greater number of shares on margin than by buying a smaller number for cash—if the stock goes up in price. Table 10-3 shows the rate of return (or loss) you will reap, with and without using margin, when the stock price increases (or decreases). In our example, we assume the stock was held for one year and we ignored brokerage commissions and the effect of taxes. The example shows that by trading on margin, an investor would realize forty percent more return than would be realized through a cash transaction (without margin). But leverage works both ways. If the stock declined to $40 per share, as shown in the example, an investor would have incurred 160 percent more loss using margin.

The general rules regarding margin trading are established by the various provincial exchanges where the stock is being traded and are binding on all brokers. Although the exchanges set the *minimum* amount the investor has to put up when buying stock on margin, brokers may and often do set their margin requirements substantially higher. The prescribed margin requirements vary with a security's selling price. For example, the Toronto Stock Exchange requires the investor to put up at least fifty percent of the purchase price of securities selling at $2.00 and over. A higher percentage is required for securities selling for less than $2.00.

One of the potential drawbacks of buying stocks on margin is that if a stock price subsequently declines, an investor may become "undermargined" (meaning that the investor's margin—down payment—plus the maximum margin loan his broker may credit to the investor on the current value of the stock falls under the original price of the stock). If this occurs, the broker would make a margin call to the investor requiring him to make up the deficiency in cash or to sell his stock.

Using our example in Table 10-3, the account of the investor who buys 200 shares at $50, putting down only the minimum fifty percent margin, and then subsequently sees the shares fall to $40, would receive a margin call for another $1,000 computed as follows:

TABLE 10-3
INVESTMENT RETURNS (OR LOSSES) BUYING ON MARGIN

	With Margin	Without Margin
Dollars Invested		
Your funds	$ 5,000	$ 5,000
Broker's funds	5,000	0
Total purchases (per share price $50)	$10,000 (200 shares)	$ 5,000 (100 shares)
1. Sale of stock for $60 per share		
Gross proceeds	$12,000	$ 6,000
Less repayment of borrowed funds	(5,000)	0
Less interest on borrowed funds at 12%	(600)	0
Net proceeds after repayment of borrowed funds	$ 6,400	$ 6,000
Return of original dollars invested	(5,000)	(5,000)
Net profit (or loss)	$ 1,400	$ 1,000
Return on your investment	$ 1,400 ÷ $5,000 = 28%	$ 1,000 ÷ $5,000 = 20%
2. Sale of stock for $40 per share		
Gross proceeds	$ 8,000	$ 4,000
Less repayment of borrowed funds	(5,000)	0
Less interest on borrowed funds at 12%	(600)	0
Net proceeds after repayment of borrowed funds	$ 2,400	$ 4,000
Return of original dollars invested	(5,000)	(5,000)
Net profit (or loss)	$(2,600)	$(1,000)
Return on your investment	$(2,600) ÷ $5,000 = (52%)	$(1,000) ÷ $5,000 = (20%)

MINIMIZING RISK

Eventually, you will have to choose between the various investment alternatives available to you and judge the risk inherent in each type of investment. You will have to decide what investment risks you are willing to take. If you are in your twenties, for example, and trying to save enough money for a down payment on a house, you will probably want to avoid investments with high financial and market risks. If, on the other hand, you have already bought your own house and are earning more than your current expenditures, and you have money put away for emergencies, then you may be quite willing to accept high financial and market risks in hopes of getting a high return.

MARGIN CALL

Total purchase (original price $50 X 200 shares)		$10,000
Less: Maximum margin loan from broker		(4,000)
(50% X $40 X 200 shares)		
Investor's original deposit		(5,000)
(50% X $50 X 200 shares)		
Margin deficiency for which a margin call would be issued		
($10,000 – $9,000 = $1,000)		$ 1,000

As your needs and economic status change, so will your investment objectives and the risks you are ready to take. Regardless of such changes, however, good investment strategy will dictate that you minimize overall risks through knowledge and diversification.

As a rule, the people who are successful investors know more than the average person about specific investments, about particular types of industries, about economic cycles, and about diverse factors of the economy. If you understand an investment opportunity and study its future potential, you should be able to reduce your risks substantially.

You will minimize risk by diversifying your investments so that they will not all be open to the same risks. Then, for example, if rising inflation and high interest rates decrease the value of your bonds, they will also increase the returns on your money market funds. You spread your risk by having various types of investments.

FORM 20—INVESTMENT OBJECTIVES

Now that you have an overview of the various types of investment objectives and risks, you can evaluate the relative importance that each of the listed investment objectives has for you. Once you have forced yourself to become clear about your priorities, you will have a sound basis for your investment decisions. On Form 20 the objectives we discussed earlier in the chapter are listed.

Figure 10-3 is an example of a couple in their mid-forties with significant employment income. They are primarily concerned about investments with growth potential and tax advantages that do not require a lot of time and effort to manage. They are also interested in using leverage and having diversification in their investment programme. They are not very concerned about safety, liquidity, and current income.

FORM 21—REVIEW OF YOUR PRESENT INVESTMENTS

The next step in your investment analysis is to review your present investments using Form 21. Before you complete this form, it might be helpful to look at the example in Figure 10-4 of the couple whose investment objectives are shown in Figure 10-3. Once you have completed Form 21, you can evaluate your present investments in terms of your objectives and see what changes should be considered.

- In the first column, list all the types of investments that make up the total of your liquid and investment assets on your net worth statement (Form 4).
- In the second column, enter the current value of each investment. The totals should agree with the amounts shown on your net worth statement (Form 4). In our example, total liquid assets are $33,500; other investments are $262,800; total investments are $296,300.
- In the third column, determine how diversified your present investment programme is by dividing the amount of each investment by the total amount of your investments. In our example, real estate of $90,000 is thirty percent of the total investments of $296,300.
- In the fourth column, list the investment objectives shown on Form 20 that each of your investments is to accomplish.
- Next, compute each investment's current yield before taxes as a percentage by dividing the income you received from it in the last year by the current value as listed in column 2.
- For those investments that had either a growth or a loss in value, enter the estimated annual percentage of gain or loss in column 6 using the following

FIGURE 10-3

File under INVESTMENT STRATEGY   Date: _May 5_

FORM 20   INVESTMENT OBJECTIVES

Indicate the relative importance you attribute to the following considerations by placing the appropriate number after each statement.

NOT IMPORTANT -- 1
MARGINALLY IMPORTANT -- 2
REASONABLY IMPORTANT -- 3
DEFINITELY IMPORTANT -- 4
MOST IMPORTANT -- 5

Diversification	How important is it for you to hedge against big losses by spreading your risks?	_3_
Liquidity	How important is it that you have cash available for emergencies or investment opportunities?	_2_
Safety	If we went into a deep economic depression, how important would it be for you to sell your investments at about the price you paid for them?	_2_
Current Income	How important is it that you get maximum income from your investments this year and next?	_1_
Future Appreciation	How important is it that your investment dollars keep pace with inflation or do better than inflation?	_5_
Tax Advantage	How important is it that you get all the tax relief that may be available to you?	_4_
Leverage	How important is it for you to use borrowed money in hopes of reaping a higher return on your investment?	_3_
Ease of Management	How important is it for you to have investments you do not have to watch or worry about?	_4_

---

simple formula: [Current value (in column 2) minus purchase price] ÷ [the number of years you have owned the asset times the purchase price] times 100. This formula is a simple way to approximate annual gain or loss. There are other more sophisticated ways to compute the annual gain or loss in value, and if you know one, use it, by all means.

• To compute the total annual return for each investment, add the percentages in columns 5 and 6.

Now that you have completed Form 21, you are in a position to evaluate your present investments in light of your objectives. The data on your form should tell you a lot about your present investment behaviour and is the starting point for making any changes in your investments.

1. How important is diversification? Look at the percentages in column 3. If a particular investment is thirty percent or more of the total, you might want to consider further diversification. In our example in Figure 10-4, one of the seven investment categories is thirty percent of the total.

2. How important is liquidity? Look at the total of your liquid assets and compare it to your employment income. If the total is more than fifty percent of your employment income, you probably have too much liquidity.

3. How important are safety and current income? These two objectives are closely related. Add up the current values of those investments for which you listed safety and current income as objectives under column 4. If these objectives are very important, the current value of investments providing safety and current income should exceed seventy percent of the total investment assets.

4. How important is growth? Add up the current values of those investments for which you listed future appreciation (inflation hedge) as an objective. If

FIGURE 10-4

File under INVESTMENT STRATEGY   Date: _**May 6**_

FORM 21   REVIEW OF YOUR PRESENT INVESTMENTS

TYPE OF ASSET COL. 1	CURRENT VALUE COL. 2	% OF TOTAL COL. 3	INVESTMENT OBJECTIVES COL. 4	CURRENT INCOME COL. 5	APPR'N (LOSS) COL. 6	ANNUAL RATE OF RETURN COL. 7
Savings Account	$9,100	3%	Liquidity & Safety	5%	—	5%
Money Market Funds	24,400	8%	Liquidity & Safety	8.5%	—	8.5%
Shares in Cdn. Public Companies	84,400	28%	Growth, Tax Savings	5%	10%	15%
Bonds	43,000	15%	Current Income	10%	(0.1%)	9.9%
Real Estate	90,000	30%	Growth	5%	10.3%	15.3%
Flow-through Shares	20,000	7%	Growth, Tax Savings	—	Too Early To Tell	—
R.R.S.P.	25,400	9%	Tax-deferred Growth	12%	—	12%
TOTAL	$296,300	100%				

appreciation is very important to you, the current value of investments providing appreciation should exceed seventy percent of the total investment assets. In our example in Figure 10-4, those investments for which appreciation is listed as one of the objectives comprise seventy-four percent of the total.

5. What about tax shelters? Often an investor interested in appreciation is also interested in tax-saving investments. If tax shelter is important, evaluate those investments in which tax advantage is a factor—real estate, oil and gas and mining shares, Canadian securities and retirement funds. If saving tax is important to you, probably at least thirty to forty percent of your investment funds should be invested in tax-advantaged investments. In our example in Figure 10-4, those investments for which tax advantage is an objective comprise forty-four percent of the total.

6. What about leverage? Are you interested in using borrowed money to make money? If so, analyze your investments to see to what extent you are using borrowed funds. Leverage is frequently used in investing in real estate, stocks, and bonds, where growth is a primary objective.

7. What about ease of management? If you believe it is important for professionals to assist you in selecting and managing your investments, then many of your investments should be made with the advice of investment counsellors or purchased through mutual funds. If you want to spend your time managing your own investments or if you are interested primarily in safety and current income and can easily find investments providing such objectives, then select and manage your investments yourself.

Rate of Return Analysis

In column 7 of Form 21, you should have entered the total annual rate of return before taxes that you achieved on each of your investments. How have you done? One measure of performance is inflation. Did you stay ahead of last year's increase in the Consumer Price Index (a widely used measure of inflation) in each of your investments? If not, which ones lagged behind inflation? Does it concern you to have some investments not keeping up with inflation?

Another measure of performance is the index in Table 10-1. How well did your stocks, bonds, real estate, and other investments compare with the average rate of return for similar investments listed in Table 10-1?

You should evaluate your total rate of return against some commonly used measures of performance to see how your present investment programme stacks up.

After you have completed the analysis of your present investments, you are ready to evaluate investment alternatives and consider changes in your present investment strategy.

ALLOCATION OF INVESTMENT DOLLARS

There are many investments to which you can allocate your investment funds, but the best way is to allocate your funds according to investment objectives appropriate for you. What is appropriate is related to your stage in life. Normally, safety, liquidity, and current income are important when you are young and interested in acquiring a car, furnishings, a home. As your employment income increases and you have additional funds for investment, growth and tax savings become of primary importance. As you approach retirement, safety and current income along with some inflation hedge usually become the important investment objectives.

Because of the large number of variables involved, such as health, employment stability, divorce, and inheritances, it is important to individualize an investment strategy, usually with the help of someone who can take an informed, unbiased view of your financial situation and objectives. With the information on Form 21, the independent advisor can review your present programme and help you allocate your investment funds to meet your objectives.

The following guidelines can help you develop an investment plan that is appropriate for your particular stage in life.

Before Marriage

As a financial stage in your life, this period begins with the first paycheque you receive in your first full-time job, and it lasts until you acquire family responsibilities. You may have a student loan to repay, but apart from that, you can probably do as you please with what is left after you've paid for your living expenses.

One of the best investments at this stage is in additional education or self-improvement programmes that will raise your professional prospects and your earning potential. This calls for some extra effort, of course, and takes up some of your precious spare time; but it pays off very handsomely, as a rule.

It is also sensible at this stage to establish a cash reserve in a savings account. This should be primarily for emergencies; but it can also help one over the common discomfort of being high and dry on Thursday and standing in a huge line at the bank on Friday.

It is probably not necessary to buy life insurance at this stage in your life. You do not need it unless you are supporting someone other than yourself.

If, like many young people nowadays, you are making quite a lot of money, and if you can keep your expenditures fairly low, you may be able to save substantial amounts that you can put into long-term investments. Given a reasonable housing market, you might use them to start acquiring a home of your own. In recent years such an investment has been an excellent hedge against inflation, and generally any gain realized on its eventual sale will be tax-free.

In addition to this, or as an alternative, you could look for investments with a potential for growth. A growth-oriented mutual fund might be your best investment of this type, since it allows you to diversify even when you do not have a lot of capital to invest. It is, moreover, managed for you, which is important to you at this stage in your life, when you should be spending your time and energy promoting your career prospects.

Before You Have Children

In our current social environment, it has become quite common for young couples to wait several years before they have children, or to decide not to have any children at all. With both spouses working, you have the income and opportunity to build up your net worth before you start to assume financial responsibility for children. Insurance is not a big factor yet, since there is little need for such protection when both spouses are working and the survivor can continue to work after the death of his or her spouse.

If the couple can keep their committed expenses at a reasonable level, then significant sums may be available for an investment programme. Of course, in the early years of marriage, there may be tremendous pressure to spend money on furnishings for a house or apartment, to have two cars if both spouses are working, and to buy labour-saving appliances because both spouses go out to work. Nonetheless, one should start on some careful budgeting during this period in order to ensure that funds are set aside for investment.

Before Your Children Are In University Or College

From the time that your first child arrives to the time that your youngest child has become self-supporting, financial considerations will have a high order of importance.

The first and most compelling aspect of financial planning then will be the protection of the spouse and children in case the primary wage earner should die, and this protection will have to be increased as the size of the family increases. Your need for life insurance should be analyzed carefully during this period, to determine the length of time for which insurance will be needed and how to obtain that coverage in the most economical way.

Aside from that, this is a time for living—a time when spending money may be the best way of using it. There are the obvious needs for additional clothing, housing and food, which raise your basic committed expenses. There is also a need for vacations and travel, and maybe for private school fees as well.

Fortunately, your income, too, is likely to go up quite a lot in this period, and therefore tax planning will become a critical aspect of your overall financial planning. And if your spouse is also working, tax planning will be much more critical. If your spouse has been primarily a homemaker, he or she may decide to enter or return to the job market when the children begin school. But before you become a two-income family, there may be some education expenditures if the non-working spouse needs to prepare for a career change.

The financing of children's university or college costs is something that parents should start to consider a great many years ahead of time. No matter how you finance these costs (the options that have some tax advantages will be discussed in Chapter 11), you will need to have fairly substantial funds available as your children reach university or college age.

When Your Children No Longer Require Support

The time when your earning power is at its highest will usually start when your children's education has been completed and you and your spouse are in your late forties or early fifties (maybe even the sixties for couples who delayed having children). That time should be used to establish your retirement income. Once your children need little or no financial support, your committed expenses decline, and you will have funds to invest in income-producing assets. You may also be able to spend more time managing your investments, which usually means that you can accept higher risks.

At this stage, you should review your life insurance. Taking your total resources into consideration, you may find that your need for insurance has become minimal. If so, the money you save by reducing or even eliminating insurance premiums can be used to build up your retirement fund.

As you get close to retirement, your investment strategy can still be aimed at building capital, but risk should be viewed as a more negative factor than it was in the earlier stages of your life. You may now want to start shifting your capital to investments that will provide income during retirement and will also provide a hedge against inflation. At this point, it will probably be advisable to get financial counselling to help you develop an effective investment strategy and assess the tax aspects of the various ways you might be paid your retirement funds.

Retirement

A comfortable income during retirement is one of the primary goals of financial planning and investment decisions. Financial independence during retirement is the result of planning and self-discipline in the earlier stages in one's life. For most people, it requires an early start, investments suitable to the various stages in one's life, an intelligent compromise between too much and too little insurance, and a great deal of determination.

It would be correct to conclude from the foregoing discussion that your investment objectives will and should change as your life situation changes. One thing that will not change is the need to keep your objectives clearly in mind as you formulate your investment strategies and make your investment decisions.

INVESTMENT MIX

An investment programme has to be related to the major periods of a planner's lifetime. In Table 10-4 we have provided some guidance as to how one might allocate investment funds in different periods of a lifetime to reflect changing investment objectives. As the table indicates, the need for safety and current income is usually greater in one's twenties and sixties than in one's thirties and forties. Also, the table reflects only selected investments—four traditional ones, and precious metals, which have become more important as Canada has experienced high levels of inflation.

ASSESSING YOUR INVESTMENT STRATEGY

Just as the different stages in your life should be reflected in your investment strategies, so there are some specific events—a new child, a higher-paying job, a large bonus, an inheritance, a large capital gain, a higher tax bracket, a change in the tax laws—that may call for modification of your investment strategy. Given such specific events as well as the overall changes, it is imperative that once, or better twice, a year you reassess your status, your investment objectives, and your investment strategy. We also recommend a minor review monthly or quarterly, or whenever there has been some change that will have financial consequences.

TABLE 10-4
SUGGESTED INVESTMENT MIX AMONG SELECTED INVESTMENTS

	Allocation in Percentages			
Age	Liquidity (Savings and Money Market Investments)	Current Income (Bonds, Low-Leverage Real Estate)	Growth (Common Stocks, Leveraged Real Estate)	Purchasing Power Hedge (Precious Metals)
20s	40-50%	20-30%	20-35%	5-10%
30s	10-20	10-20	60-80	10-15
40s	5-10	10-15	70-90	10-15
50s	5-10	15-20	55-70	10-15
60s	20-30	20-30	25-40	5-10

FORM 22—YOUR INVESTMENT STRATEGY

We strongly believe that you will achieve the best investment results by setting specific investment goals and then following an investment programme that is designed to accomplish your goals.

On Form 20, you assessed your current investment objectives. You then completed Form 21, *Review of Your Present Investments*. Now it is time for you to select from among your objectives those that will be the most important to you over the next three years. When that is clear to you, determine what changes you want to make in your present investment position.

- The first step in formulating your investment strategy is to review Form 20, *Investment Objectives*, and enter those objectives most important to you during the next three years under question 1 on Form 22.
- Next, enter your estimation of the inflation rate during the next three years. One of the measures of performance you should consider in targeting an overall return on your investments is the inflation rate.

- In light of your estimation of inflation and your past investment performance, enter your target overall annual return for the next three years under question 3 on Form 22. Be realistic in setting this target return; take into consideration your objectives and the time and effort you will devote to your investments.

- Under question 4, list the specific changes, if any, you want to make in your present investments. If you desire a higher return than you are presently achieving, you may have to reallocate some investment funds presently in safe, liquid investments to investments with greater growth potential.

- Another important factor in your investment programme is to determine what annual amount you can set aside from your current employment income during each of the next three years. For example, you and your spouse may plan to set aside $4,000 a year for investment in an RRSP. Or you may be planning to set aside $5,000 a year for an investment in a mutual fund. Try to set a goal for investing some amount of your employment income each year and enter that amount under question 5.

- Under question 6, list those investments you will make with the funds you have identified under question 5. These investments should be related to your objectives as well.

Figure 10-5 illustrates a completed Form 22 for the mid-life couple we used as an example in Figures 10-3 and 10-4.

MUTUAL FUNDS

Before we leave the general topic of investments, let's look briefly at the subject of mutual funds, a type of investment which has become increasingly popular in recent years. Mutual funds are professionally managed pools of investments which provide an individual investor with an opportunity to invest in the stock market or other areas without the responsibility of making specific investments. Mutual funds also allow individuals with limited funds to invest their money, together with a large number of other individuals, in many different investments, thereby "spreading the risk". When you buy units of a mutual fund, you own a share of all of the investments made by the fund, and as income is earned by the fund (dividends, interest, or capital gains), your portion is reinvested in additional units of the fund.

Mutual funds are sold by trust companies, banks, brokerage houses, insurance companies and by mutual fund managers. There are many different funds available. You can choose a fund that invests in the Canadian, U.S. or other countries' stock markets, Treasury bills and other money market instruments, corporate or government bonds, mortgages, precious metals, other commodities, or a combination of some or all of these. Some funds invest primarily to achieve capital appreciation, while others concentrate on earning current income. Many funds, often called "balanced funds," aim for both moderate capital appreciation and current income. Depending on the types of investments made by the mutual fund, a fund can qualify as an investment for your RRSP. You should be able to determine the type of fund that is best for you by matching the kind of investments it makes with your investment objectives identified earlier in this chapter.

Mutual funds are best for investors who want an easily managed investment with the potential for a higher return than other such investments, like Canada Savings Bonds. The reliability of the return from a mutual fund is, of course, dependent on its underlying investments—funds which invest in precious metals or other commodities will be more risky investments than those which invest in preferred shares or government bonds. Your mutual fund investment is also not covered by Canadian deposit insurance, unlike investments such as guaranteed investment certificates.

FIGURE 10-5

File under INVESTMENT STRATEGY

Date: *May 7*

FORM 22   YOUR INVESTMENT STRATEGY

1   What investment objectives (see Form 20) will be most important for you during the next three years? _____

Growth, Tax Shelter

2   What do you assume the inflation rate will be during the next three years?

4-6 %

3   What overall annual pre-tax return on your investments do you want to achieve in the next three years? *10-12 %*

4   What specific changes do you have to make in your present investments to achieve your objectives and overall rate of return in the next three years?

Decrease real estate investments to less than 30% of total investments

5   What annual amount do you believe you can set aside for investment during the next three years? *Very little except through tax savings and investment income of approximately $10,000*

6   What investments will you make with your additional investment dollars?

Growth stocks, mutual funds

If you are interested in investing in a mutual fund, there are several factors you should consider in choosing between the various funds which match your investment objectives. The single most important criterion for choosing a fund is the quality of its investment counsel, and this is usually best measured by past performance. Compare the funds' performance in the last year and over the previous five to ten years. Look for sustained performance. A fund with a tremendous gain in the last year, but mediocre performance over the last five years, may not be able to repeat its recent success. You can get information about a fund's performance directly from the fund manager or from regular surveys of registered fund performance in the financial press. See Chapter 15, *Keeping Up with Current Financial Information*, for some sources.

You should also consider the costs of investing in the various funds. Many funds charge substantial commissions (from one to nine percent) when you purchase units—these are often referred to as "front-end load" funds. All funds charge an annual management and administration fee, usually between one-half and two percent of the current value of the fund's assets. There may also be fees to withdraw money from the fund or to transfer to another fund. These fees will reduce the growth in value of your investment, but in the long term (five to ten years or more) a well-managed fund should realize a better rate of return, even after deduction of fees, than most people could achieve on their own.

11

EDUCATIONAL FINANCING

Education is a very special investment. It can introduce you to an entirely new way of looking at things. It can open up new directions and options in life. It can be a rare period of unencumbered time to pursue ideas for their own sake, to reflect, and to philosophize; and like many other special investments, it requires significant financial resources.

Although the most important considerations in choosing a school programme are educational, there are financial considerations also, and these have become a matter of concern for a great many families. Educational expenditures are no longer confined to four years of university. Many families have children attending private preschools, elementary schools, and secondary schools, where tuition and fees may approach or exceed $5,000 a year per child. On the other side of undergraduate school, there may also be masters' and doctoral programmes that require additional years of funding.

In this chapter, we will discuss the costs of education and how to meet them. We will focus on university costs, but much of this discussion will also be applicable to the costs of graduate schools and colleges.

HOW MUCH WILL UNIVERSITY OR COLLEGE COST?

Typically, university or college costs consist of the following major items:

- Tuition fees
- Books and supplies
- Room and board
- Transportation
- Personal expenses

University or college fees are a major, although not necessarily the largest, component of educational cost. Although costs vary among provinces, you can expect to pay approximately $1,300 per year.

The costs of books and supplies do not vary much from one university or college to the next. However, certain fields of study, such as engineering and the physical sciences, will generally require more expensive books and supplies than other fields of study. You should anticipate spending at least $200 to $300 on books and supplies.

Room and board costs vary considerably. For students who live at home and commute to school, room and board will be considerably less than for students who live on or near campus. For students who do not live at home, the costs vary with the type of residence chosen, which might be a dormitory on campus, or a privately owned apartment or rooming house. But, in general, you should expect to pay about $3,000 per year for room and board.

Transportation expenses for students who attend school a great distance from home are often considerable at the beginning and end of an academic year or term, while students who commute will have small daily transportation expenses.

Personal expenses include such items as laundry, toiletries, recreation, and furnishings for the student's "home away from home."

More accurate information about the cost of a particular school can be obtained from the school's admissions office.

FORM 23—UNIVERSITY, GRADUATE SCHOOL AND COLLEGE COSTS

University or college costs can be very high. It is therefore a good idea to do some planning ahead of time, and the first step in that process is to estimate what those costs are likely to be. Before or while you are filling in this form, it might be helpful to look at Figure 11-1, which shows you an example of the filled-in form.

- On line 1, list your children's first names.
- On line 2, list your children's present ages.
- On line 3, list how many years from now each child will be starting university or college. If a child is already in university or college, put a zero on line 3.
- On line 4, enter the estimated number of years each child will attend university or college and graduate school. If a child is presently in university, college or graduate school, enter the number of years required to complete his or her education.
- On line 5, compute the number of years to be used in an inflation adjustment. This number is determined by adding the years on line 3 to fifty percent of the years on line 4.
- On line 6, estimate the average annual inflation rate between now and the end of the child's educational programme.
- On line 7, enter the compound factor from Table 1 in Appendix I for the number of years on line 5 and for the estimated inflation rate on line 6.
- On line 8, enter for each of your children the present cost of one year's attendance at university or college. Obtain the approximate figures from the relevant institution's catalogue or use the approximate amounts discussed above.
- On line 9, estimate the inflation-adjusted annual university or college costs for each child by multiplying the amount on line 8 by the factor on line 7.
- On line 10, calculate the total estimated university or college costs for each child by multiplying the amount on line 9 by the number of years on line 4.
- On line 11, estimate the annual after-tax rate of return on educational funds invested.

- On line 12, enter the compound factor from Table 1 in Appendix I for the number of years on line 5 and for the estimated rate of return on line 11.
- On line 13, enter the amount of funds presently set aside for the education of each child.
- On line 14, calculate the estimated future value of the present educational funds by multiplying the amount on line 13 by the factor on line 12.
- On line 15, calculate the annual amount to be invested for each child's education.
    - (a) First subtract the amount on line 14 from the amount on line 10.
    - (b) Divide the result in 15a by the compound factor from Table 2 in Appendix 1 for the estimated rate of return on line 11 and the number of years on line 5. The result is the annual amount to be invested for each child, to be entered on line 15(c).

Now that you have picked yourself up off the floor after the fainting spell induced by the grand total of your children's estimated university or college costs and the annual amount to be invested, let us consider the various means of financing these costs.

WHO PAYS?

Most universities, colleges, and grantors of financial aid have developed guidelines for determining how much a student's family can pay for education and how much financial aid may be needed. They start with the premise that the responsibility of paying university or college costs falls on the student's parents and the student to the extent of their ability to pay them.

Financial Aid

The provincial governments have programmes which provide students with financial assistance in the form of loans and grants. Qualification for these programmes is based on a means test and examines the financial resources of both the student and the parents. Details of the programmes and applications are available through universities, high schools or by contacting the Ministry of Education.

There are many scholarships available through both the universities and colleges and private foundations. Again you should contact the universities, colleges or high schools for information. Many companies have educational assistance programmes for children of their employees. The personnel office should be able to assist you in this matter.

If you or your children do not qualify for financial assistance, you should investigate other ways of reducing your costs such as the Registered Education Savings Plan, loans or gifts, and investment of family allowance payments.

Reducing the Cost of an Education

The benefits of a Registered Education Savings Plan and other income-splitting methods result from tax-planning techniques discussed in Chapter 6. Shifting income from the parent who is in a high tax bracket to the student who is in a low tax bracket will reduce the taxes paid by the family as a whole, thereby providing the same kind of financial relief as a scholarship grant.

Now let us see how income shifting might work for you if your child is attending a school that costs $5,000 a year. We will assume that your child has agreed to earn and pay $1,000 of that cost and you have agreed to pay the remaining $4,000. If you are in

FIGURE 11-1

File under EDUCATIONAL FINANCING   Date: _June 11_

FORM 23   UNIVERSITY, GRADUATE SCHOOL AND COLLEGE COSTS

1	Children's Names	_Sue_	_John_	_Elizabeth_
2	Ages of Children	_20_	_19_	_10_
3	Number of Years until University	_in university_	_in university_	_8_
4	Estimated Number of Years in University and Graduate School	_4_	_5_	_6_
5	Number of Years for Inflation Adjustment	_2_	_2.5_	_11_
6	Estimated Annual Inflation Rate between Now and End of Education	_8_	_8_	_6_
7	Inflation Factor	_1.17_	_1.21_	_1.90_
8	Estimated Annual University Costs in Today's Dollars	_$5,000_	_$5,000_	_$5,000_
9	Estimated Annual Costs Adjusted	_5,850_	_6,050_	_9,500_
10	Estimated TOTAL Costs Adjusted	_$23,400_	_$30,250_	_$57,000_
11	Estimated After-Tax Rate of Return on Educational Funds	_8%_	_8%_	_9%_
12	Compound Factor for Rate of Return on Line 11	_1.17_	_1.21_	_2.58_
13	Present Value of Funds Set Aside for Education	_$10,000_	_$8,000_	_0_
14	Future Value of Funds Set Aside	_$11,700_	_$9,680_	_0_

FIGURE 11-1 CONT'D

15 | Annual Amount to be Invested for Education

a) total needed:

$11,700 $20,570 $57,000

b) compound factor

2.08   2.68   17.56

c) annual amount required:

$5,625 $7,675 $3,246

the fifty percent tax bracket, you would have to earn $8,000 to have $4,000 left after taxes, and that is a very expensive way to go.

Now let us look at the child's tax bracket. With an income of $1,000 for the year, the child will not be taxable. Even if the child had income that amounted to $5,000, the child would pay no tax. But you would have paid $4,000 in taxes to generate the same $4,000 after-tax income. Therefore, if you can manage to transfer sufficient income to your child to finance education costs, significant tax savings can result.

Registered Educational Savings Plans

A Registered Educational Savings Plan (RESP) can be a useful tool for parents or grandparents who wish to set aside funds to help their children finance their post-secondary education.

A parent or grandparent sets up the RESP by making a contribution and designating a child or grandchild as beneficiary. Depending on the plan, contributions may be made in lump sums or as a series of regular payments. There are limits on the amount that can be contributed to a plan. The contributions are not tax deductible but income earned on the contribution accumulates tax-free in the plan. The contributions may be refunded tax-free to the contributor. The timing of such refunds depends on the terms of the particular RESP.

The major restriction with RESPs is that the accumulated income must be used to finance the beneficiary's post-secondary education. Therefore, if the child chooses not to continue his or her education after high school, the income in the plan cannot be paid to the child or the contributing parent. For this reason, it is preferable to choose a plan which will allow you to change the beneficiary so that the income can be used by another child instead. Plans with flexibility in the choice of beneficiaries are available through several major investment dealers, mutual fund managers and life insurance companies.

Education costs are very broadly defined and include room and board as well as tuition and books. As long as the child is going to school, income can be distributed from the plan to finance some or all of the child's reasonable education costs. The child will pay tax on such income received in the year only if it, plus any other income earned in the year, generates taxes payable which exceed the child's tuition and education tax credit, basic tax credit and any other credits the child is entitled to.

In summary, the advantages of RESPs are that:

1. they allow income to accumulate tax-free; and
2. the income is ultimately taxed in the hands of the child who should pay tax at a lower rate than the parent and should have available substantial credits that could not otherwise be claimed by the parent.

There have been very few RESPs offered in the past and these have been very restrictive. However, a few new plans are now being offered which are more flexible with respect to investments held by the plan, subsequent changing of beneficiaries, refunds of contributions, academic requirements and eligible schools. But, before you invest in one of these plans, you should be aware of all of its terms and how they may affect you.

Loans or Gifts

As discussed in Chapter 6, opportunities for income splitting with spouses or minor children have been severely restricted in recent years. However, as most post-secondary age students are eighteen years or over, income splitting is still possible. The student may be loaned or given funds for investment. The income generated by the funds will be taxed in the hands of the student who usually has a lower marginal tax rate than his or her parents. The result is that from the same income, more after-tax dollars will be available for financing the child's education.

Family Allowance

Family allowance is taxed in the hands of the person who claims the children as dependents. Provided that the payments are deposited in a separate account and invested for the child's benefit, the income earned will be attributed to the child rather than to the parent. As a result, this income can often be received tax-free for eighteen years.

12

RETIREMENT PLANNING

Until they retire, people who have been working most of their adult years are usually unaware of how much their jobs and their work environments mean to them. Unprepared, many of them experience a tremendous sense of loss, emptiness and uselessness. Some companies now hold pre-retirement clinics to help their employees make the transition from organizational life to private life. Essentially, such clinics tell the impending retirees to do the following:

- Evaluate your accomplishments; assess your strengths and weaknesses, your likes and dislikes; and envisage your activities during your retirement years.
- Widen your personal interests. Explore pursuits from which you would derive great satisfaction—a hobby, a service project, an autobiography.
- Analyze your financial requirements and the sources of your retirement income.

There are regrettably few retirees whose financial provisions for retirement prove to be adequate. Retirement planning is essential if you are to reach the goals you have set for that period of your life. To do this effectively, you should start to work on your retirement programme at least ten to fifteen years before you expect to retire.

You will have to work out what your financial requirements will be at retirement and then plan to have the necessary financial resources available.

FORM 24—ESTIMATED BASIC LIFESTYLE EXPENDITURES AT RETIREMENT

Before you can estimate your financial needs and resources at retirement, you must set a time frame for your projections by deciding at what age you want to retire. Most people think of sixty-five as retirement age, but you may want to retire earlier or later than that, or maybe plan on partial retirement instead of complete retirement.

The simplest way of estimating your financial needs at retirement is to begin with your present pattern of expenditures, and then to visualize in what respects the pattern will be different once you have retired.

- Begin by completing the first column, *Current Year*, with the figures you listed on Form 7, *Basic Lifestyle Expenditures*, filed under *Financial Profile*.
- In the second column, *At Retirement*, complete lines 1 through 18 by putting your estimated expenditures in terms of today's dollars (present-day prices). In some categories, such as medical care, it may be wise to allow for greater expenses than those you have at present. In other categories, such as housing, clothing, and transportation, you are likely to have smaller expenses than at present. Your home mortgage, for example, may be completely paid off by the time you retire.
- On line 19, enter the total of your estimated annual expenditures in retirement. This will not be your final forecast, because so far it has not taken inflation into account.
- On line 20, list in how many years you plan to retire.
- On line 21, estimate the average annual rate of inflation for the years before you retire.
- For line 22, select the right figure from Table 1 in Appendix I. Choose the column with the same percentage as the one you listed on line 21. Then go down that column until you get to the number of years you listed on line 20, and there you have your compound factor.
- For line 23, multiply the total on line 19 by the inflation factor on line 21.

FORM 25—ESTIMATED DISCRETIONARY EXPENDITURES AT RETIREMENT

In completing this form, you will essentially do the same things you did to complete the previous form.

- Begin by completing the first column, *Current Year*, with the figures you listed on Form 8, *Discretionary Expenditures*, filed under *Financial Profile*.
- In the second column, *At Retirement*, use today's dollars (present-day prices) for your estimates on lines 1 through 12.

In some categories, such as vacations or hobbies, you may want to spend more in retirement than you do now; but in others, such as support of relatives or contributions to retirement plans, you might be spending much less or nothing at all.

- On line 13, add up the amounts on lines 1 through 12 in the second column.
- On line 14, list the same inflation factor you listed on line 22 of Form 24.
- For line 15, multiply the total on line 13 by the factor on line 14.

FORM 26—ESTIMATED RETIREMENT NEEDS, INCLUDING TAXES

- On line 1, list your total from line 23 of Form 24, *Estimated Basic Lifestyle Expenditures at Retirement*.
- On line 2, list your total from line 15 of Form 25, *Estimated Discretionary Expenditures at Retirement*.
- On line 3, put the sum of lines 1 and 2.

The Impact of Taxes

So far, none of your estimates have taken income taxes into account. Therefore, the next and last step in estimating your financial needs at retirement will be to calculate the impact of income taxes on your retirement needs. It is likely that some, if not most, of the income you will receive during retirement will be taxable. The federal and provincial governments expect their share of your retirement income. Due to inflation, you may actually find yourself in quite a high tax bracket after you retire. A "rule of thumb" that can be used to estimate your tax requirements during retirement is to assume that taxes will constitute thirty-five percent of your estimated needs. Although this may seem lower than the average tax rate you are currently paying, remember that some of your income during retirement may not be taxable or may be taxed in a favoured way.

- To estimate retirement expenditures including taxes using an estimated average tax rate of thirty-five percent, put a tax factor of sixty-five percent on line 4 of Form 26.
- Then, on line 5, compute your total estimated retirement needs including taxes by dividing the amount on line 3 by the tax factor of sixty-five percent.

If you would like a more accurate estimate of taxes payable on your retirement income, fill out Form 11 assuming you were already retired. Include all your expected sources of income as listed in Form 19 and any expected deductions. Use the resulting taxable income figure calculated on Form 11 to estimate your total taxes payable by referring to Appendix II. Your total retirement needs including taxes will then be the sum of your estimated basic and discretionary lifestyle expenditures on retirement (lines 1 and 2 on Form 26) plus this estimated tax amount.

RETIREMENT INCOME

To have sufficient income to meet one's retirement needs requires some long-term planning. Although most people have an employee retirement plan, these plans are not necessarily designed to provide all your needs at retirement. The remainder of your needs may not be adequately covered by Old Age Security or the Canada or Quebec Pension Plan. So it is up to you to have sufficient investment income to make up any deficiency.

We have counselled some people who did not realize the importance of investment income to their retirement dreams until they were just a few years away from retirement. They were then faced with the need either to continue working or else to scale back their retirement lifestyle. The need to start serious retirement planning at least ten to fifteen years before you wish to retire cannot be emphasized enough. Ten to fifteen years before retirement, you have probably completed the children's education, settled comfortably into your dream house, and stopped your "accumulating phase." You have completed phases of your life that require heavy expenditures, so you will probably have more funds available for investment and should concentrate on funding your retirement.

Allocate your funds to investments with a solid growth potential. You should now avoid investments with a high risk because you do not have much time to recover from substantial losses. As you near retirement, you should continue to invest primarily in quality, growth-oriented investments; but start to look for quality income-oriented investments as well. You should, however, also be concerned about the impact of inflation during retirement, so investments that provide a hedge against inflation should be a substantial part of your investment programme.

Below is a brief description of the more common sources of retirement income.

COMPANY RETIREMENT PLANS

Companies in Canada generally provide two basic types of retirement plans: registered pension plans or Deferred Profit Sharing Plans. A registered pension plan can be either benefit-oriented or contribution-oriented. A pension plan is registered if it complies with certain conditions and limits and has been accepted for registration by the Minister of National Revenue. Virtually all pension plans in Canada are registered because only registered pension plans qualify for the special tax advantages described below.

With a *defined benefit plan*, the amount of the benefits you will be paid at retirement has been set in advance, and the company's contributions to the plan are actuarially determined to give the plan the assets necessary for paying these predetermined benefits. Often, retirement benefits are set according to a formula related to your earnings (for example, seventy-five percent of the average of your highest five years' earnings).

With a *defined contribution or money purchase plan*, the company's contribution on behalf of its employee is either a flat dollar amount or a percentage of the employee's compensation. Here, the amount of the employee's retirement benefits will depend on how much capital has been contributed on the employee's behalf, on how much this capital has earned, and on how large an annuity can be purchased with the accumulated funds, given prevailing interest rates at the time of retirement.

Deferred Profit Sharing Plans, which are contribution-oriented, are funded by the company according to a formula based on a percentage of the company's profits. The level of these contributions varies with the company's profits, and if there are no profits, there are no contributions. As is the case with pension plans, a Deferred Profit Sharing Plan must also be registered as complying with certain terms and conditions, in order to qualify for the special tax advantages described below. Deferred Profit Sharing Plans tend to be used much less than registered pension plans as retirement plan vehicles by Canadian companies.

Tax Advantages

The money you have in a company's Deferred Profit Sharing Plan (DPSP) or registered pension plan (RPP) does not become taxable until you receive it upon retiring or leaving the company for some other reason. It can therefore accumulate and gather a compound rate of return untaxed, and this is a tremendous advantage. A given sum of money invested at eight percent untaxed will double itself in nine years; but it will take about sixteen years for that sum to double itself if your eight percent return is taxable every year and you are in the forty percent tax bracket.

Let's look at these two tax situations further by comparing two people, Joe and Fred. Each sets aside $3,000 a year from current compensation for a retirement plan. Let's say that in Joe's case, this is done by his employer contributing $3,000 on his behalf to the company's RPP. Because the pension plan is registered, Joe does not have to pay tax currently on this $3,000. Fred, however, operates on a do-it-yourself basis; he has to include his $3,000 of compensation in taxable income, then takes what is left of it after taxes and invests it. If both Joe and Fred are in the thirty percent tax bracket, Joe's $3,000 can all be invested (in the company's RPP) because he has paid no tax on that portion of his compensation. Fred has only $2,100 to invest, because thirty percent of his $3,000 has to be paid to Revenue Canada. Further, the income on Joe's annual $3,000 pension contribution is tax-deferred because it is in an RPP; the income on Fred's investment will be taxable. Assume that the RPP holding Joe's pension contributions gets ten percent on its investments and that Fred finds a similar type of investment that yields ten percent before taxes. Joe's funds compound tax-free: Fred's compound annual rate will only be seven percent because of his thirty percent tax bracket. After the first year, Joe's $3,000 has earned $300 in the RPP. Fred's $2,100 has earned $210, but after he pays his tax, only $147 is left for reinvestment. After one year, Joe has

$1,053 more than Fred. If they continue on the same basis, after a period of thirty years, the difference is even more impressive.

If you use a calculator and punch in the data for the annual amount invested ($3,000 versus $2,100) and rate of return (ten percent versus seven percent), the results after thirty years of steady investing will be:

Joe $493,500

Fred $198,400

The difference between the retirement funds of Joe and Fred, about $295,000, is due to the tax-free compounding of $3,000 per year at ten percent on Joe's behalf in his employer's RPP versus the after-tax compounding of $2,100 per year at seven percent in Fred's account. Well, you say, that's not a fair comparison because Joe's funds will be taxed when he receives them during retirement. That's right—your retirement benefits are taxed when received, at your applicable marginal tax rate of up to approximately forty-five percent or higher. Fred would not be taxed on any of his $198,400 at the end of thirty years, since he has already been taxed on the capital he invested and on the earnings of this invested capital. However, there are tax-favoured ways of receiving your retirement payments that we will discuss in a few pages, which allow you to spread the tax impact throughout your retirement years, and minimize the total tax paid.

And even if Joe took all his pension funds out in a lump sum and paid tax at a rate of forty-five percent, he would still have about $271,400 after tax, or over $73,000 more than Fred.

This example assumed Joe accumulated his retirement funds in an RPP; the same tax advantages would have resulted if his employer's contributions had instead been invested in the company's DPSP.

This example also assumed only the employer contributed to the RPP. If the terms of the RPP also required contributions by employees, Joe's contributions would have enjoyed special tax treatment. Joe's contributions would have been deductible from his taxable income (subject to certain limits already discussed in Chapter 6) and income on these contributions would also accumulate tax-free, giving the same special tax treatment as provided for employer contributions.

Retirement Plan Terms and Conditions

Retirement plans (RPPs, DPSPs and other unregistered plans) are generally administered by a trustee or several trustees, such as a trust company or the employer (usually represented by a group of the company's executives resident in Canada). As already discussed, most companies have retirement plans that comply with terms and conditions required for registration by the Department of National Revenue, in order to take advantage of the tax benefits described above. As well, there are provincial or federal standards under applicable *Pension Benefits Acts* which must be met.

The standards for all pension plans governed by federal legislation were significantly changed in 1986, effective 1 January 1987. Similar changes have been introduced for pension plans governed by legislation in Ontario and Alberta (effective in 1987) and Nova Scotia (effective in 1988) and are proposed in New Brunswick and Quebec. These changes will improve employee pension benefit entitlements by providing for earlier entitlement for membership in employer pension plans, earlier vesting of pension benefits, minimum rates of return on employee contributions and greater transferability of pension benefits on ceasing employment. The equal division on marriage breakdown of pension benefits which accrued during the marriage is also provided for.

The present reform of pension benefits standards has been underway for several years, and will probably take several more years to complete. But given the significant action taken by the federal government plus the five provinces mentioned above, similar legislation will likely apply to all public and private pension plans in Canada by 1990.

If you are covered by a company retirement plan, make sure you understand the details of the plan and know your rights and benefits. Ask for an annual update on the details of your retirement accounts; in particular, find out what monthly benefit you will receive at retirement and what vested benefits you have.

To assist you in better understanding your retirement plan and the potential effect of pension reform, the more important and common terms in such plans are discussed below.

Eligibility Requirements

Normally, there is a waiting period before a new employee is eligible for coverage under a plan. You should find out how long this waiting period is with your company.

After pension reform, full-time employees and some part-time employees (if they have sufficiently high earnings) will generally be eligible for membership in the company pension plan after two years service. In some provinces where the pensions benefits standards have not been amended recently, there are no rules limiting the length of time an employee must wait before being eligible for membership.

Contributions to the Plan

Contributions to finance a pension plan can be made in several ways:

- The company contributes all the funds.
- The company and the employees share in the contributions on some predetermined basis.
- The employees can make voluntary contributions in addition to their regular contributions. The ability to make tax-deductible additional voluntary contributions has been severely restricted as a result of tax changes introduced in October 1986. Refer to Chapter 6 for details.

One of the major changes introduced in the current round of pension reform is the so-called "fifty percent rule". Under this rule, the employer must pay for fifty percent of the employee's accrued benefits on termination, death or retirement. Any excess payment by the employee to the time of his termination may be refunded, used to fund increased pension benefits or transferred to the pension plan of his new employer, depending on which legislation applies. This rule is waived under the federal *Pension Benefits Standards Act* if the pension plan provides sufficient inflation protection. A version of the fifty percent rule applies in some, but not all of the provinces, whose *Pension Benefits Standards Acts* have not been recently amended.

Retirement Date

Most pension plans specify a retirement age for their employees, such as the first day of the month after which the employee reaches the age of sixty-five. An employee may be able to retire earlier, but that will usually reduce the employee's retirement benefit according to a formula outlined in the plan.

Under the Ontario and the proposed Quebec changes, an employee must retire not later than the age of 65 or 65½, respectively. In other jurisdictions, there are no rules for determining normal retirement age.

Under the federal, Alberta, and Ontario legislation, an employee can retire early within ten years of normal retirement. Under the proposed changes in Quebec, early retirement will be allowed within five years of normal retirement.

Resignation or Dismissal

Pension benefits for employees who leave the company for reasons other than retirement are computed according to the amount of employee's own contributions to the plan and to the pension's *vesting rules*. Whatever amount the employee has contributed is returned with interest when the employee leaves. (See also the discussion of the fifty percent rule under *Contributions to the Plan*.)

Under pension reform, a minimum interest rate must be paid on refunded employee contributions.

Vesting Rules

Whether an employee will receive some part of the company's contributions upon dismissal or resignation is determined by the vesting rules set out in the company's benefit package. Under these rules, the percentage of the company's contributions to which the employee is entitled will increase with the number of years of employment. A company might have a vesting schedule that fully vests its employees after ten years with the company. In that case, upon retiring or leaving for other reasons after ten years, the employee is entitled to 100 percent of the contributions made on his or her behalf. Pension plans have a deliberate bias in favour of employees who stay with the company for a long time.

The changes introduced in the current round of pension reform will significantly reduce the time period necessary for vesting. Under the federal, Nova Scotia, Ontario and the proposed Quebec legislation, full vesting will occur after only two years of membership in the pension plan. Full vesting will occur after five years of employment under the Alberta and the proposed New Brunswick legislation.

Death Benefits Prior to Retirement

Your retirement plan will outline what benefits, if any, will be available to your survivors, should you die before retirement age. Retirement plans will often provide for the return of any employee contributions, but may not make any further provisions, assuming the employee to be adequately covered under the company's group life insurance plan.

Death benefits prior to retirement will be significantly increased under pension reform, to reflect the value of vested pension benefits rather than just employee contributions. Under federal legislation, your surviving spouse will be entitled to the commuted value of the amount you would have been entitled to had you left your job at death, including any additional value resulting from the fifty percent rule. Under Ontario legislation, your spouse or your estate will receive 100% of the commuted value of your vested benefits. Under Nova Scotia, Alberta, and the proposed New Brunswick legislation, the mandatory pre-retirement death benefit will be at least sixty percent of the commuted value of the deferred pension, rather than the 100% Ontario requires.

Indexation of Pension Benefits

Both the Ontario and the Nova Scotia legislation include requirements for inflation-adjusted pensions, although details of how this is to be accomplished are not yet known. The federal legislation also encourages employers to provide inflation protection by granting an exemption from the fifty percent rule if acceptable inflation protection is provided.

Retirement Payments

Retirement benefits from an RPP are paid out in the form of an annuity for the remaining life of the retired employee. The annuity may have different features, including a guaranteed minimum term, survivorship options or guarantees of the payout of employee contributions in the event of early death.

You should take great care in choosing your RPP annuity. If you choose a simple life annuity, with no guaranteed minimum term and no survivorship options, your survivors will receive nothing from the annuity after your death, even if you die shortly after its purchase. This is not a prudent way to invest the retirement benefits you have worked so hard to earn, unless you are leaving your dependents other substantial assets.

If you choose a guaranteed minimum term of say, ten years, the annuity payments will continue for the greater of ten years and the number of years you live after retirement. If you choose a joint-and-last survivor option, the annuity will continue to pay throughout your lifetime and that of your spouse, should he or she live longer. These options will reduce somewhat the amount of your monthly pension benefit (because the life insurance company expects to have to pay benefits for a longer time) but will give you much more certainty in planning for your retirement and for those you may leave behind.

Under the revised federal *Pension Benefits Standards Act* and under several existing and proposed provincial acts, RPP annuities must provide benefits for surviving spouses (for example, 60 or 66⅔ percent of accrued benefits at the time of death of the first spouse).

The benefits paid by the various life insurance companies for otherwise similar life annuities can vary substantially. You should take the time and trouble to get several quotes from different suppliers, and if possible, consult an independent advisor (one who does not sell only one or two companies' products!) who can evaluate the different products available without bias.

Funds accumulated in a DPSP can be used on retirement to purchase an annuity (with or without a guaranteed minimum term, which cannot exceed fifteen years, or survivorship options), but may also be received in installments payable not less frequently than annually for a period of not more than ten years. As well, although lump sum payments are generally not allowed from RPPs, they can usually be made from DPSPs.

Flexibility in timing of retirement payments will be discussed more fully under *Taxation of Retirement Payments.*

Taxation of RPP and DPSP Payments

Because payments from RPPs and DPSPs are taxed in essentially the same manner as payments from Registered Retirement Savings Plans (RRSPs), taxation of these payments will be discussed together after the following general description of RRSPs.

REGISTERED RETIREMENT SAVINGS PLANS

Registered Retirement Savings Plans (RRSPs) are very flexible vehicles which can be used to build up retirement funds for those who are self-employed, as well as providing employees covered by company pension plans an opportunity to augment their retirement income. In essence, your RRSP is your own individual pension plan account. Unlike an RPP or a DPSP, there is no employer to fund the plan—all contributions must come from you. (This is not true in the case of an employer-funded group RRSP, but such plans are not common and will not be discussed further here.)

RRSPs are allowed generous tax treatment, similar in many ways to that provided to RPPs. Up to specified limits, contributions to an RRSP are deductible from the contributor's taxable income. (These limits are discussed in Chapter 6.) As well, income earned in the RRSP on these contributions accumulates tax-free as long as it remains in the plan. This tax-free compounding of tax-deductible contributions allows the RRSP contributor to accumulate a significantly higher retirement fund by using an RRSP instead of another savings plan. (See the "Joe and Fred" example discussed earlier in this chapter under *Company Retirement Plans* for more details.) Examples of possible accumulations within an RRSP are outlined in Table 6-1 in Chapter 6.

Table 6-1 clearly demonstrates the advantage of starting your retirement savings as early as possible. The benefits of tax-free compounding of income within an RRSP are not earned evenly over time. Instead, the benefits are much greater in later years because income is earned not just on the initial contribution but on the continually growing pool of previously-earned income. You may need to be a mathematician to understand exactly how this happens, but a quick look at Table 6-1 indicates the potential benefits. For example, after ten years of contributing $7,500 each year, assuming a ten percent rate of return, your RRSP will contain $119,510. If you continue the same contributions for another ten years, earning the same rate of return, your RRSP will have grown to $429,560. After another ten years of the same contributions at the same rate of return, your RRSP will have grown to $1,233,710. These are very impressive numbers!

There are RRSPs which should suit any kind of investor, although the types of investments that can be made in an RRSP are limited by the *Income Tax Act*. RRSPs are offered by banks, trust companies, life insurance companies, most stock brokerage firms, credit unions, *caisses populaires* and mutual funds. For more conservative investors, there are RRSPs which invest in low-risk investments such as guaranteed investment certificates, money market funds and savings accounts. More speculative investments such as Canadian corporate bonds and equities are also available. And for those who like to make their own investment decisions, self-administered RRSPs are also available. In deciding the appropriate type of investments for your RRSP, consider the discussion of *Investment Objectives* in Chapter 10. As well, before choosing a plan offered by a particular bank, trust company, etc., compare the features of the plan to similar ones offered by other companies. For example, you should compare fees charged to purchase, transfer and withdraw funds from the plan, administration fees, expected rates of return, frequency of compounding, length of time the rate of return is guaranteed and portability (the ability to transfer funds from one plan to another).

You may also make contributions to an RRSP for the benefit of your spouse. The tax advantages of this have already been discussed in Chapter 6.

Taxation of Retirement Payments

Let's assume now that you have accumulated substantial retirement funds in your company's RPP or DPSP, or in your own RRSP. How can these funds be received and what are the tax consequences on receipt?

Retirement benefits from an RPP will generally start as regular monthly receipts as soon as you retire, although they may be delayed until you reach age sixty-five in the case of early retirement. The amount of your monthly benefit will be affected by the various options you choose—guaranteed periods of payment, survivorship options, etc.

Retirement benefits from a DPSP can be paid to you on retirement as an annuity payable monthly, although you can choose instead to receive your benefits in installments (paid no less frequently than annually) for a period of not more than ten years or in a lump sum payment. Receipt of retirement benefits from your DPSP can also be delayed until age seventy-one if desired, to prolong the advantage of tax-free compounding of income in the DPSP.

Your choice in timing the receipt of your retirement funds accumulated in an RRSP is even more flexible. As with RPPs and DPSPs, you can choose to receive monthly payments for life, with or without a guaranteed term or survivorship options. You can also choose to receive your funds as a fixed term annuity payable to age ninety (or alternatively until your spouse is ninety). You may also elect to receive your RRSP funds in a lump sum or use them to invest in a Registered Retirement Income Fund

(RRIF). A RRIF is similar to a term annuity to age ninety, but instead of the monthly payment remaining constant during the annuity term, it increases with time. This pattern is intended to help retired people better cope with rising living costs due to inflation.

Effective for 1986 and subsequent years, individuals will be allowed even more flexibility in timing the receipt of RRSP and RRIF retirement funds. It will be possible to cancel and withdraw a lump sum payment (i.e. commute) from a term or life annuity under an RRSP. As well, payments from a RRIF, which previously were based on set formulae, can now be increased as desired beyond required annual minimums.

If you can't decide which is the single best choice for your RRSP funds, you can invest your funds in a combination of the options available.

RRSPs allow contributors another option in timing the receipt of their pension income. Unlike retirement funds accumulated in RPPs where benefits must generally commence at the time of retirement, your RRSP does not have to mature (i.e. be converted into an annuity, RRIF or cash) until the end of the year in which you turn seventy-one.

No matter how you choose to time the payments of your retirement benefits from an RPP, RRSP, or DPSP, these payments will be included in your taxable income in the year received as pension income, and will therefore be subject to tax at that time. (There are certain exceptions to this general rule. For example, the repayment from a DPSP of an employee's contributions to the plan are not taxed when received, as these contributions are not deductible for tax purposes by the employee when originally made.)

There are several opportunities to delay the tax bite. If you do not need all the retirement benefits you have received in the year for current living expenses, you may be able to delay the payment of tax on this excess by contributing it to your RRSP (although such RRSP contributions will not be allowed after the year in which you turn seventy-one). Old Age Security and Canada or Quebec Pension Plan benefits plus RPP benefits and certain DPSP payments can be "rolled over" to an RRSP, over and above your annual RRSP contribution limit. These funds can then continue to accumulate tax-free. Such contributions can only be made to an RRSP for your own benefit, and cannot be contributed to a spousal RRSP.

Beginning in 1990, the transfer of pension benefits to an RRSP will not be available. However, for 1990 to 1994, up to $6,000 a year of RPP payments can be rolled into a spousal RRSP if your RPP does not provide for survivor benefits. In the meantime, if you are sixty or over, and are receiving pension payments eligible for the $1,000 pension income credit (see Chapter 6) and decide to defer tax on this income by making rollover contributions to an RRSP, you should generally transfer at least $1,000 less than the maximum, leaving sufficient pension income (net of the rollover) to take advantage of the $1,000 annual pension income credit. If you are under sixty and are receiving income otherwise eligible for the $1,000 pension income credit, this credit will not be available if, for the same year, you deduct any amount for a rollover contribution of pension benefits to an RRSP.

You can also defer payment of tax on your retirement income by making a regular RRSP contribution of up to $7,500 in 1988 and 1989. You will only be able to make regular RRSP contributions to your own plan up to the year you turn seventy-one but you can continue contributing to your spouse's plan, if your spouse is younger, until he or she turns seventy-one. Until 1990, pension benefits from an RPP and a DPSP which have not been rolled over to an RRSP, as just discussed, qualify as earned income. (Your regular RRSP contribution cannot exceed twenty percent of earned income).

We should make one other comment on deferring receipt of all or part of your retirement income. The longer you can delay payment of funds from your RRSP, the longer they can accumulate tax-free and the more retirement benefits you will ultimately have. But it may not be a good idea to delay until the last possible moment converting your RRSP into an annuity or RRIF (assuming you will not want to receive all of it in a lump-sum cash payment). The amount of benefits you will receive in the future from your RRIF or annuity will depend, among other things, on the interest rates prevailing at the time of your RRSP conversion. If they are temporarily low in the year in which you turn seventy-one, some of the benefit of delaying receipt of your retirement benefits will be offset by unnecessarily low annuity or RRIF payments. So watch the interest rates during your retirement years and if you believe they are higher in a year than you expect in the future, that may be the best time to convert your RRSP (or at least a portion of it) even though it accelerates, to some extent, receipt and taxation of your RRSP funds. And if you don't feel competent to make this kind of decision, consult investment advisors you trust for their views.

As you can see, there are several opportunities to delay taxation of retirement benefits and earn tax-free income in the meantime by deferring their receipt. But although your retirement benefits will be taxable when eventually received, the tax cost may not be high. When you retire, your primary source of income usually ceases, and is replaced with pension and investment income. This replacement income is generally lower than your pre-retirement employment or business earnings, and therefore you should be paying tax at a lower marginal rate. You have an additional personal tax credit when you turn sixty-five and may be able to claim the pension income tax credit to further reduce your tax bill. Many kinds of investment income are taxed in a favoured way as already discussed in Chapter 6. All this should help to keep the tax costs down in your retirement years.

You can receive a tax credit on up to $1,000 of certain types of pension income each year. (The types of pension income which are eligible are described in Chapter 6.) Where only one spouse will be entitled to pension benefits from an RPP or DPSP, both spouses may still be able to take advantage of the annual pension income tax credit by doing some advance planning. Annuity payments from an RRSP received by a person sixty-five or older are eligible for this $1,000 tax credit. Therefore, the spouse who will be receiving other eligible pension income should contribute, if possible, to a spousal RRSP on behalf of the spouse who will not otherwise receive eligible pension income. Enough contributions should be made so that there are sufficient funds to purchase an annuity when that spouse turns sixty-five which will pay at least $1,000 annually. Then both spouses can take advantage of the pension income tax credit.

PERSONAL RESIDENCE

For many people, retirement signals a major change in lifestyle, with a corresponding change in housing needs. If you have considerable equity in your home, a change in your personal residence may create a substantial pool of capital that will generate additional retirement income.

As a general rule, gains realized on the disposition of your principal residence will be exempt from tax and will not affect the cumulative amount of your lifetime capital gains exemption.

The principal residence exemption is based on a formula, under which the tax-free portion of the gain is calculated as the number of years (plus one) for which the property qualified and was designated as a principal residence over the number of years it was owned after 1971.

If the property did not qualify as a principal residence for two or more years during the period of ownership, part of the resulting gain may be subject to tax.

Before 1982, it was possible for a family to obtain an exemption from capital gains tax for more than one residential property, by designating each property as the principal residence of a different member of the family. For example, if one spouse owned the family home, the other owned the summer vacation property.

Now, each family unit, consisting of a taxpayer, his or her spouse (unless legally separated and living apart throughout the year) and any unmarried children under eighteen years of age, is collectively entitled to designate only one property as a principal residence. Where a second property was also designated as a principal residence before 1982, only gains accruing after 1981 will be taxed when that property is eventually disposed of.

Although it is not necessary to designate which property is the principal residence (and for how many years) until one of the previously eligible properties is sold, it may be prudent to determine (and record for future reference) the values of each of the properties at the end of 1981, so that you will be in a position to make the appropriate decision when a disposal occurs sometime in the future.

To the extent that the principal residence exemption does not apply, any gain you realize on disposal of your residential or vacation property is generally subject to the normal capital gains rules. Two-thirds of the gain must be included in income, and taxed at regular rates unless you choose to exclude all or part of it from taxable income by applying any available portion of your capital gains exemption for this purpose. Accordingly, the decision as to which property to designate as your principal residence is still relevant and will likely depend on which property reflects the greater increase in market value—particularly after 1981.

INVESTMENT ASSETS

As mentioned earlier, retirement planning should include the buildup of your investments during the ten to fifteen years before you retire. Investment assets can be used to provide income during your retirement. To build up your investment funds prior to retirement, you need to manage your present investment assets effectively (see Form 21, *Review of Present Investments*). Try to boost the return on your investments. That generally means sacrificing some safety in order to be more aggressive. But you can go from a yield of eight percent to eleven or twelve percent without unreasonably endangering your capital.

Another way to increase your investment assets at retirement is to put aside each year more income for investment. Maximize your RRSP contributions and take advantage of any other tax-deferred programmes available to you.

As you approach retirement, you will probably have current income as your primary investment objective. Such an objective can be achieved through quality bonds, dividend-paying stocks, and income-producing real estate You should still keep up to forty percent of your investments at retirement in something with growth potential, such as growth stocks or real estate.

Another way of getting retirement income is to sell those investments that have increased in value. Consider, for example, two retirement funds of $250,000 each. If one fund consisted of bonds yielding ten percent and maturing in ten years, the annual income would be $25,000—all fully taxed—and the $250,000 capital amount would not increase in value if the bonds were bought at face value and held to maturity; thus, no inflation protection. If the other fund consisted of growth stocks paying no dividends but appreciating at an average rate of twelve percent per year over the ten years, you could sell $25,000 of the stocks the first year. The fund would have grown to $252,500 at the end of the first year and to $254,200 at the end of the second year, after you sold another $25,000. Thus, even though you were deriving current income from it, your retirement fund would be appreciating and providing some hedge against inflation, and on top of that, your income from it would be taxed as capital gain (only two-thirds taxed, or tax-free to the extent of any unused capital gains exemption limit).

OLD AGE INCOME SECURITY

The Canadian and provincial governments provide some financial assistance to retired persons through the Old Age Security programme, the Canada or Quebec Pension Plans, the Guaranteed Income Supplement programme and provincial supplementary programmes in many provinces.

Old Age Security benefits are paid to all persons sixty-five years or older who satisfy certain Canadian residency requirements, regardless of their income level. These payments are taxable. In 1987, the maximum benefits available were $3,629.

Benefits paid by the Canada or Quebec Pension Plan are funded by both employer and employee contributions. Your benefits after retirement at age sixty-five are determined by the amount of contributions you and your employer made during your working life. In 1987, the maximum benefit available was $6,258 ($6,517 in 1988). These benefits are included in your taxable income.

Beginning in 1987, retired persons can choose to start to receive Canada Pension Plan benefits at anytime between age sixty and seventy. Their retirement benefits will be increased by six percent for each year receipt is delayed beyond sixty-five, (to a maximum of 130 percent) and will be reduced by six percent for each year receipt is accelerated (to a minimum of seventy percent).

Also beginning in 1987, spouses can choose to share their CPP (but not their QPP) retirement pension payments. Both spouses must be at least 60 years old and have applied for any CPP benefits to which they are entitled. Each spouse will receive a portion of the other's CPP retirement pension, if any. The shared portion is calculated based on the length of time the couple have lived together compared to the total CPP contributory period. The total CPP benefits received do not change, but this presents an opportunity to transfer some income to a lower-income spouse who will pay tax at a lower rate. As well, the lower-income spouse could contribute his portion of the CPP benefits to an RRSP (assuming he has not reached his 71st birthday in a previous year), which will eventually generate income eligible for the $1,000 pension income credit when the RRSP is converted into an annuity or RRIF.

The Guaranteed Income Supplement is only paid to retired persons with limited income and is not subject to tax. The maximum benefit for a single person in 1988 is $4,430. As well, the province you live in may pay a further supplement to those who qualify for the federal supplement.

Income security legislation may change from time to time and cost-of-living increases and indexing computations can make it difficult to calculate the exact amount of your government-provided retirement benefits. You should contact the local Health and Welfare Canada office and ask for specific information on benefit payments, eligibility and how to apply as you near retirement.

WILL YOUR RETIREMENT INCOME MATCH YOUR EXPENDITURES?

You began by setting the date at which you might like to retire. Then you estimated how much an enjoyable retirement and its less enjoyable taxes might cost you. But none of this has yet been measured against the financial resources you expect to have at retirement.

Now the moment has come to probe the feasibility of your various retirement objectives. Will the annual income from your retirement plans and present investments cover your anticipated expenditures? If not, will your retirement plans, your present investments, and the investments you will make before retirement give you an annual income that will cover your retirement expenditures? If not, there are some more questions to ask yourself. Could you step up your investment schedule by earning more or spending less? Were you too extravagant when you forecast your retirement expenditures? Should you retire later than you intended?

FORM 27—RETIREMENT INCOME

On this form, you will relate your retirement needs to your retirement sources. We have provided an example of Form 27 in Figure 12-1. You might want to review it before you complete your own.

FIGURE 12-1

File under RETIREMENT PLANNING   Date: _November 1_

FORM 27   RETIREMENT INCOME

Projected Retirement Age: _62_   Number of Years to Retirement: _7_

| 1 | Estimated Annual Retirement Needs | | | _$ 90,200_ |

2   Estimated Annual Income from Retirement Plans
    (other than lump-sum distributions)

  a. Old Age Security and Canada or Quebec
      Pension Plan   _$11,000_

  b. Company Retirement Plan   _$37,200_

  c. Deferred Compensation   _—_

  d. Other Retirement Plans   _—_

3   TOTAL Annual Income from Retirement Plans   _$48,200_

4   Annual Income Gap   _$42,000_

5   Retirement Capital Required to Fill Gap

  a. Estimated Pre-Tax Rate of Return   _8%_

  b. Retirement Capital Required   _$525,000_

6   Sources of Retirement
    Capital

		INVESTMENT ASSETS	LUMP SUMS FROM RETIREMENT PLANS	RRSPs	TOTAL
a.	Value of Present Investment Assets and Retirement Accounts	_$165,000_		_$54,700_	_$219,700_
b.	Estimated Rate of Return from Now until Retirement	_10%_		_12%_	
c.	Years until Retirement	_7_		_7_	
d.	Compound Factor from Table 1 (in Appendix I)	_1.95_		_2.21_	
e.	Estimated Value of Your Investment Assets and Retirement Accounts at Retirement	_$321,800_	_0_	_$120,900_	_$442,700_

FIGURE 12-1 CONT'D

		INVESTMENT ASSETS	RRSPs	OTHER	TOTAL
7	Additional Capital from Annual Investments You Are Planning to Make				
a.	Annual Amount to Be Invested Between Now and Retirement	$4,000	$3,500	_____	$7,500
b.	Estimated Rate of Return on Annual Investment	10%	12%	_____	_____
c.	Years until Retirement	7	7	_____	_____
d.	Compound Factor from Table 2 (in Appendix I)	9.49	10.09	_____	_____
e.	Estimated Value of Additional Capital from Your Annual Investments	$38,000	$35,300	_____	$73,300
8	TOTAL Estimated Retirement Capital				$516,000
9	Additional Capital Needed, if Any, to Provide Retirement Income				$9,000
10	Additional Annual Investment Needed to Provide Capital on Line 9				
a.	Estimated Rate of Return from Now until Retirement			10%	
b.	Years until Retirement			7	
c.	Compound Factor from Table 2 (in Appendix 1)			9.49	
d.	Annual Amount Required				$950

- On line 1, enter the annual amount you listed on line 5 of Form 26.
- On lines 2a, 2b, 2c, and 2d, enter the annual amounts you are likely to receive after retirement from sources that will distribute payments in forms other than a lump sum. You may have to get the required information from your company's personnel office, your local Health and Welfare Canada office, and other sources from which retirement funds will come. Do not include projected RRSP income in this section of Form 27. You will consider this source of retirement income further down on the form.
- Total the estimated annual income from all your retirement plans on line 3.
- Subtract the total annual income from your retirement plans (line 3) from your estimated annual retirement needs (line 1) and enter the result on line 4 of the

worksheet. If the estimated income from your retirement plan exceeds your requirements, you could consider retiring earlier or look forward to a more comfortable retirement period. If you still need additional sources of retirement income, go on to the next step.

- Convert the annual income still needed on line 4 into a capital amount that will yield the annual income required. Perform these steps:
  - On line 5a, enter the estimated pretax rate of return on your investment capital when you retire.
  - On line 5b, enter the estimated capital required at retirement by dividing the amount on line 4 by the rate on line 5a.
- The next step on Form 27 is probably more complicated because it involves making judgements about your present investment assets, RRSP funds, and any lump sum retirement plans. It also involves forecasting what the value of these assets might be at retirement.
  - Enter on line 6a the present value of your investment assets and RRSP funds. Most of this data will come from your net worth statement (Form 4).
  - Enter on line 6b the estimated rate of return you think you will get on your investment assets and RRSP funds between now and your retirement. Refer to Form 22, *Your Investment Strategy*, for your estimates.
  - Enter on line 6c the number of years from now to retirement. Next, enter the approximate factor from Table 1 in Appendix I on line 6d.
  - On line 6e, estimate the value of your investment assets and retirement capital at retirement by multiplying the amount on line 6a by the factor on line 6d. You are getting really good at these calculations! Also enter on 6e, under the "Lump Sum" column, the amount to be paid in a lump sum, at retirement, from retirement plans.
  - Finally, add the totals across on line 6e to get the total estimated value of your capital at retirement.
- Compute the additional capital you will obtain by making annual additions to your investment funds and annual contributions to your RRSPs.
  - Enter on line 7a the annual amount to be invested between now and retirement.
  - On line 7b, enter the estimated rate of return on your annual investments.
  - On line 7c, enter the number of years from now until retirement.
  - On line 7d, enter the appropriate factor from Table 2 in Appendix I.
  - On line 7e, estimate the value of additional capital by multiplying the amount on line 7a by the factor on line 7d.
  - Finally, add the totals across on line 7e to get the total estimated value of your additional capital at retirement.
- On line 8, enter your total estimated retirement capital from lines 6e and 7e.
- On line 9, enter the amount that results from subtracting the amount on line 8 from the amount on line 5b. If the amount is negative—because your estimated retirement capital exceeds your requirements—consider early retirement or look forward to a much more comfortable retirement lifestyle, or plan a really big retirement party. If you need additional capital to meet your needs, go to the next and final step.
- If the result on line 9 of the worksheet suggests you will need additional investment capital at retirement, then you will need to start putting even more funds aside each year for investment. How much you need to set aside can be computed on the worksheet.
  - On line 10a, enter the estimated rate of return on your investments from now until retirement.

- On line 10b, enter the number of years between now and retirement.
- On line 10c, enter the compound factor from Table 2 in Appendix I.
- On line 10d, compute the annual amount of additional funds required by dividing the amount of capital required on line 9 by the factor on line 10c.

In our example in Figure 12-1, the individual would have to invest about $950 for seven years at ten percent to have the additional capital needed at retirement. Some clients with whom we have worked have a much greater annual investment requirement and say, "Are you kidding me?" If this is your case, you will need to reevaluate the variables in your plan and consider the choices you have.

YOUR RETIREMENT PLANNING CHOICES

What choices do you have between now and retirement that will help you meet your estimated retirement needs? Here are several you should consider:

- You can manage your investments and retirement funds more effectively to get a greater annual return.
- You can set aside more funds for annual investment by decreasing your current expenditures.
- You can plan to sell your personal residence at or before retirement and move into something less expensive to provide additional investment capital.
- You can plan to use some of your investment capital during retirement to handle your needs. Maybe the easiest estate planning is to spend your last dime as you take your last breath! Systematic use of investment capital during retirement may, in fact, be a very good choice for some people.

If, after considering the above choices, you still do not think it will be feasible to retire when you want to and still maintain a desired standard of living, you may have to hang in there and continue to work for your living.

THINKING OF EARLY RETIREMENT?

Many people think about retiring at an early age, such as fifty or fifty-five. It's an appealing idea, but one that should be considered carefully if you want to avoid frustration, anger, and financial problems. The advice we would give to anyone who is not independently wealthy is the following:

- Do not retire early unless you are free of major financial obligations, such as putting your children through university or college or paying off your mortgage.
- Do not retire early unless you have a vested pension—meaning one that belongs to you—as well as substantial savings or investments.
- Be wary if your retirement benefits are heavily dependent on the stock market.
- Try to negotiate any extra benefits your employer may be willing to give you because you take early retirement.
- Make sure the terms of your retirement plan will not prevent you from working elsewhere if you so desire.
- Have a plan to use your time effectively.

A RETIREMENT PLANNING CHECKLIST

As you approach your retirement date, you should do the following:

- Call your local Health and Welfare Canada office to find out what you must do to apply for benefits.
- Make an appointment with the official in your company who is responsible for your pension and profit-sharing benefits. Find out what payment plans are available to you, and consider which of the payment options would be most beneficial to you.
- Discuss the tax consequences of your retirement payment options with your tax advisor.
- Review your life insurance coverage. In retirement you may need less than your present coverage. If you have and want to keep a company-paid or company-sponsored group policy, check the options available to you.
- Review your health care coverage. Find out what your provincial medical insurance plan provides. If you need supplemental coverage, shop around. If you have a company plan, find out whether you can convert it to an individual plan.
- Review your will and your estate plan. You may wish to meet with your lawyer or chartered accountant to evaluate estate-planning ideas.
- Find out about senior citizens' programmes and discounts in the area you choose for your retirement.

13

RISK MANAGEMENT AND THE ROLE OF INSURANCE

Personal financial planning is a process which includes steps to help you minimize your income taxes and select the right tax shelter or mutual fund. But if you fail to properly evaluate and insure risks that create uncertainty or financial loss, you have not completed the financial planning process. Protecting your financial well-being is as important as the planning and implementation process you use to accumulate your wealth.

In this chapter, we discuss the concept of risk management and how the orderly approach to identifying and analyzing risks enables you to make more informed and financially sound decisions for meeting your insurance needs, whether for life, property-casualty, or health insurance.

RISK MANAGEMENT

Risk management includes all the efforts necessary to conserve assets by controlling the uncertainty of financial loss. This concept is readily applied to all forms of insurance whether it is homeowners, auto, personal and professional liability, life, disability, or medical insurance. In fact, the risk management approach can be applied in all personal and business circumstances where there is uncertainty about the risk of financial loss from the partial or complete decline in value in an unexpected or unpredictable manner. Risk of financial loss is the basis for the need for risk management evaluation and the purchase of the necessary insurance. Simply stated, insurance reduces or eliminates the uncertainty by transferring it to a large group of insured people who have uncertainties of loss, just as you do.

Deciding how much insurance you need is the end product of a decision making process that includes objective analysis, characterization of possible losses and determination of the financial impact of financial loss based on a risk analysis.

Risk analysis is very important and involves the following three factors:

- Identification of risks (assets and activities risk analysis)
- Measurement and evaluation of potential losses
- Evaluation and implementation of alternative techniques for handling the various risks

Let's consider each of these elements more closely.

Identification. The risk of financial loss must be identified before any other steps in risk management can be taken. The following three questions should be asked:

- What could happen to your assets?
- What accidents could impair your assets or your earning power?
- What activities could create liabilities to others due to personal injury or damage to property?

The answers to these questions can provide broad guidelines on vulnerability to financial losses for both assets and activities.

Measurement and evaluation. After identifying the exposures to financial loss, it is crucial to evaluate the nature of possible losses and the degree of control you may exert over their occurrence. This is also known as risk-treatment planning. Methods for dealing with risk management fall within one of the following basic techniques:

- *Avoiding risk.* Simply put, risk avoidance minimizes the possibility of risks by removing their causes. For example, if one does not skydive, the possibility of an accident from that cause has been completely eliminated.
- *Risk reduction.* Beyond taking measures to prevent a calamity from happening, this technique involves recognizing the potential for damage and keeping it to a minimum. The installation of a smoke-and-fire alarm system in your home is a risk-reduction technique. If a fire breaks out, there should be less property damage or personal injury because you have this early warning system.
- *Risk retention.* Once a risk is properly evaluated and every effort is made to diminish it, then the question becomes one of how much risk you can afford to retain or assume yourself—also known as self-insurance. As we will see, the cost of sharing or transferring that risk (insurance) may be too expensive, or coverage may not even be available for a given calamity. Increasing or decreasing insurance deductibles is one form of risk retention. In other words, once you have evaluated an insurable risk and its possible economic consequences, you can then decide how much risk of loss you want to retain before acquiring insurance coverage.
- *Risk transference.* This is the best understood technique of personal risk management. Simply stated, you remove the risk of loss from yourself and transfer it to a third party, namely an insurance company. In exchange for relieving you of this risk of loss, the insurance company receives a premium from you to cover the costs of assuming that risk.

Evaluation and Implementation of Alternative Techniques. Ideally, you should retain as much risks you yourself can handle financially and then acquire insurance to cover the risks of loss that are beyond your means. At this point, you should ask yourself

- What risks am I willing to accept?
- What measures for controlling risks are available?
- Can the risk be eliminated or avoided?

You now decide how to deal with the risk and uncertainties of loss either by insuring or not insuring. The key is that you are making your insurance decision based on the results of the information you have gathered and evaluated. Your insurance will be systematic and organized, not merely a haphazard, inefficient patchwork of coverages. The result is that your personal financial management plan is comprehensive and has a much greater assurance of being completed as planned rather than being vulnerable to risks and uncertainties.

The following discussion is divided into these categories:

- Life insurance
- Property and liability
- Health insurance
- Selecting the insurance company and agent

LIFE INSURANCE

Most of our financial planning is based on the assumption that we will continue to live for a long time and thus can earn an income for as long as we choose. There is a possibility, though, that we won't live to a ripe old age and good planning must take this risk into account. If premature death would disrupt or dry up the income stream needed to maintain our dependents, then life insurance should be used to prevent such financial disruption.

Our insurance needs will go up and down as our income and responsibilities go up and down and as our investments grow. Without children, insurance requirements are not great. Children and a mortgage mean increased responsibilities and a greater need for insurance protection. As children are born, insurance needs normally reach a maximum. As the children become financially independent, the need for insurance declines. At retirement, insurance may not be a big factor either, except for providing the necessary liquidity when it comes to settling the decedent's estate. At that point, your investment assets should be sufficient to provide your surviving spouse with the required income.

Because the need for protection changes, we strongly recommend that you evaluate your insurance at least every three years and that you buy insurance policies that allow you to change your protection coverage.

In essence, all life insurance policies say the same thing: In return for premiums duly received, the insurance company will pay the *face amount* (the promised benefit) of the policy to the beneficiary upon receiving proof of the insured person's death. The death benefits are paid out very quickly and are generally not taxable to the beneficiary.

In order to assess whether your present life insurance coverage is adequate, inadequate, or excessive, you have to envisage the needs and resources of your dependents in the event of your or your spouse's unexpected death. Which dependents, if any, will require financial support? When will they need it, how much will they need, and for how long? What income will be available from other sources? How much income will the proceeds of the life insurance have to provide?

DO YOU REALLY NEED LIFE INSURANCE?

The only purpose of insuring your life is to provide income for your dependents after your death. Therefore, the first question to ask yourself is, "Do I have any dependents for whom I should provide after my death?"

FIGURE 13-1
CHANGING NEED FOR LIFE INSURANCE

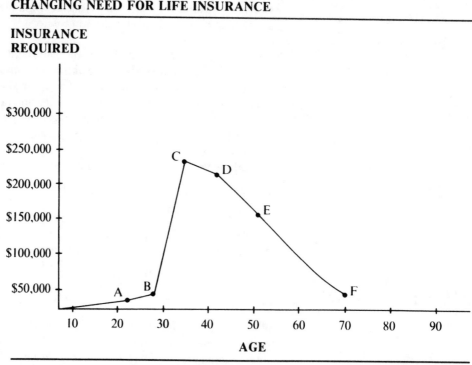

INSURANCE
REQUIRED

There may be none, and therefore little or no need for life insurance, if you are single, or married but without children or mortgage and both of you are working. Similarly, there may be little or no point in paying for the safety net of life insurance once your children are independent and you have ample net worth. However, if your spouse, children, or parents depend on your earnings, you may have to insure your life quite heavily.

As your financial responsibilities and circumstances change, so will your need for life insurance. You can see this illustrated in Figure 13-1, which shows the life insurance needs of people at different life stages. The six selected points on the graph correspond to the following stages:

- **Point A:** Single young person. Normally, this person has no dependents, and therefore little or no need for life insurance. About the only things that may have to be covered by life insurance are funeral expenses or loans outstanding, such as education loans.

- **Point B:** A childless couple. When both spouses are employed, they each have the best kind of insurance—a job; but if they have purchased a home, insurance to cover the mortgage would be a good idea. If their lifestyle depends on their combined incomes, they may want $25,000 to $50,000 of insurance on each other's life. Often this can be provided through a group term policy offered by their employers.

- **Point C:** A thirty-year-old couple with two small children and a heavily mortgaged house. There are three good reasons why the amount of life insurance needed is relatively high:

1. The investment assets of a couple at the age of thirty are usually not sufficient to cover the living expenses of the surviving spouse and two small children.

2. The living expenses are relatively high because the surviving spouse, aged thirty, has many more years to live, so the lump sum required to pay his or her expenses for a long time is large.

3. The cost of raising and educating the children adds significantly to the required living expenses of the surviving spouse; it may be desirable to set up an education fund from the insurance proceeds.

- *Point D*:   A forty-year-old couple with dependent children and dependent parents. They have relatively high life insurance needs for much the same reasons as the thirty-year-old couple. They still have to cover significant living expenses for the surviving spouse (usually the wife) and for dependent parents; in addition, there are the costs of educating the children. Most couples of this age and in this situation have not amassed enough investment assets to cover these various requirements.
- *Point E*:   A fifty-year-old couple whose two children have completed their formal education and will soon be financially independent. The surviving spouse does not have as long to live as a spouse at the age of thirty or forty, and child-rearing expenses are few. In addition, a fifty-year-old couple will usually have greater investment assets than a couple of thirty or forty, so their investments can provide some of the needed income.
- *Point F*:   A seventy-year-old couple whose children are financially independent. The amount needed for the living expenses of the surviving spouse is relatively small because there are not as many years for which provision must be made and the investment assets of the couple may be sufficient to cover those needs.

FORM 28—YOUR PRESENT LIFE INSURANCE COVERAGE

The obvious way to begin your insurance review is by listing the significant aspects of any insurance you presently carry on your life and the life of your spouse. You will be able to obtain the necessary information from the actual policy or policies or from your insurance agent.

Under *Type of Policy*, identify each policy as either whole life, individual term, group term, endowment, or whatever other description is appropriate. Under *Cash Surrender Value* and *Loan on Policy*, the total amounts should agree with those on your net worth statement (Form 4). Under *Owner of Policy*, indicate who owns the policy. Usually, the insured is the owner. Under *Beneficiary*, identify the person who is entitled to receive the face amount of the policy on your death.

HOW MUCH INSURANCE DO YOU NEED?

Before you can tell how much life insurance you should carry, you have to forecast the financial needs of your dependents and have a good idea of the amount and liquidity of your assets.

Your dependents' financial needs will normally fall into the following categories:

- Cash to pay immediate obligations, including potential taxes at the time of your death (see Chapter 14 for a discussion of these taxes)
- Money to pay the mortgage
- Money for education
- Cash to cover living expenses

It may be a good idea for the survivors to set up four separate funds in separate accounts to cover these four different needs.

Immediate Cash Requirements

Many of the expenses that come into existence at death are expenses that simply did not exist before. Cash is required for funeral expenses, for current bills (including medical bills and administrative expenses), for an emergency fund, and possibly for taxes. Funeral costs vary depending on whether you want your ashes spread at sea or wish to be buried with your ship and other accessories for the life hereafter, as the Vikings were. The average cost of death is about $5,000, which includes the funeral and burial in a cemetery.

An emergency fund is required to cover living expenses during the period when the estate is being settled and the nature and amount of assets to be received by the survivors may be uncertain. Since most of us do not plan to die soon, there may not be enough liquid assets available to your survivors to take care of the cash requirements in the first months following your death, and life insurance could fill this gap.

Mortgages

In this age of buying expensive homes and financing the purchase with a large mortgage, many breadwinners die leaving their families indebted to a lending institution. From a purely financial perspective, it may not make much difference whether the mortgage is paid off immediately or is covered by a "living expenses fund" in the insurance; but for the peace of mind of the survivors, it may be important to have a mortgage insurance fund for clearing your home of debt.

If your mortgage interest rate is low—say seven or eight percent—the survivor should consider keeping the mortgage, because the cost of the mortgage may be significantly lower than the after-tax return from employing the funds elsewhere. Suppose the survivor is in a forty percent tax bracket and has a mortgage rate of seven percent. If the funds can be invested to yield more than 11.7% (i.e. seven percent after-tax), then it makes sense not to pay off the seven percent mortgage. If this high a yield cannot be reliably obtained, then the funds should be used to pay off the mortgage.

Education Costs

Education, like a mortgage, can be paid for from the living expenses fund; but your children may find it reassuring to have a specific fund set aside for educational purposes. The amount of the fund will depend on several factors: location of university or community college; length of education; the children's ability to generate money for their education; availability of scholarships; and your views on providing support for the children after you die.

Living Expenses

The calculation of living expenses raises the fundamental question of how well the family should be provided for. Most of us would like our dependents to maintain the standard of living to which they are accustomed. Maintaining this same standard of living should not, however, require the same level of expenditure. With one member of the family gone, some expenses will either be reduced or eliminated, since this person will no longer need any clothes, transportation, or food. Some life insurance premiums will also be eliminated. Income taxes will be lower, and mortgage payments will be eliminated if insurance proceeds have been used to pay off the balance.

If the mortgage is paid off or is paid from a separate mortgage fund, the surviving spouse and children will need less gross income for living expenses (as a general rule of thumb, about sixty percent of the gross income that the family needed before the spouse's death). If the mortgage payments are still a part of the general living costs, then the family will need more gross income—perhaps seventy-five percent of the complete family's former gross income, as a rule of thumb. To more accurately estimate the expected reduction in living expenses after one spouse dies, Forms 7 and 8 can be redone to reflect anticipated changes in basic and discretionary expenditures, and Form 11 can be filled out to estimate the remaining family's tax burden.

Some families may be able to meet their expenses with the income from accumulated assets, government assistance (Canada or Quebec Pension Plan, Old Age Security), and the surviving spouse's income. A housewife who survives her husband may need to find a job outside the home after her husband's death. Some income may also be generated by teenage children. Consider also the reverse situation where the homemaker dies leaving small children. The surviving spouse may need substantial funds to hire a housekeeper or make other child-care arrangements.

FORM 29—TOTAL LIFE INSURANCE REQUIRED

Before or while you complete this form, it might be helpful to look at an example of the completed form as shown in Figure 13-2.

- *Line 1a*: The average present cost of a funeral and burial is about $5,000.
- *Line 1b*: If you frequently have large debts outstanding on your credit cards, take that into consideration.
- *Line 1c*: The cost of administering your estate will generally amount to one-and-a-half to two percent of your net worth (see Form 4), although fees can vary substantially based on the complexity of your estate.
- *Line 1d*: Enter fifty percent of the insured spouse's annual gross income. (You can adjust the percentage depending on your individual circumstances.)
- *Line 1e*: If, upon death, the decedent's entire estate will be passed to the other spouse, put zero on this line. If not, refer to the discussion of potential taxes on death in Chapter 14 to prepare an estimate, or you might ask your accountant for an estimate.
- *Line 2a*: Enter the lump-sum total of life insurance benefits to be paid when the insured spouse dies, as shown on Form 28.
- *Line 2b*: Enter the death benefits payable from retirement programmes or a group life insurance plan or both. Most retirement programmes do not provide significant death benefits until the employee reaches a certain age, such as fifty-five years or older; so check out the death benefits of your retirement programmes. Certain death benefits can be received free of tax. Payments by an employer in recognition of an employee's service (provided the payments are made from an employer's fund that is separate from the company pension plan) qualify for special tax treatment. Up to $10,000 of any such payments received will be tax-exempt.
- *Line 2c*: Enter your liquid assets total, as shown on your net worth statement, Form 4, but don't include the cash value of the insured spouse's life insurance.
- *Line 3*: Subtract line 1f from line 2e. If you get a negative figure, indicate this by showing it in parentheses. Most people who have any life insurance programme or liquid assets will get a positive figure here.
- *Line 4a*: Discuss with your spouse whether, when you die, the mortgage should be paid off. If you have a low balance on your mortgage, this might not be a priority. If the mortgage balance is large and the rate of interest fairly high, it is probably better to pay off the mortgage.
- *Line 4b*: Use today's dollars, and base your figures on your estimates on Form 23, *University and Graduate School Costs*.
- *Line 5a*: Include investment assets as shown in your statement of net worth (Form 4), but exclude any assets already included on line 2C.

FIGURE 13-2

File under INSURANCE

Date: *Sept. 25*

FORM 29   TOTAL LIFE INSURANCE REQUIRED

1   Cash Required Immediately

    a.   Funeral *$5,000*

    b.   Current bills .... *—*

    c.   Administrative *9,000*

    d.   Emergency fund *36,000*

    e.   Taxes on death .... *—*

    f.   TOTAL .... *($50,000)*

2   Cash Available Immediately

    a.   Insurance proceeds *$155,000*

    b.   Death benefits from retirement
        programmes or group life insurance
        plan *10,000*

    c.   Liquid assets *26,500*

    d.   Other .... *—*

    e.   TOTAL *$191,500*

3   Net Cash Available (or Required) *$141,500*

4   Assets Required for Mortgage and Children's Education

    a.   Mortgage outstanding *$50,000*

    b.   Education *45,000*

    c.   TOTAL .... *($95,000)*

5   Assets Available for Mortgage and Children's Education

    a.   Investment assets *$262,800*

    b.   Personal assets convertible into
        cash .... *—*

FIGURE 13-2 CONT'D

   c. Other   —

   d. TOTAL $262,800

6   Net Resources Available (or Required) $167,800

7   Total Resources Available (or Required)   309,300

8   Annual Living Expenses   54,000

9   Annual Income Available for Living Expenses

   a. Income from assets $30,900

   b. Employment income of spouse $10,000

   c. Other   —

   d. TOTAL $40,900

10   Annual Income Excess (or Deficiency) $(13,100)

11   Additional Insurance Required

   a. Negative amount from line 7   —

   b. Negative amount from line 10
       divided by 10% $131,000

   c. TOTAL $131,000

- *Line 5b*: Consider such items as a second car, a boat and the odd Rembrandt you may own and are willing to sell.
- *Line 6*: Subtract line 4c from line 5d. If you get a negative figure, indicate this by showing it in parentheses.
- *Line 7*: Add lines 6 and 3. If the result is a positive figure, there are some resources to cover the annual living expenses. If the result is a negative figure, then additional insurance is needed equal to the negative amount on line 7. Additional insurance will also be needed to cover the annual living expenses, which will be the next thing you assess.
- *Line 8*: If your living expenses will include mortgage payments, use seventy-five percent of the gross income presently earned by the family as an estimate of total living expenses for the remaining family. If mortgage payments will not be part of annual living expenses, use sixty percent of the gross income presently

earned by the family as an estimate of total living expenses. For a more accurate estimate, refer to the Forms 7 and 8 you have already completed and revise them to reflect anticipated changes in expenditures after your death.

- *Line 9a*:   If you have a positive figure on line 7, estimate the annual pretax income these assets might generate.

- *Line 9b*:   If your spouse is employed, or would, in the event of your death, be able to work, estimate the annual income from such employment.

- *Line 10*:   Subtract line 8 from line 9d. If the result is a positive figure, you probably have too much insurance. To determine how much excess insurance you have, multiply the amount on this line by ten (assuming a ten percent rate of return on invested funds). If the result on line 10 is a negative figure, you need additional insurance, and should now determine how much more.

- *Line 11a*:   Enter the amount on line 7 if that is a negative amount.

- *Line 11b*:   Enter ten times the negative amount on line 10, again assuming a ten percent rate of return on invested funds.

- *Line 11c*:   Add lines 11a and 11b. The resulting sum is the additional insurance you need.

Once you have completed this analysis and determined that you are either overinsured or underinsured, you should review your analysis with your insurance agent and then take the appropriate action.

LIFE INSURANCE POLICIES

There are two basic types of life insurance policies: pure insurance, called *term insurance*, and life insurance combined with a savings or investment programme. These two basic types can be further subdivided according to some of their special features.

Term Insurance

Term life insurance is like the automobile, fire, and health insurance you have in that it protects you for a limited specified time. If, as you hope, you are still living at the end of the specified time, your protection ceases, just as a fire insurance policy expires, and there is no residual value in that policy. Term policies are ideal for providing a large amount of protection for a limited time at the lowest premium outlay.

By paying an additional premium, term insurance may be renewable or convertible or both. If the policy is renewed or another term policy is issued to replace it, a higher premium is charged because the policy holder is now older and has a greater chance of dying than in the previous period.

Renewable term policies include an option permitting you to renew the contract for a number of specified periods—five, ten, fifteen, or twenty years, or to a certain age, such as sixty, sixty-five, or seventy—without further medical examination. Term policies may allow you to convert the full amount of insurance to a *whole life* or *endowment policy* without medical reexamination at any time while your insurance is still in force.

Term policies have several advantages. Term offers the lowest cost for pure protection. The needs of a family tend to change over the years, so term insurance can be very useful for providing the funds for temporary needs, such as university education or mortgage payments. With the flexibility of its renewable policies and its low premiums, term insurance has a definite place in all well-planned life insurance programmes.

There are three basic kinds of term policies: *annual renewable term, decreasing term*, and *level term*.

Annual Renewable Term

With an annual renewable term policy, the face amount of your insurance remains the same, and premium increases every year.

Decreasing Term

Your premium remains the same with a decreasing term policy, but the face amount of the insurance decreases. Typically, your insurance needs decline as you grow older, so decreasing term insurance can fit that situation very well. Mortgage insurance, which some people buy, is really a decreasing term policy.

Level Term

With a level term policy, the face amount of the policy remains the same for a chosen period—five, ten, fifteen, twenty, twenty-five, or thirty years, or until you reach the age of sixty-five. The premium remains level throughout the period, and it approximates the average of the annual renewable term rates for the specified number of years. If you chose a twenty-year level term policy, for example, the insurance company would essentially add up the renewable term rates for twenty years and divide the total by twenty, and you would pay the same annual rate for each of the twenty years.

Life Insurance Combined with an Investment Programme (Whole Life)

Some policies provide an investment programme as well as protection. With such policies, you normally buy a level face amount of insurance—say, $10,000—but the premiums you pay go for protection *and* for an investment account. In reality, you are buying a form of decreasing term insurance, for as your investment account increases, your insurance protection goes down, but the combined value of your savings and your insurance protection remains the same.

You can obtain the cash from your investment account in two ways. You can stop paying premiums at any time, take the cash surrender value (i.e. the current realizable value of the investment account) and terminate the policy. Alternatively, you can borrow from the cash surrender value. Then your insurance coverage will be reduced by the amount you borrowed until the loan is repaid. You can repay your policy loan at any time, but you are not required to do so. On older policies, the cost of borrowing against the cash value of insurance policies can range from five to eight percent and is much lower than the cost of borrowing from a bank. On newer policies, the interest rates are more similar to a bank's.

When you hold a life insurance policy that has a cash surrender value, you can do any of the following things with your cash surrender value:

- You can convert the contract to paid-up life insurance for a lesser amount than the original face amount.
- You can have the original face amount continued as term insurance for a specified period. The length of the period will depend on the amount of the cash surrender value and on the face amount of the original policy.
- You can arrange for a minimum deposit plan that will allow you to take part of your annual dividend in the form of additional term insurance, instead of taking it all as cash. The additional term insurance is sold at a lower price than regular term insurance.

Other Types of Life Insurance Policies

Two other insurance products have recently been introduced and deserve some mention. One is universal life insurance, which is similar to conventional whole life insurance with one important exception. The investment portion of a universal life insurance policy earns income at a variable rate, which fluctuates with prevailing interest rates. There may be a minimum guaranteed rate of return, but otherwise your investment income will not be fixed, as is the case with most conventional whole life policies. Because you are bearing more of the investment risk with a universal life insurance policy, these policies usually provide cheaper insurance coverage than the other whole life policies.

Another relatively new product is variable whole life insurance. Here cash values are invested in either a money market fund or a common stock fund, and both the return on the cash value and the amount of the death benefit vary with investment performance.

Tax Considerations for Life Insurance Policies

Generally, there is no tax on life insurance proceeds received when an insured person dies. We have said "generally" because there are two types of life insurance policy— *exempt* and *non-exempt* policies. There is no tax payable on insurance proceeds received when a person insured under an exempt policy dies and there is no tax payable on investment income earned by an exempt policy prior to the death of the insured. Taxation of non-exempt policies is not so generous, however.

Insurance policies where there is a substantial degree of savings in addition to insurance protection may be non-exempt policies (unless they were issued before December 1982). Investment income earned on such policies is accrued for tax purposes and an individual must pay tax on this accrued income at least every three years. An individual policy owner may also elect to report the accrued income on non-exempt policies annually if this is more beneficial. When the person insured under a non-exempt policy dies, any accrued investment income which has not yet been taxed must be brought into income. Only the pure insurance element of the policy will be tax-free.

Tax may also be payable if an insurance policy (exempt or non-exempt) is disposed of. A disposition would include such things as surrender of a policy, conversion of a policy to an annuity or a transfer of ownership. If a policy is disposed of, the policy owner must include in income the amount by which the proceeds of disposition exceed the adjusted cost basis of the policy. Proceeds of disposition will generally be the cash surrender value of the policy. The adjusted cost basis is generally the total of premiums paid less dividends and loans received by the owner. Premiums paid after 1 May 1985 must exclude the insurance portion of the premium and will effectively represent only the portion of the premium designated for savings.

Dividends and loans also have tax consequences, in that they reduce the adjusted cost basis of your policy. However, tax will not be payable at the time the dividend or loan is received unless the adjusted cost basis of the policy becomes negative as a result.

This is a very brief summary of the more common tax issues involving insurance policies. The taxation of life insurance policies is extremely complex and you should usually ask for professional tax advice before making any major change in your insurance coverage.

SHOULD YOU DISCONTINUE OR REPLACE OLD POLICIES?

Should you discontinue old policies? If your insurance analysis indicates that you have too much insurance, the answer is yes. When you decide to drop some of your policies, drop those with the highest cost per $1,000 of insurance protection—a calculation discussed in the next section.

As for replacing old policies with new ones, you should know that the cost of new policies has dropped substantially in recent years. You should, therefore, analyze the cost per $1,000 of benefits of your old policies and compare them with the costs of new policies, but don't inadvertently convert a tax-exempt policy to a non-exempt policy or the tax consequences may be very costly.

Determining the cost per $1,000 of benefits for term insurance is quite easy. Merely divide the annual premium by one-thousandth of the face amount. For example, if you have a group term policy with a face amount of $100,000 and your premium is $600 a year, then the cost per thousand is $6 ($600 ÷ 100). For whole life policies, it is a little more complicated to determine the cost per thousand—but by completing Form 30, you can do so.

FORM 30—WHOLE LIFE POLICY: INSURANCE COST PER $1,000

- *Line 1*: Enter the face amount of your present policy as listed on Form 28.
- *Line 2*: Enter the cash surrender value for the policy as listed on Form 28.
- *Line 3*: Subtract line 2 from line 1 to get the net insurance protection provided by your policy.
- *Line 4*: Enter the present gross premium amount before dividends on your policy.
- *Line 5*: Enter the increase in the cash value of your policy during the current year. This can be determined by looking at the cash value table in your policy contract or by asking your agent.
- *Line 6*: Enter the dividend you received for the current year. This is normally shown on your premium payment notice.
- *Line 7*: Enter five percent (assumed after-tax rate of return) of the amount on line 2.
- *Line 8*: If you have borrowed your cash value and are investing the funds, enter five percent (assumed after-tax rate of return) of the borrowed cash value.
- *Line 9*: Add line 7 to line 4; then subtract lines 5, 6, and 8 from the result. You now have the total annual cost of your present policy.
- *Line 10*: Divide line 9 by one-thousandth of line 3.

PROPERTY AND LIABILITY INSURANCE

Even though you may have thoroughly planned all other aspects of your personal financial plan, you can still encounter ruinous setbacks if you suffer a catastrophic loss for which you are inadequately insured. Today, it is more important than ever to protect yourself against financial liability caused by your acts or those of your family.

Two Broad Property Coverage Types

There are two broad types of property coverage—named-peril and all risks. "Peril" coverage protects you against loss stemming from a named and specific calamity. Common named perils include fire, theft and collision.

The second type of property coverage coverage is "all risks." This insurance typically covers property against loss from *any* source of "peril." Be forewarned: Not all policies cover all perils; there are usually exclusions from coverage. It is important to review your current policies to identify the specific exclusions and decide whether you want to assume the risk of loss from the excluded events. When considering policies from different companies, you should compare the specific perils excluded from each policy and determine how those exclusions bear on your specific situation. Since coverage is generally broader under an all-risks policy, the cost is generally more expensive.

Homeowner's Insurance

A homeowner's policy is actually a collection of coverages combined into one policy. This covers the dwelling and its contents, liability, and medical payments for personal injury.

Perhaps one of the most important concepts of homeowners insurance is that of replacement cost riders. Without these you may recover only up to your original cost—and sometimes just the depreciated value. Thus, a replacement cost rider can be quite valuable since, with adequate coverage, you can recover the full replacement cost of an entire lost structure—or part of it—without any reduction for depreciation. You should be sure that your coverage will at least equal the replacement cost as values increase, and this can be achieved with an automatic escalator.

If you don't have adequate replacement cost coverage, you may not collect the full amount of the loss even if it is less than the policy's face amount. Recovery for a loss under an 80 percent co-insurance clause—the most common one used—is determined using this formula:

$$\frac{\text{Face amount of the insurance policy}}{80\% \text{ x full replacement cost}} \quad \text{x} \quad \begin{array}{l}\text{Cost of} \\ \text{replacement} \\ \text{or repair}\end{array}$$

An example can best illustrate how a co-insurance clause works.

Example: You bought a house in 1974 for $100,000, exclusive of the land. Over the years, you increased the coverage on the house from $100,000 to $160,000. However, the cost to replace the house in 1987 is $300,000. A kitchen fire has resulted in a $30,000 repair cost and the formula determines how much you recover under your policy:

$$\frac{\$160,000}{80\% \text{ x } \$300,000} \text{ x } \$30,000 = \$20,000$$

The $10,000 difference would come out of your pocket simply because you had failed to keep up with the required replacement-cost provision.

Had you suffered a total loss, the formula indicates that you would recover $200,000:

$$\frac{\$160,000}{80\% \text{ x } \$300,000} \text{ x } \$300,000 = \$200,000$$

but this is limited, of course, by the $160,000 face amount of your policy. By maintaining at least $240,000 coverage (80% of full replacement value), recovery would be the full $240,000 face value.

How do you maintain adequate coverage? First, by having your insurance agent recommend coverage based on construction costs and real estate values for your area. Then, you can add to your policy an inflation rider that automatically increases your coverage. This additional "endorsement," however, does not automatically guarantee adequate coverage, since it is based on a broad-based inflation factor and does not necessarily reflect the replacement-cost increases for your geographic area.

Furthermore, homeowner's policies contain built-in ceilings on the amount of personal property that can be covered under the basic policy. For example, you may have a rare stamp collection worth $50,000. If nothing is done to cover that item specifically, it will be insured with all other personal property, with a limit of perhaps $500. Therefore, it is very important to add specific floaters to the general policy that will cover more valuable items like jewelry, stamps, cameras, furs, and artwork.

Since under any policy, part of the problem in collecting after a loss is proving the existence of an item, it is highly advisable to maintain a current pictorial inventory of insured assets. More and more people, for example, are photographing or videotaping their home and its contents and writing detailed descriptions of jewelry, clothes, antiques, collections, artwork, furniture, silver, and so on. Photographs, accompanied by complete descriptions, are also a good form of identification. Of course, it goes without saying that this pictorial evidence should be kept in a safe location outside the home, preferably in a vault.

Your homeowner's insurance policy should also include adequate liability insurance to cover any losses or damage caused by your negligence. As an example, any homeowner with a pool should have insurance to protect against any injuries a visitor might suffer while using the pool. Coverage usually includes the amount stated in the policy as well as costs of defence. It is very important that you understand and comply with all the conditions in the policy. Liability coverage is relatively inexpensive and is one of the best bargains in the insurance insurance industry. Most homeowners can have the comfort of carrying $1,000,000 or more in liability coverage at a very reasonable price.

Automobile Insurance

Generally speaking, automobile insurance covers liabilities stemming from accidents, medical payments, damage or destruction to vehicles, theft of vehicles, etc. Ancillary costs, such as renting a car if yours is stolen, towing charges, and glass coverage may also be covered. Depending on provincial law and your own needs, there are specified limits in the policy for each category. For instance, there may be a $350,000 liability limit or a $5,000 medical-payment ceiling for any person injured in an accident. These restrictions on liability are very important. Here, as with the homeowner's policy, it is very important to review the coverage exclusions specifically mentioned in the policy.

For your coverage to be more cost effective, you should get the answers to certain questions to determine the cost of your automobile and homeowner's coverage. Since risk retention is one technique of risk management, by selecting a deductible on a policy, you are deciding how much of the risk you are willing to assume. The higher the deductible, the higher the risk retention and the lower the premiums.

It is possible to get better overall coverage on a policy for the same dollars if you are willing to pay a higher deductible. Then, too, the need for collision coverage decreases as your car gets older. For example, after four years, the value of a vehicle is so much less than you originally paid that collision insurance coverage may not be cost effective.

Excess Liability or "Umbrella" Coverage

It is frequently said that Canada is becoming a more litigious society, and the astonishing size of some awards in recent liability trials should make you think twice about your liability coverage.

Suppose you had done a painstaking job of financial planning for retirement, which is a month away. Unfortunately, however, you have an automobile accident and injure someone. You settle out of court for $500,000. The automobile insurance company pays its share up to the $350,000 liability limits of your policy. Where does the remaining $150,000 come from? You guessed right. It comes out of those assets you so diligently saved for a comfortable retirement.

This would be a financial disaster for most people. If you had an excess liability policy in place, you could have averted this financial calamity. Excess liability policies are sometimes referred to as "umbrella" policies. They are designed to provide you with coverage over and above the liability limits of your homeowners and automobile policies.

The cost of these umbrella policies is miniscule compared with what you'd have to pay in a lawsuit. One of these policies belongs in everyone's insurance portfolio.

HEALTH INSURANCE

Under the broad category of health insurance there are two distinct and critical areas of coverage needs: disability income and medical expenses.

Without comprehensive coverage in each area, the best planning can be devastated due to financial losses from sickness or accidents.

Disability Income Insurance

Perhaps no other area of personal risk management is so often neglected. Part of this neglect—and sometimes confusion—may arise from uncertainty over the range of eligibility and adequacy of coverage, which varies greatly from insurer to insurer. Scrupulous review of existing disability policies is in order before you can reach a conclusion on the proper choice of policy.

The following four definitions should help you decide on the coverage you need:

1. **Elimination period.** This is the period from the onset of the disability until the benefits begin under the policy. The shorter the elimination period, the more costly the premiums. It might be possible under a policy to extend the elimination period and increase the monthly disability benefits while keeping the cost of the policy (that is, the premiums) even. The question involving the elimination period is: How long can you live on your savings before the benefits start?

2. **Period of benefits.** This is the length of time over which the benefits may be payable. It can be expressed in terms of months, years, a specified age or a lifetime. The period of the benefit selected generally depends on, among other things, cost of premiums, other assets, and other income. The longer the period, the more benefits to be received and the higher the premium.

3. **Reason for disability.** Some policies cover disability only from accidents as opposed to disability from a prolonged illness. Coverage for accidents alone is somewhat limited, and coverage for both types of disability should be sought.

4. **Disability defined.** Perhaps nowhere else is there more confusion and potential for problems than in the definition of disability. The definition under which each insurance company will pay benefits differs greatly from policy to policy. If you are totally disabled, any company will pay benefits.

The greatest differences come about in those circumstances when you are partially and permanently disabled, or disabled with symptoms that will ultimately go away. Some policies may say that an injured person able to work at "any occupation" is not disabled and thus no benefits should be payable. At the other end of the spectrum, some companies say that if you cannot work at "*your* own occupation," you are considered disabled.

For example, if a surgeon hurts his hands and cannot operate but can teach in a medical school, is he disabled? Under a strict interpretation of the word "disabled," the insurance company could answer no, since he can work at "any occupation." Under more liberal policies, the answer would be yes, since his specialty was surgery, which he can no longer perform. Read the definitions of "disability" very carefully when comparing policies from different carriers.

Be aware, too, that although your employer provides a long-term disability policy as part of your benefits program, that does not necessarily mean that you are adequately covered. Study the coverage for elimination periods, benefit periods, causes of disability, and the definitions of disability and partial disability. You may need to buy additional disability income coverage from an outside insurance company.

Also consider the tax treatment of payments from your disability plan. Where you have paid premiums out of your own after-tax income, any benefits will be received tax-free. But if your employer has paid all or a portion of the disability insurance premiums, any benefits you receive will be taxed, so that only a portion of these benefits will be available to cover your living expenses.

Medical Expense Coverage

Many Canadians do not carry additional coverage for medical expenses because most basic medical procedures are provided under the various provincial health care plans. Additional private coverage can be purchased to supplement this basic level of coverage. Typically, this coverage could include semi-private or private rooms for hospital stays, extended services such as eye-glasses and prescription drugs, and dental plans. Many employers provide additional private medical insurance on a group basis. Employees do not pay tax on the value of the extra coverage. If you are not covered at work, consider buying additional coverage on your own, although the cost will be considerably higher for an individual subscriber, compared to that for members of a group plan.

Health care costs outside Canada can be very expensive and may not be fully covered by provincial health care plans. If you have private health insurance through your employer, you may be adequately covered. If not, you can purchase additional protection for health care costs while you are travelling outside Canada at very reasonable rates.

SELECTING THE INSURANCE COMPANY

There are generally two types of insurance companies: those that generate a profit and those that are "not for profit." Carriers owned by shareholder/investors are for-profit companies. They pay a portion of their profits to the shareholders as dividends. Because the policyholders do not share in the company's earnings, premiums on policies are generally level.

There are many life insurance companies in Canada. Carriers owned by the policyholders themselves are mutual insurance companies. The earnings of a mutual are returned to the policyholders. So it is not always easy to find out what the premiums on a policy will be, since the earnings for the year can only be projected.

Selecting the one that is right for you requires evaluation of three important factors:

- The financial strength and integrity of the company
- Service
- The cost of the policy

Financial Strength and Integrity

Insurance involves a long-term financial guarantee, so you should be concerned about the company's ability to fulfill its obligations to you whenever it is called upon to do so —tomorrow, or fifty years from now.

For information on the financial strength and integrity of insurance companies, we suggest that you look at a copy of *Best's Insurance Reports*. This hefty volume is available in the reference rooms of most metropolitan public libraries, and contains a report on many Canadian life insurance companies. It will give you detailed financial information about a company, an analysis of the company's investments, a brief history of the company and its growth, and a description of the company's method of operation.

Best's Insurance Reports also includes a policyholder's rating for most insurance companies. The classifications used are

A+ and A	Excellent
B+	Very Good
B	Good
C+	Fairly Good
D	Fair

As an alternative, ask for financial information about the insurance companies whose products you are considering. Look at their annual financial statements—is the company currently profitable? Does it have a history of profits, or is its performance record up and down? See if you can find any reports on the company in the financial press.

Service

If you are not able to plan and maintain your insurance programme yourself, you will probably rely on the advice of an insurance company's local representative. You should seek an agent who has competence and integrity. Ask your friends, associates, or trusted business advisors whether they can recommend any such person working for companies that you know have financial strength and stability. Talk to several agents and find out about their experience and approach to determining your needs. Obtain a proposal and a sample policy; then study their provisions thoroughly at your leisure. Make sure you understand what insurance policy you are buying, and why, before you sign the application.

Cost

Cost is probably the most important factor in deciding from which company you will buy your insurance. In any company, the cost of a policy depends on such factors as the company's investment performance, its selection of policyholders, its efficiency of operation, and its costs of acquiring new policyholders. These factors have to be managed, and the net result of company management is the cost of the insurance policy. Since management performance differs from company to company, so do costs. As more than one consumer-oriented insurance publication has suggested: Shop around for your insurance!

To help you compare the net costs of different insurers' policies, insurers provide interest-adjusted cost estimates, which apply an interest factor to the yearly premiums, dividends, and increases in cash value. When you are shopping for life insurance, ask the insurance agents to provide you with interest-adjusted cost estimates for any policy you are considering, and don't do any business with an agent who refuses to supply such indexes.

The interest-adjusted cost estimates given by different insurance companies can differ greatly for the same benefit and type of policy. A recent study published by the American Institute for Economic Research, *Life Insurance from the Buyer's Point of View*,* included a cost ranking of companies that had a Best's rating of A or A+ (excellent) and insurance contracts totalling $1 billion or more. To rank the companies, this study used the interest-adjusted annual cost of a $25,000 whole life policy for a man 35 years of age. The findings showed a difference of $4,505 between the least costly and the most costly company. This study only included those companies that were rated excellent. If all companies had been analyzed, the cost difference would have been even greater.

---

*Available from the American Institute for Economic Research, Great Barrington, Massachussetts 01230.

Choosing the Agent

A competent insurance agent often makes the choice of a qualified insurance company much easier. When you select an agent, be sure that person has had extensive experience with the particular type of insurance you are shopping for. The agent should be involved not only in the original sale of coverage but also in monitoring and updating it. References from existing clients are an excellent way of checking the service and professionalism of a prospective broker. Remember that, at all costs, you should *buy* insurance, not *be sold* insurance.

Another factor involved in your selection should be a review of the professional designations they have earned. This is often a sign of the professionalism and commitment they have made to their careers. The designation important in the property-casualty field is the chartered property casualty underwriter (CPCU). In the life and health areas, the designations to look for are chartered life underwriter (CLU), or chartered financial planner (CFP). Each of these designations demonstrates a willingness to provide competent service. Obviously, this does not imply that individuals without these designations are not competent.

Remember, you should purchase insurance only after you have completed the risk management process. This offers the assurance that you are making informed, knowledgeable, and sound decisions about your insurance coverages.

CLOSING OBSERVATIONS

Knowing that there really is a logical and comprehensive way to tackle the task of risk management in your complete personal financial management strategy should assure you that your insurance needs can be met in an understandable, straightforward fashion. The primary purpose of this chapter has been to give you the insight necessary to take action rather than just react in determining where insurance in its myriad forms may be used to your best benefit.

No personal financial management process would be complete without a thorough application of the risk-management process described here. Simply stated, we cannot plan with assurance unless we adequately protect ourselves from financial loss due to risks we overlook, neglect, or cannot escape.

14

ESTATE PLANNING

"You can't take it with you"—so goes the adage on worldly wealth that we've all heard. But you may not have heard the punchline, "The reason you can't take it with you is that *it* goes before *you* go." Assume though, with the help of this book, that yours won't go before you go—you will want your heirs to receive the maximum of your estate with a minimum of aggravation.

Since a smooth transfer of your property is by no means automatic, you should plan and organize your estate now in order to prevent needless delays and losses later on. The preparation of your Financial Planner should be very helpful in estate planning.

WHAT IS ESTATE PLANNING?

Estate planning is the process of providing for the orderly transfer of all your assets at death to your chosen beneficiaries in the time frame you select. For example, you may wish to leave all of your assets to your minor son on the condition that he obtain full control of these assets only when he reaches twenty-five years of age.

WHY DO IT?

One of the major reasons people plan their estates is to reduce taxes payable on death. This is certainly an important motive but appropriate estate planning can also minimize some of the problems and disruptions that often arise when a family member dies. Cash flow problems between the time of death and the settlement of the estate can be prevented. The length of time necessary to settle the estate can be minimized.

Planning your estate will also ensure that your assets are distributed according to your wishes, based on your intimate knowledge of your family situation, rather than being distributed as dictated by provincial statute. As well, both the emotional and monetary cost of administering your estate can be reduced by pre-planning, lessening some of the burden on your executors and beneficiaries who must deal with the consequences of your death, and get on with their own lives.

TAX CONSEQUENCES ON DEATH

Before we discuss the process of estate planning, let's first consider the potential tax consequences of your death.

You will, of course, be subject to tax on any salary, wages, investment income, etc., received in the year before you die. These will be reported in your final tax return. Income such as interest or dividends which have accrued up to the date of death are included in taxable income, even though they are not received until after death. For example, any accrued interest on compound savings bonds will be included in taxable income. But you may have income in addition to this to be reported on your final return.

There are no longer any estate or gift taxes payable in Canada. There are, however, additional income taxes that may be payable just as a result of your death. When you die, the *Income Tax Act* deems you to have disposed of all your non-depreciable capital assets (stocks, bonds, etc.) at their fair market value immediately before your death. Therefore, if you own investments or other non-depreciable capital property with gains accrued since you acquired them, these gains will become taxable on your death. These gains are determined in the same manner as ordinary capital gains, as discussed in Chapter 6. To the extent you have accrued losses on non-depreciable capital properties, you will be able to offset these losses against any gains in the year of death to reduce the amount of the net capital gain reported in your final return.

There are additional special rules to govern the taxation on death of depreciable property, eligible capital property, resource properties and other special business assets. If you have significant holdings in these types of property, you probably need some expert tax advice to formulate an appropriate estate plan.

The tax payable on accrued gains at death can be deferred by leaving these assets unconditionally to your surviving spouse or to a trust which cannot benefit anyone other than your spouse during the remainder of his or her lifetime (spousal trust). Tax on the accrued gains will be deferred until the subsequent death of your spouse or until the property is sold by your spouse. This deferral can allow time for an orderly disposal of assets to minimize tax or to spread its payment over several years.

Capital gains triggered on death may also be offset by any unused capital gains exemption, as previously described in Chapter 6. Since each spouse has their own lifetime capital gains exemption, total taxes may be reduced if you leave some assets with accrued gains directly to your children in order to trigger sufficient gains to use up your remaining exemption limit, rather than deferring these gains by leaving the assets to your spouse. Your unused exemption limit cannot be transferred to your spouse or anyone else—it expires on your death.

Additional income taxes may also be triggered if you have unmatured RRSPs at the time of death. (An unmatured RRSP is one which you have not yet converted to an annuity, RRIF or cash). In general, the current value of investments and funds held in any unmatured RRSPs will be included in the taxable income reported in your final return. If you designate your spouse as the beneficiary of your RRSP, however, tax will only be payable when funds are actually received from the RRSP by your spouse. Your spouse will also be able to transfer tax-free your RRSP funds to his or her own RRSP. All or part of the tax payable on your unmatured RRSPs can also be deferred if you designate as beneficiaries dependent children or grandchildren (dependent by reason of mental or physical infirmity, or dependent and twenty-five years of age or younger). You can also choose, in certain conditions, to have all or part of an unmatured RRSP taxed in the hands of your spouse or a dependent child or grandchild, rather than in your final return.

An estate plan (or any other plan, for that matter) should not just be considered from a tax viewpoint. If, in order to save tax, you inadvertently deprive your spouse of a reasonable income after your death, it cannot be considered a successful plan. Tax savings are often the reason for choosing a particular method of estate planning, but they should never be the single determining factor.

The above discussion of the potential tax consequences on death is very simplified and general, and it does not include details relating to the filing of special returns, certain elections available, etc. An in-depth discussion of all these items could fill many chapters of this book and would probably not be of much interest to many readers. This discussion, along with the completion of Form 31 (discussed below), should allow you to come up with a fairly accurate estimate of potential taxes on death and you can use this as a first step in formulating your estate plan. A more detailed analysis of your potential tax situation should be done with the help of a qualified tax advisor.

FORM 31—POTENTIAL INCOME TAX LIABILITY ON ASSETS OWNED AT DEATH

Form 31 can be used to estimate your potential tax liability at death on non-depreciable capital assets and unmatured RRSPs. Form 13B will supply you with most of the information required to determine accrued gains or losses on the non-depreciable capital properties you currently hold. Information on the current value of your unmatured RRSPs can be obtained from the financial institution that administers your plans.

FORM 32—AFTER-TAX VALUE OF ESTATE

Form 32 is provided to help you determine the after-tax value of your estate, drawing from information contained in other forms in this book.

Start with Form 5, *Analysis of Net Worth*. If this has been recently up-dated, it will provide you with an accurate estimate of the pre-tax value of your estate excluding insurance. Put the amount of your total net worth, excluding insurance, as determined on line 10 of Form 5, onto line 1 of Form 32. Add to this the amount of insurance that will be paid to your estate on your death as indicated on Form 28. The after-tax value of your estate can then be obtained by deducting the estimated potential tax on death determined on Form 31, as well as estimated funeral expenses and administration costs for your estate.

STEPS TO IMPLEMENT YOUR ESTATE PLAN

All the steps which follow apply equally to both husband and wife. For simplicity, the completion of each step has only been described for one spouse. Obviously, it is important to consider an estate plan for both spouses, particularly when each own significant assets independent of one another.

Decide How You Would Like The After-Tax Value Of Your Estate Divided

Think carefully about how you would like to divide your assets. If your spouse is still alive and will not have sufficient income of his or her own to live comfortably after your death, estimate how much of your estate will be needed to make up this income gap. If your estate cannot provide sufficient assets to fund this income gap, you should consider additional life insurance (discussed in Chapter 13). If there is any excess, consider how you would like this divided among your children, other family members, friends, and charitable organizations. If you have changed your original allocation of assets to your spouse and others, reflect this by adjusting the potential taxes payable you estimated on Form 31 and recalculating the after-tax value of your estate.

Remember that, in general, tax can be deferred on assets left to your spouse, while there is usually no deferral on assets left to others.

In some circumstances, you may not be able to divide your estate exactly as you wish. All provinces have family law legislation that deals with the division of assets acquired during the marriage between spouses in the event of marriage breakdown. The legislation may also extend to the division of assets on death of a spouse. For example, in Ontario, the surviving spouse is entitled to one-half of assets accumulated during the marriage (with some exceptions). If the deceased spouse's will bequeaths less than this amount to the surviving spouse, he or she has a legal right to demand an equalizing payment from the estate. Therefore, if you live in Ontario and wish to leave the bulk of your estate to someone other than your spouse, your will may not be followed, unless you and your spouse have previously agreed in a valid domestic contract to forego your rights under the *Family Law Act* to vary the division of assets on death. The lawyer you consult to draft or revise your will should be able to explain your rights and obligations to your spouse under the applicable provincial legislation. It may be that you need not only an updated will, but a marriage contract as well.

Consider Reviewing Your Situation with a Tax Specialist

Particularly with the introduction of the lifetime capital gains exemption and the minimum tax, estate tax planning can be complex. If you have a substantial estate or investments with large accrued gains, investments in private companies, partnerships or other business interests, or investments in foreign properties such as U.S. real estate, it is almost certainly worth your while to invest several hundred dollars or more in the services of a tax specialist. There may be legitimate opportunities for you to reduce tax, opportunities which you might otherwise be unaware of. For example, a business owner who intends to eventually transfer ownership of his company to his children could reduce future taxes on death (or retirement) by "freezing" the value of his company at its current value, with future growth accruing to shares held by his children. In the meantime, the business owner could retain control of the company, if he wishes. The lawyer you consult to draft your will may have this specialized tax knowledge, or you may wish to consult a C.A. with expertise in estate planning to work along with your lawyer.

Consult a Lawyer to Draft or Review Your Will

This is such an important step that it's hard not to put it before the previous two steps. (It's only placed here because you really need to decide on the division of your estate and consult a tax specialist before you can provide your lawyer with the information needed to draft or revise your will.)

Should everyone have a will? Maybe not. But anyone with a spouse and children, or some interest in the disposition of their property after death, should definitely make a will. It is *essential* unless you want your assets distributed according to the intestacy law of the province in which you live, and your minor children placed under a guardianship determined by the courts. A will allows you to consider the special needs of your family members. For example, you may wish to delay the time at which your children unconditionally receive their inheritance until they turn twenty-five. Without a will, they would automatically receive their share of your estate at the age of majority (generally eighteen).

Without a will, you cannot choose the executors (administrators) of your estate— they will be selected by the court. If you die intestate, there will be a period immediately after your death (until the court appoints the executors of your estate) when no one has the legal authority to administer your estate. This can be inconvenient for your survivors, and cause them cash flow problems. Failure to draft a will almost certainly will delay the distribution of your estate and will result in higher administration costs. As well, most opportunities to defer or reduce taxes on death will be lost if you do not have a will.

In some cases, you can control the transfer of your assets without a will. For example, property owned in joint tenancy with the right of survivorship will pass automatically on death to the surviving joint owner. As well, you can name a beneficiary under an insurance policy or an RRSP, so that on your death the property passes to that beneficiary.

However, even if you can structure all your assets to pass automatically to specified beneficiaries on your death, it is still prudent to have a will to provide alternative beneficiaries should you and your specified beneficiaries die in a common disaster.

TERMS OF YOUR WILL

For people of modest wealth with relatively straightforward estate plans, their needs can be met by a simple will. The following points should be remembered in drawing up a will:

- your (testator's) identity and address.
- revocation of prior wills and codicils (revisions to prior wills).
- burial instructions or other disposition of your body (such as donating it for medical purposes).
- specific bequests (gifts) of identifiable real or personal property, sums of money or shares of stock to a specified beneficiary, such as your spouse, your children, or charities.
- bequests of tangible personal property, such as personal and household effects, jewellery and cars, to family members, friends or charities.
- establishment of trusts to hold specific or residuary bequests for certain beneficiaries who may need ongoing assistance in handling their bequests. Trusts are particularly common for minor children, and for spouses not experienced in financial matters.
- residuary bequests of assets that have not been specifically bequeathed. In small estates, such assets are usually left outright to the surviving spouse or children. In large estates, the residual assets are more important and their disposition is more complicated, often involving trusts and other matters requiring legal advice. When there is no close family or surviving spouse, the residual assets are often left to charities.
- survivorship provisions that establish a presumed order of death in case you and your spouse or other beneficiary die in the same accident and there is no proof of which one died first. This component in the will should also include provisions that will serve to avoid the expense of double administration in case two parties, one inheriting from the other, die within a short time of each other.
- appointment of a guardian for your minor children in the event you and your spouse die at the same time.
- appointment of executor(s).
- appointment of trustee(s) when the will contains a trust.
- payment of funeral expenses, administration costs of the estate and debts of the estate, including income taxes payable as a result of your death.
- provision for contingencies. For example, you should select alternate beneficiaries in the event the expected beneficiaries die before you.

CHANGING YOUR WILL

Keep your will in a safe place where your executor, spouse or closest beneficiary can get to it quickly and easily. The original will might best be kept by your lawyer. Another copy can be kept in your safety deposit box but, if you plan to do so, find out first what procedures would have to be followed to open the box after your death. Keep another copy with your financial records at home for easy reference. It might be a good idea also to summarize and discuss the important provisions of your will with the persons affected by it.

Once you have a will, you should review it every few years to make sure it still fits your situation and have it adjusted, if necessary. Substantial changes in your financial situation, such as a large inheritance, may necessitate changes in the provisions of your will. There may also be changes in the tax law that affect your will and if you marry or divorce, you will almost certainly wish to make changes in your will. (Your existing will may be automatically revoked if your marital status changes.)

WHO WILL BE YOUR EXECUTOR?

What could be better than to have your spouse or other close relative serve as the executor of your estate? After all, he or she is most likely to know exactly what you would have done if you were still alive. However, you might be better off having a professional take on the job of executor.

The job of executor is complicated because of tax laws, inheritance rules and probate regulations, although much of the paperwork involved (including the filing of tax returns) can be dealt with by a family member executor with the help of a lawyer and a chartered accountant. This is particularly true when the estate is left outright to a spouse or other family member. But make sure any executor you select is willing to take on the responsibility.

When more complex estates are involved, for example, or when your will establishes trusts to invest funds bequeathed to minor children or other family members, it may be prudent to choose someone other than a family member as executor. One solution is to name a trust company and have your spouse or a relative as co-executor.

CLOSING OBSERVATIONS

You work hard—maybe a total of 80,000 hours during your lifetime—to earn your money and invest it wisely. It would be a shame if, at your death, your nearest and dearest were to suffer financially because you did not give sufficient consideration to the transfer of your estate. We hope you have taken time to estimate the existing value of your family's estate, to forecast how the estate will be divided on your death, and to estimate the potential tax consequences of your death (as well as consider ways to reduce this potential tax, where possible).

We know that estate planning can sometimes become quite complicated. If that's how it seems in your case, we suggest that you seek some good professional advice to help you conserve the maximum amount of your estate.

15

TAKE ACTION

This book has given you a structure for analyzing your personal finances, for forecasting your financial future, and for identifying the financial steps that can bring you closer to your various objectives in life. This, in itself, may well prevent you from taking some ill-considered step you might have taken without it; but to reap major benefits from the knowledge and insight you have acquired, you must apply it by taking the appropriate positive action.

The first thing to do is to ask and answer questions such as:

- How much do you want or can you afford to put aside for your long-term objectives of education, retirement, extended travel, remodelling, and so forth?
- Do your current and projected budgets permit you to set aside for your long-term objectives?
- What are the trade-offs to make between your current lifestyle and future objectives?

Before you answer such questions and prepare a projection for next year, here are some general guidelines for people of varying ages.

IN YOUR THIRTIES

Take care of the four firsts: an annual income, normally secured by a job; a place to live; a reserve fund that can be used in an emergency; and low-cost life insurance—a source of future income for your dependents should you die.

The first two, an annual income and a place to live, have far-reaching implications for long-term financial planning. Income obviously is a big factor in providing sufficient resources for accumulating assets and establishing a comfortable standard of living. However, it is not necessarily true that the larger the income, the larger the resources accumulated or the estate developed. Maintaining an income level sets in motion complicated problems of living up to one's career position. Many people of significant income have lifestyle expenses as great, if not greater, than their income, and they never seem to accumulate assets for future needs.

So during your thirties, concentrate on your income and basic lifestyle expenditures—housing, transportation, food, and clothing. Resist the instant gratification craze and get in the habit of saving something for investment. Consider starting an education fund if you have children.

Remember that the cash reserve fund should be kept in liquid, low-risk investments such as Canada Savings Bonds. Try to attain a level of three months' take-home pay for this reserve. Life insurance is usually an easy goal to achieve at this age because most employers offer group term insurance at little or no cost. If this is the case in your situation, you won't have to purchase additional coverage from an independent agent. Make sure that you have adequate disability coverage, as this is the most important aspect of insurance planning at this time in your life.

IN YOUR FORTIES

Control the increase in lifestyle expenditures. Look for investments, other than your personal residence, that the family can use and enjoy—vacation property, a boat, a computer. Concentrate on education funds and try to shift income to your children to pay for their education. Start a retirement programme. Focus on growth and tax savings in selecting your investments.

IN YOUR FIFTIES

The children, you hope, are educated and on their own. You might even be able to decrease your basic lifestyle expenditures at this stage. Focus on new personal growth activities, such as travel, photography, or art collecting. Concentrate on retirement planning and increasing your investment assets and retirement funds to make your retirement years golden. Pay off your home mortgage. Concentrate your savings and investment dollars in instruments of moderate to low risk.

IN YOUR SIXTIES

Pare your basic lifestyle costs. Get those retirement activities lined up and going. Concentrate on being active and continue your zest for life. Get out of debt and manage your investment assets to stay even with inflation. Get your estate in order and keep your financial affairs simple.

FORM 33—INCOME AND EXPENDITURE PROJECTION

To complete this form, you need to refer to forms you previously completed about your objectives and to follow the steps below:

- Enter in the *Last Year* column your actual income and expenditures from Forms 6, 7, 8, and 9.
- Enter on lines 1, 2, 3, and 4 in the *Next Year* column your estimates of next year's expenditures for long-term objectives.
- On line 1, enter the amount for each of your children from line 15(c) of Form 23, *University, Graduate School and College Costs.* Using the example shown in Figure 11-1 for Form 23, you would enter $16,546 on line 1 of Form 33.
- On line 2, enter the amounts from lines 7a and 10d of Form 27, *Retirement Income.* Using the example in Figure 12-1 for Form 27, you would enter $8,450 on line 2 of Form 33.

- On line 3, enter your answer to question 5 of Form 22, *Your Investment Strategy*. Using the example shown in Figure 10-3 for Form 22, you would enter $10,000 on line 3 of Form 33.
- On line 4, enter the amounts for the next year of the major discretionary expenditures you listed on Form 17, *Income and Expenditure Objectives*.
- On line 5, enter the totals of lines 1 through 4 to get the amount you would like to set aside next year for long-term objectives.
- On line 6a in the *Next Year* column, enter your estimate of employment income for next year. Review lines 1 and 2 of Form 17 for the estimate you previously prepared.
- On line 6b, enter your estimate of investment income for next year. Review information on Form 11, *Tax-Planning Worksheet*, as a starting point here. Total your estimated income for next year on line 6c.
- On line 7, enter your estimate of basic lifestyle expenditures for next year. Review Form 7, *Basic Lifestyle Expenditures*, as a starting point; remember that some very significant basic expenditures may not increase—for example, your mortgage payment. Remember also that whether these expenditures increase is up to you—the quality of your future lifestyle is not necessarily dependent on more quantity, more expenditures.
- On line 8, enter your estimate of discretionary expenditures. Review Form 8, *Discretionary Expenditures*, as a starting point.
- On line 9a, enter your estimate of income taxes for next year. Use your estimate of taxable income from Form 11, *Income Tax-Planning Worksheet*, and refer to Appendix II for the taxes payable on this amount.
- On line 9b, enter your estimate of other payroll deductions, including Canada or Quebec Pension Plan contributions, Unemployment Insurance premiums, and any provincial health insurance payments. Total your estimated income taxes and other deductions on line 9c.
- On line 10, enter the totals from lines 7, 8, and 9c.
- On line 11, enter the amount that results from subtracting line 10 from line 6c.

At this point, compare the amount on line 5 to the amount on line 11. If the amount on line 11 is less than the amount on line 5, determine what changes you need to make in your financial situation to achieve your long-term objectives. Can you increase your income? Can you reduce your discretionary expenditures? Can you manage your taxes more effectively? These are choices you can make to increase the amount available for long-term objectives. If you are unwilling or unable to increase the amount on line 11, then you will have to revise the amounts you can set aside next year for long-term goals.

Once you have evaluated your choices and trade-offs, get the amounts on line 5 and line 11 in balance. Then commit yourself to making your projections a reality. The income and expenditure projection then becomes a blueprint for the first year of your financial future.

FORM 34—YOUR ACTION STEPS

Have you been noting your potential action steps for next year as you were working on various other forms? If not, let us remind you of the planning areas into which they might fall.

- Net worth planning
- Controlling or reducing expenditures

- Increasing earned income
- Reducing taxes
- Increasing investments and return on investments
- Financing your children's education
- Retirement planning
- Life insurance
- Estate planning

In listing steps on Form 34, try to be as specific as you can. Decide on the type of action to take, on the amount of money involved, and on the date by which the action should be accomplished. Something vague like "My wife and I want to set aside some funds for retirement this year" is less likely to be translated into action than "My wife and I want to contribute $4,000 to an RRSP by May 31 this year," which sets you a specific and presumably well-considered target.

As has been mentioned earlier, it is unrealistic to assume that you can accomplish more than ten such action steps in one year. Therefore, select the most feasible of your proposed action steps and make a commitment to complete them.

To keep to your timetable, and to make sure that nothing is left undone because it just slipped your mind, take a look at this form once a month, and transfer the appropriate action step(s) onto your everyday list of things you must remember to do. The timely accomplishment of these goals is imperative to a successful financial management programme.

PROFESSIONAL ADVICE

As you face the increasing complexity of our tax laws and a multitude of investment opportunities, you may feel a need for professional guidance or confirmation before you make some weighty financial decision. Depending on your particular concerns— income tax planning, retirement or estate planning, investments, or life insurance—you might want to consult a professional advisor in an accounting firm, a bank, a brokerage firm, a *caisse populaire*, a credit union, a financial counselling firm, an insurance company or a law firm.

The institution or organization you consult should be experienced in the particular field of your inquiry, and you should ask how clients with problems similar to your own have been counselled. Get references on the quality of the organization's work in this field, and find out what professional training your prospective counsellor has had.

The majority of these counselling services will charge you a fee. Certain accounting firms, banks, trust companies, brokerage firms, insurance companies, credit unions and *caisses populaires* may provide some financial counselling. Some of these organizations may be primarily in the business of selling products and they may offer free counselling services in order to make their products more attractive or to promote their sale.

Any professional advisor you choose will find the analyses you have made of your financial holdings, needs, objectives, and expectations enormously helpful; and wherever the advisor's fee is determined by the time spent on your behalf, the work you have done on your forms will reduce such a fee, perhaps by forty to fifty percent. If there is going to be a fee, agree on the terms of it beforehand and make sure you will get an itemized bill.

Except in matters of law, rules, and regulations, which the advisor should know insofar as they relate to the advisor's specialty, the professional guidance you receive will not be based on certainties but on estimates of probabilities. On the whole, the professional's estimates should be correct more often than your own. Even so, any professional advice that is based on an estimate of probabilities should not be followed blindly, nor should you ever take financial action on the basis of rationales that you do not understand. A good advisor will be ready to explain the reasons for any advice or recommendation.

For those who might want to consult an advisor, the following paragraphs give a brief description of the organizations that provide various types of financial advice.

Accounting Firms

Personal financial planning services are offered by some medium-sized accounting firms and by all of the large ones. As well as helping you to formulate financial plans and goals, they can advise you on particular concerns like tax planning, tax shelters, investment planning and performance, educational financing, and retirement and estate planning. Their unique expertise lies in the field of taxation, and this is quite crucial, since tax considerations enter into just about every phase of financial planning and management. To determine which combination of variables will be the most advantageous for you, they make extensive use of computer analysis, in addition to their knowledge of the tax laws.

The advice you get from an accounting firm will not be coloured by self-interest. Accounting firms don't act as brokers or sell insurance on the side. If they suggest that you buy or sell some product, it will not be because they receive a commission on it. They don't. They work for a fee based on hourly rates, and before entering into an engagement with you, they should give you an estimate of their fee. They will also be able to put you in touch with competent and reliable firms of stockbrokers, insurers, or whatever else you may need to put your financial plans in action.

Banks, Credit Unions, and Trust Companies

Recently some banks, credit unions and trust companies have started to provide a variety of financial planning services. These services may include tailor-made loans, estate planning, asset management, trust services, stock purchases, and financial counselling.

Investment Counsellors

Most investment counsellors provide investment management of a portfolio of securities. Many firms will not handle portfolios below some minimum size—from $100,000 to $250,000. Investment counsellors charge a fee for their financial advice based on some percentage of the value of the portfolio. This percentage may run from one or two percent of the minimum portfolio to one-half a percent of larger portfolios.

In using an investment counselling firm, it normally makes sense to give the professional manager the power to buy and sell investments without your consent. Remember, the professional counselling firm is being paid for its judgement. If you do not want the firm to exercise its judgement, you should probably not pay for investment management. If you do choose to let an investment counselling firm handle your investments, you should review its performance quarterly or semi-annually and either retain or dismiss the firm, based on its performance.

Since there are many investment counselling firms available, one of the biggest problems is to select the right firm for you. One approach is to check the banks and trust companies in your area to see if they provide an investment counselling service. Often they do. If they do not, they might be able to give you a list of investment advisors who may help you. In addition, your CA and lawyer should know of investment counselling firms they can recommend to you. Usually stockbrokerage firms know of investment firms, since investment counselling firms have to work through a stockbroker in order to buy and sell securities for their clients. And many stockbrokerage firms have their own affiliated investment advisory services.

Mutual Funds

For those who do not have sufficient investments to interest a personal investment counsellor, consider mutual funds. A mutual fund is an enterprise that obtains money from institutional and individual investors and invests the money in securities selected to achieve certain financial objectives. By pooling the funds of many investors, the mutual fund provides diversification, professional management, and continuous supervision of investments.

There are hundreds of mutual funds from which to choose, varying in size, purpose, and policy. Refer back to Chapter 10 for a general description of mutual funds.

Brokerage Houses

In recent years, some brokerage houses have established financial planning departments staffed with investment counsellors, CAs, lawyers, and insurance specialists. They provide comprehensive services and charge a fee for the services. Some of them arrange that if the client buys investment products from the brokerage house, the brokerage commissions are deducted from the financial planning fees.

Of course, brokerage houses are organized primarily to provide investment products, ranging from money market funds, stocks and bonds to real estate or oil and gas tax shelters. A good broker should first perform an analysis of your investment needs, including your present assets and your investment objectives. The broker should know whether you wish to emphasize capital gains or income, short-term or long-term investments, safety or speculation, and so forth. In essence, the broker attempts to find out what types of investments you feel comfortable with. After reviewing your personal data, present financial situation, and investment objectives, the stockbroker should develop an appropriate investment plan based on what you consider to be a desirable or acceptable rate of risk and return.

Full-service brokerage houses provide research reports on specific securities, reference libraries, and safekeeping services for your securities. Of course, they buy and sell securities, for which they charge a commission. A full-service brokerage house charges a higher commission than a discount brokerage house because of the extensive services it offers. Discount brokers do nothing more than buy and sell securities.

Financial Planners

In recent years, two new designations in the financial planning field have emerged. One is the Certified Financial Planner (CFP); the other is the Registered Financial Consultant (RFC). Both of these designations are awarded to people who have completed a comprehensive educational programme in areas of financial planning. Typically, a CFP or RFC has experience in a specific financial field such as selling stocks, mutual funds or insurance. Some financial planners are independent and objective in their analyses and recommendations and charge a fee for their services; others do not charge a fee and hence will tend to recommend the products that they sell on commission.

Insurance Advisors

Primarily, insurance advisors provide professional assistance in the broad area of insurance—health, disability, casualty, and life insurance. Such an advisor often acts as a catalyst in the financial planning process, bringing the client together with other experts—a CA, a lawyer, or an investment broker.

A good insurance advisor will review the client's financial affairs and will call in these other financial advisors when appropriate. If the client's business transactions are too complex for the insurance agent to handle, the agent should consult the proper specialist—a CA about possible tax advantages, a trust company or lawyer about changing a client's will or the setting up of a trust.

The role of the life insurance agent as a financial advisor is a difficult one because of the obvious conflict of interest. The insurance agent is expected to make an objective analysis of the client's needs and to recommend the appropriate insurance coverage, but the agent is compensated on a commission basis: The more insurance the agent sells, the greater the agent's income.

KEEPING UP WITH CURRENT FINANCIAL INFORMATION

Periodicals

There are several sources of financial information and analyses.

Canadian Sources:

1. *The Globe & Mail*, Report on Business section (daily)
   Canadian Newspapers Company Limited
   444 Front Street West
   Toronto, Ontario
   M5V 2S9

   (a good source of general business information, along with recent developments in taxation and personal finance)

2. *Financial Post* (daily)
   Maclean Hunter Limited
   777 Bay Street
   Toronto, Ontario
   M5W 1A7

   (concentrates on reporting developments in the business world, including stock market information, but has regular features on personal tax and financial planning matters. Also has quarterly reviews of mutual fund performance)

3. *Financial Times* (weekly)
   Southam Inc.
   920 Yonge Street
   Suite 500
   Toronto, Ontario
   M4W 3L5

   (also concentrates on general business and investment information but with regular personal financial management features and monthly reviews of mutual fund performance)

4. *Canadian Business* (monthly)
   CB Media Limited
   70 The Esplanade
   2nd Floor
   Toronto, Ontario
   M5E 1R2

   (reports on many business topics, including personal tax and financial planning)

5. *Your Money* (monthly)
   CB Media Limited
   56 The Esplanade
   2nd Floor
   Toronto, Ontario
   M5E 1A7

   (deals exclusively with personal finance topics)

U.S. Sources:

6. *The Wall Street Journal* (daily)
   200 Burnett Road
   Chicopee, Massachusetts 01021

   (in every Monday issue is a column entitled "Your Money Matters")

7. *Business Week* (weekly)
   McGraw-Hill Inc.
   1221 Avenue of the Americas
   New York, New York 10020

   (has a "Personal Business" column, in addition to articles covering many economic areas)

8. *Forbes* (bi-weekly)
   60 Fifth Avenue
   New York, New York 10011

   (includes a "Personal Affairs" column as well as several money and investments columns in each issue. Also has an annual mutual fund analysis in August or September issue)

9. *Fortune* (bi-weekly)
   541 North Fairbanks Court
   Chicago, Illinois 60611

   (has a "Personal Investing" column, in addition to comprehensive business articles)

10. *Money* (monthly)
    Time, Inc.
    541 North Fairbanks Court
    Chicago, Illinois 60611

    (Includes articles on many personal financial matters with a how-to-do-it approach; it includes a regular article on "one family's finances" that discusses specific financial recommendations)

Newsletters

There are many newsletters available. Many brokerage houses provide letters to their clients, as do investment counselling firms. Some specialize in certain kinds of investments. Many of these newsletters are advertised by direct mail. If you are interested in one that seems to fit your objectives, we suggest you write and ask for a sample copy.

Television

There are television news programmes and talk shows that stress money matters. Global TV has a weekly programme, "Everybody's Business," that covers current issues. Canadian public television also has programmes dealing with personal finances, including TV Ontario's "Money$worth." "Wall Street Week" is a half-hour U.S. Public Broadcasting System production that covers a variety of current investment ideas and products primarily in the U.S. market.

Seminars

There are a variety of financial planning seminars—some free, some expensive—offered by universities, community colleges, banks, investment firms, trust companies and accounting firms.

16

YOUR ANNUAL FINANCIAL CHECKUP

Congratulations to all of you who have worked your way through this book and filled in all its forms. At this point, you know what you own, what you need, what you want, what you can reasonably expect, and what you can do. You have made some choices, evaluated the consequences, committed yourself to some action, and are in control of your financial affairs. In addition, you have saved $2,000 to $3,000 in professional fees by putting your Financial Planner together. You have earned the laurels and might like to wear them around the house for a month or so.

Beware of resting on your laurels, though. Time marches on, and some of your current records and plans will inevitably become out-of-date. So you should periodically update everything that has some bearing on your financial plans and decisions.

Some of the forms you have completed may merely need to be reviewed and amended where necessary. Others should be completed anew.

Because few people can or want to update their affairs in one sitting, we suggest that you do your updating systematically and do it over the course of the year. In our experience, the following timetable is the best and most convenient.

JANUARY—FEBRUARY

In these first months of the year, make some inroads on the tax returns due on April 30 by assembling all data pertaining to your financial transactions in the last calendar year.

When you have finished with that, review and update the following forms:

- *Form 1*, *Personal and Family Data* (Chapter 2), filed under *Personal Data* in your Financial Planner. The information listed here will not change greatly from year to year, so merely check your completed form and amend it as necessary.

- ***Form 2***, *Financial Documents* (Chapter 2), filed under *Financial Documents* in your Financial Planner. Use your completed form. Make sure the listings are complete and that the documents are in their stated locations. Go over this list with your spouse and also let someone else in your family know that this list exists and where to find it.
- ***Form 3***, *Financial Advisors* (Chapter 2), filed under *Financial Documents* in your Financial Planner. Use your filled-in form. Evaluate your original choices and amend them if that seems advisable.
- ***Form 4***, *Statement of Net Worth*, and Form 5, *Analysis of Net Worth* (Chapter 3), filed under *Financial Profile* in your Financial Planner. Here your filled-in forms are out-of-date by up to one year. Since you can now take some of the required data from your original form and the rest from the data collected for your tax return, this second time around will be much easier than the first.
- ***Form 6***, *Income Sources* (Chapter 4), filed under *Financial Profile*. Take a copy of this form and complete it with the information you have collected for your tax return. Compare it with your original form and set some goals for the current year.
- ***Form 7***, *Basic Lifestyle Expenditures*, and Form 8, *Discretionary Expenditures* (Chapter 4), filed under *Financial Profile*. Update these forms with data for the last calendar year. Then challenge your expenditure patterns and set some goals for the current year.

MARCH

Focus on completing your tax return for last year by the end of March. If you want a tax accountant to review or prepare your return, stay away from the April 30 scramble. You are likely to get much better service before April, and to obtain that, you must give your accountant the necessary data by early to mid-March. Be sure to keep a copy of your tax return.

When you have mailed your tax return to Revenue Canada, update the following forms:

- ***Form 9***, *Income Taxes and Other Deductions* (Chapter 4), filed under *Financial Profile* in your Financial Planner. Use a duplicate of this form, and take your figures from your newly completed tax return. Find your top tax rate from the appropriate schedule in Appendix II. Find your average tax rate by adding lines 2 and 3 and then dividing the result by line 1.
- ***Form 10***, *Analysis of Earned Income and Expenditures* (Chapter 4), filed under *Financial Profile* in your Financial Planner. Use a copy of this form, and take your figures from your newly completed Form 6, Form 7, Form 8, and Form 9.

Now, after either updating or completing anew Forms 1 through 10, you have an updated financial profile and are again in a position to do some planning for the future.

APRIL—MAY

Now that you have completed and mailed your last year's tax return, prepare a tax plan for this year on Form 11, *Income Tax Planning Worksheet*. You may wish to use a tax professional to help you prepare your plan and to identify tax-saving ideas (Form 12).

Finally, you should prepare an estimate of this year's tax liability. Make sure you understand how much tax will be withheld from your paycheques and the estimated tax payments, if any, you will need to make on March 31, June 30, September 30, and December 31 of this year.

Before the summer rolls around, you can do a little more reviewing and updating of the following forms:

- *Form 16, Financial Security* (Chapter 9), filed under *Financial Objectives* in your Financial Planner.
- *Form 17, Income and Expenditure Objectives* (Chapter 9), filed under *Financial Objectives* in your Financial Planner.
- *Form 20, Investment Objectives* (Chapter 9), filed under *Investment Strategy* in your Financial Planner. Review your completed form and amend it as necessary.
- *Form 21, Review of Your Present Investments* (Chapter 10), filed under *Investment Strategy* in your Financial Planner. Review your completed form and amend it as necessary.
- *Form 22, Your Investment Strategy* (Chapter 10), filed under *Investment Strategy* in your Financial Planner. Review your completed form and amend it as necessary.
- *Form 33, Income and Expenditure Projection* (Chapter 15), filed under *Action* in your Financial Planner. Use the copy of this form and update your projections for this year.

JUNE—AUGUST

Even the most conscientious financial planners must take time off to recharge their batteries. Try to relax during these months and temper your financial planning with lots of sunshine, hikes, vacation trips, sailing, or whatever gives you a break from work and gets you closer to your family and friends.

SEPTEMBER—OCTOBER

Imagine how boring fall would be if you had no financial planning to do—nothing but falling leaves, apples, pumpkins, and football games! As a change from all that, you will want to update the following forms:

- *Form 28, Your Present Life Insurance Coverage* (Chapter 13), filed under *Insurance* in your Financial Planner. Review your completed form and amend it as necessary.
- *Form 29, Total Life Insurance Required* (Chapter 13), filed under *Insurance* in your Financial Planner. Review your completed form and amend it as necessary.
- *Form 13, Capital Gains and Losses* (Chapter 8), filed under *Tax Planning* in your Financial Planner. Use a copy of this form and complete it with your transactions for the current year.
- *Form 14, Year-End Tax Plan* (Chapter 8), filed under *Tax Planning* in your Financial Planner. Use a copy of this form and complete it with your data for the current year.
- *Form 15, Year-End Tax Action* (Chapter 8), filed under *Tax Planning* in your Financial Planner. Use a copy of this form, and try to render as little as possible unto Caesar—legally, of course.

NOVEMBER—DECEMBER

Continue to implement your year-end tax action steps through December.

If you have had any second thoughts about your financial retirement needs, make the appropriate changes in your completed Form 24, *Estimated Basic Lifestyle Expenditures at Retirement* or Form 25, *Estimated Discretionary Expenditures at Retirement* (Chapter 12), filed under *Retirement Planning* in your Financial Planner. If there is any change in your expected retirement income, amend your completed Form 27, *Retirement Income* (Chapter 12), filed under *Retirement Planning* in your Financial Planner.

Unless the secret of immortality has been discovered and is available to you by the time you read this, review the following forms, and use copies to complete them anew if there are any changes.

- *Form 31,* *Potential Income Tax Liability on Assets owned at Death* (Chapter 14), filed under *Estate Planning* in your Financial Planner.
- *Form 32,* *After-Tax Value of Estate* (Chapter 14), filed under *Estate Planning* in your Financial Planner.

And finally, now that you have finished updating all the forms, review your Financial Planner and complete Form 34, *Action Steps* (Chapter 15), filed under *Action* in your Financial Planner.

CONCLUDING OBSERVATIONS

You have prepared your Financial Planner and are well on your way to financial control and financial security. Spend according to your plan and invest in those assets that are tailored to your objectives. Evaluate your plan at least once a year and update it for changes in your objectives, the economic situation, and other events that affect you financially. But, by all means, remember to have a good life. May you grow old gracefully and with a good deal of prosperity.

APPENDIX I

COMPOUND INTEREST TABLES

TABLE 1
FUTURE WORTH OF ONE DOLLAR WITH AMOUNT OF RETURN COMPOUNDED ANNUALLY

Year	Annual Rate of Return										
	5%	6%	7%	8%	9%	10%	11%	12%	13%	14%	15%
1	1.05	1.06	1.07	1.08	1.09	1.10	1.11	1.12	1.13	1.14	1.15
2	1.10	1.12	1.15	1.17	1.19	1.21	1.23	1.25	1.28	1.30	1.32
3	1.16	1.19	1.23	1.26	1.30	1.33	1.37	1.40	1.44	1.48	1.52
4	1.22	1.26	1.31	1.36	1.41	1.46	1.52	1.57	1.63	1.69	1.75
5	1.28	1.34	1.40	1.47	1.54	1.61	1.69	1.76	1.84	1.93	2.01
6	1.34	1.42	1.50	1.59	1.68	1.77	1.87	1.97	2.08	2.20	2.31
7	1.41	1.50	1.61	1.71	1.83	1.95	2.08	2.21	2.35	2.50	2.66
8	1.48	1.59	1.72	1.85	1.99	2.14	2.31	2.48	2.66	2.85	3.06
9	1.55	1.69	1.84	2.00	2.17	2.36	2.56	2.77	3.00	3.25	3.52
10	1.63	1.79	1.97	2.16	2.37	2.59	2.84	3.10	3.40	3.71	4.05
11	1.71	1.90	2.11	2.33	2.58	2.85	3.15	3.48	3.84	4.23	4.65
12	1.80	2.01	2.25	2.52	2.81	3.14	3.50	3.90	4.34	4.82	5.35
13	1.89	2.13	2.41	2.72	3.07	3.45	3.88	4.36	4.90	5.50	6.15
14	1.98	2.26	2.58	2.94	3.34	3.80	4.31	4.89	5.54	6.26	7.08
15	2.08	2.40	2.76	3.17	3.64	4.18	4.79	5.47	6.25	7.14	8.14
16	2.18	2.54	2.95	3.43	3.97	4.60	5.31	6.13	7.07	8.14	9.36
17	2.30	2.69	3.16	3.70	4.33	5.05	5.90	6.87	7.99	9.28	10.76
18	2.41	2.85	3.38	4.00	4.72	5.56	6.54	7.69	9.02	10.58	12.38
19	2.53	3.03	3.62	4.32	5.14	6.12	7.26	8.61	10.20	12.06	14.23
20	2.65	3.21	3.87	4.67	5.60	6.73	8.06	9.65	11.52	13.74	16.37
21	2.79	3.40	4.14	5.03	6.11	7.40	8.95	10.80	13.02	15.67	18.82
22	2.93	3.60	4.43	5.44	6.66	8.14	9.93	12.10	14.71	17.86	21.65
23	3.07	3.82	4.74	5.87	7.26	8.95	11.03	13.55	16.63	20.36	24.89
24	3.23	4.05	5.07	6.34	7.91	9.85	12.24	15.18	18.79	23.21	28.63
25	3.39	4.29	5.43	6.86	8.62	10.83	13.59	17.00	21.23	26.46	32.92
26	3.56	4.55	5.81	7.40	9.40	11.92	13.08	19.04	23.99	30.17	37.86
27	3.73	4.82	6.21	7.99	10.25	13.11	16.74	21.33	27.11	34.39	43.54
28	3.92	5.11	6.65	8.63	11.17	14.42	18.58	23.88	30.63	39.20	50.07
29	4.12	5.42	7.11	9.32	12.17	15.86	20.62	26.75	34.62	44.69	57.58
30	4.32	5.74	7.61	10.06	13.27	17.45	22.90	29.96	39.12	50.95	66.21
31	4.54	6.09	8.15	10.87	14.46	19.19	25.41	33.56	44.20	58.08	76.14
32	4.77	6.45	8.72	11.74	15.76	21.11	28.21	37.58	49.95	66.22	87.57
33	5.00	6.84	9.33	12.68	17.18	23.23	31.31	42.09	56.44	75.49	100.70
34	5.25	7.25	9.98	13.69	18.73	25.55	34.75	47.14	63.78	86.05	115.81
35	5.52	7.69	10.68	14.79	20.41	28.10	38.58	52.80	72.07	98.10	133.18
36	5.79	8.15	11.42	15.97	22.25	30.91	42.82	59.14	81.44	111.83	153.15
37	6.08	8.64	12.22	17.25	24.25	34.00	47.53	66.23	92.02	127.49	176.13
38	6.39	9.15	13.08	18.63	26.44	37.40	52.76	74.18	103.99	145.34	202.54
39	6.71	9.70	14.00	20.12	28.82	41.15	58.56	83.08	117.51	165.69	232.93
40	7.04	10.29	14.97	21.73	31.41	45.26	65.00	93.05	132.78	188.88	267.86

TABLE 2
FUTURE WORTH OF ONE DOLLAR INVESTED EACH YEAR WITH INTEREST (RETURN) PAYABLE AND REINVESTED AT END OF EACH YEAR

Year	\multicolumn{11}{c}{Annual Rate of Return}
	5%	6%	7%	8%	9%	10%	11%	12%	13%	14%	15%
1	1.00	1.00	1.00	1.00	1.00	1.00	1.00	1.00	1.00	1.00	1.00
2	2.05	2.06	2.07	2.08	2.09	2.10	2.11	2.12	2.13	2.14	2.15
3	3.15	3.18	3.22	3.25	3.28	3.31	3.34	3.37	3.41	3.44	3.47
4	4.31	4.37	4.44	4.50	4.57	4.64	4.71	4.78	4.85	4.92	4.99
5	5.53	5.64	5.75	5.87	5.99	6.10	6.23	6.35	6.48	6.61	6.74
6	6.80	6.98	7.15	7.33	7.52	7.71	7.91	8.11	8.32	8.54	8.75
7	8.14	8.39	8.65	8.92	9.20	9.49	9.78	10.09	10.41	10.73	11.07
8	9.55	9.90	10.26	10.64	11.03	11.43	11.86	12.30	12.76	13.23	13.73
9	11.03	11.49	11.98	12.49	13.02	13.58	14.16	14.77	15.42	16.09	16.78
10	12.58	13.18	13.82	14.49	15.19	15.94	16.72	17.55	18.42	19.34	20.30
11	14.21	14.97	15.78	16.65	17.56	18.53	19.56	20.66	21.81	23.05	24.35
12	15.92	16.87	17.89	18.98	20.14	21.38	22.71	24.13	25.65	27.27	29.00
13	17.71	18.88	20.14	21.50	22.95	24.52	26.21	28.03	29.99	32.09	34.35
14	19.60	21.02	22.55	24.22	26.02	27.98	30.10	32.39	34.88	37.58	40.51
15	21.58	23.27	25.13	27.15	29.36	31.77	34.41	37.28	40.42	43.84	47.58
16	23.66	23.67	27.89	30.32	33.00	35.95	39.19	42.75	46.67	50.98	55.72
17	25.84	28.21	30.84	33.75	36.97	40.55	44.50	48.88	53.74	59.12	65.08
18	28.13	30.91	34.00	37.45	41.30	45.60	50.40	55.75	61.73	68.39	75.84
19	30.54	33.76	37.38	41.45	46.02	51.16	56.94	63.44	70.75	78.97	88.21
20	33.07	36.78	41.00	45.76	51.16	37.27	64.20	72.05	80.95	91.03	102.44
21	35.72	39.99	44.87	50.42	56.77	64.00	72.27	81.70	92.47	104.77	118.81
22	38.51	43.39	49.01	55.46	62.87	71.40	81.21	92.50	105.49	120.44	137.63
23	41.43	47.00	53.44	60.89	69.53	79.54	91.15	104.60	120.21	138.30	159.28
24	44.50	50.82	58.18	66.77	76.79	88.50	102.17	118.16	136.83	158.66	184.17
25	47.73	54.86	63.25	73.10	84.70	98.35	114.41	133.33	155.62	181.87	212.79
26	51.11	59.16	68.88	79.95	93.32	109.18	128.00	150.33	176.85	208.33	245.71
27	54.67	63.71	74.48	87.35	102.72	121.10	143.08	169.37	200.84	238.50	283.57
28	58.40	68.53	80.70	95.34	112.97	134.21	159.82	190.70	227.95	272.89	327.10
29	62.32	73.64	87.35	103.97	124.14	148.63	178.40	214.58	258.58	312.09	377.17
30	66.44	79.06	94.46	113.28	136.31	164.49	199.02	241.33	293.20	356.79	434.75
31	70.76	84.80	102.07	123.35	149.58	181.94	221.91	271.29	332.32	407.74	500.96
32	75.30	90.89	110.22	134.21	164.04	201.14	247.32	304.85	376.52	465.82	577.10
33	80.06	97.34	118.93	145.95	179.30	222.25	275.53	342.43	426.46	532.04	664.67
34	85.07	104.18	128.26	158.63	196.98	245.48	306.84	384.52	482.90	607.52	765.37
35	90.32	111.44	138.24	172.32	215.71	271.02	341.59	431.66	546.68	693.57	881.17
36	95.84	119.12	148.91	187.10	236.13	299.13	380.16	484.46	618.75	791.67	1,014.35
37	101.63	127.27	160.34	203.07	258.38	330.04	422.98	543.60	700.19	903.51	1,167.50
38	107.71	135.90	172.56	220.32	282.63	364.04	470.51	609.83	792.21	1,031.00	1,343.62
39	114.10	145.06	185.64	238.94	309.07	401.45	523.27	684.01	896.20	1,176.34	1,546.17
40	120.80	154.76	199.64	259.06	337.88	442.59	581.83	767.09	1,013.70	1,342.03	1,779.09

TABLE 3
$10,000 LUMP-SUM INVESTMENT COMPOUNDED ANNUALLY END-OF-YEAR VALUES

End of Year	Annual Rate of Return										
	5%	6%	7%	8%	9%	10%	11%	12%	13%	14%	15%
1	10,500	10,600	10,700	10,800	10,900	11,000	11,100	11,200	11,300	11,400	11,500
2	11,025	11,236	11,449	11,664	11,881	12,100	12,321	12,544	12,769	12,996	13,225
3	11,576	11,910	12,250	12,597	12,950	13,310	13,676	14,049	14,428	14,815	15,208
4	12,155	12,624	13,107	13,604	14,155	14,641	15,180	15,735	16,304	16,889	17,490
5	12,763	13,382	14,025	14,693	15,386	16,105	16,850	17,623	18,424	19,254	20,113
6	13,401	14,185	15,007	15,868	16,771	17,715	18,704	19,738	20,819	21,949	23,130
7	14,071	15,036	16,057	17,138	18,280	19,487	20,761	22,106	23,526	25,022	26,600
8	14,775	15,938	17,181	18,509	19,925	21,435	23,045	24,759	26,584	28,525	30,590
9	15,513	16,894	18,384	19,990	21,718	23,579	25,580	27,730	30,040	32,519	35,178
10	16,289	17,908	19,671	21,589	23,673	25,937	28,394	31,058	33,945	37,072	40,455
11	17,103	18,982	21,048	23,316	25,804	28,531	31,517	34,785	38,358	42,262	46,523
12	17,959	20,121	22,521	25,181	28,126	31,384	34,984	38,959	43,345	48,179	53,502
13	18,856	21,329	24,098	27,196	30,658	34,522	38,832	43,634	48,980	54,924	61,527
14	19,799	22,609	25,785	29,371	33,417	37,974	43,104	48,871	55,347	62,613	70,757
15	20,789	23,965	27,590	31,721	36,424	41,772	47,845	54,735	62,542	71,379	81,370
16	21,829	25,403	29,521	34,259	39,703	45,949	53,108	61,303	70,673	81,372	93,576
17	22,920	26,927	31,588	37,000	43,276	50,544	58,590	68,660	79,860	92,764	107,612
18	24,066	28,543	33,799	39,960	47,171	55,599	65,435	76,899	90,242	105,751	123,754
19	25,270	30,255	36,165	43,157	51,416	61,159	72,633	86,127	101,974	120,556	142,317
20	26,533	32,071	38,696	46,609	56,044	67,274	80,623	96,462	115,230	137,434	163,665
21	27,860	33,995	41,405	50,338	61,088	74,002	89,491	108,038	130,210	156,675	188,215
22	29,253	36,035	44,304	54,365	66,586	81,402	99,335	121,003	147,138	178,610	216,447
23	30,715	38,197	47,405	58,714	72,578	89,543	110,262	135,523	166,266	203,615	248,914
24	32,251	40,489	50,723	63,411	79,110	98,497	122,391	151,786	187,880	232,122	286,251
25	33,864	42,918	54,274	68,484	86,230	108,347	135,854	170,000	212,305	264,619	329,189
26	35,557	45,493	58,073	73,963	93,991	119,181	150,798	190,400	239,905	301,665	378,567
27	37,335	48,223	62,138	79,880	102,450	131,099	167,386	213,248	271,092	343,899	435,353
28	39,201	51,116	66,488	86,271	111,671	144,209	185,799	238,838	306,334	392,044	500,656
29	41,161	54,183	71,142	93,172	121,721	158,630	206,236	267,499	346,158	446,931	575,754
30	43,219	57,434	76,122	100,626	132,676	174,494	228,922	299,599	391,158	509,501	662,117
31	45,380	60,881	81,451	108,676	144,617	191,943	254,104	335,551	442,009	580,831	761,435
32	47,649	64,533	87,152	117,370	157,633	211,137	282,055	375,817	499,470	662,148	875,650
33	50,032	68,405	93,253	126,760	171,820	232,251	313,082	420,915	564,402	754,849	1,006,998
34	52,533	72,510	99,781	136,901	187,284	255,476	347,521	471,425	637,774	860,527	1,158,048
35	55,160	76,860	106,765	147,853	204,139	281,024	385,748	527,996	720,685	981,001	1,331,775
40	70,399	102,857	149,744	217,245	314,094	452,592	650,008	930,509	1,327,815	1,888,835	2,678,635

TABLE 4
FUTURE WORTH OF $1,200 INVESTED EACH YEAR AT VARYING RATES COMPOUNDED EACH YEAR

Rate of Return	End of Year							
	5	10	15	20	25	30	35	40
5%	6,631	15,093	25,894	39,679	57,272	79,727	108,384	144,960
6%	6,764	15,817	27,931	44,143	65,837	94,870	133,722	185,714
7%	6,901	16,580	30,155	49,194	75,891	113,353	165,884	239,562
8%	7,040	17,384	32,583	54,914	87,727	135,940	206,780	310,868
9%	7,182	18,231	35,233	61,392	101,641	163,569	258,853	405,459
10%	7,326	19,125	38,127	68,730	118,016	197,393	325,229	531,111
11%	7,473	20,066	41,286	77,043	137,296	238,825	409,907	698,191
12%	7,623	21,058	44,736	86,463	160,001	289,599	517,996	920,510
13%	7,776	22,104	48,501	97,136	186,743	351,839	656,017	1,216,445
14%	7,932	23,205	52,611	109,230	218,245	428,144	832,287	1,610,430
15%	8,091	24,364	57,096	122,932	255,352	521,694	1,057,404	2,134,908

TABLE 5
RATES OF RETURN AND THE INVESTMENT AMOUNTS REQUIRED TO HAVE $100,000 AVAILABLE AT END OF SPECIFIED PERIOD

Rate of Return	End of Year							
	5	10	15	20	25	30	35	40
5%	78,353	61,391	48,102	37,689	29,530	23,138	18,129	14,205
6%	74,726	55,839	41,727	31,180	23,300	17,411	13,011	9,722
7%	71,299	50,835	36,245	25,842	18,425	13,137	9,367	6,678
8%	68,058	46,319	31,524	21,455	14,602	9,938	6,763	4,603
9%	64,993	42,241	27,454	17,843	11,597	7,537	4,899	3,184
10%	62,092	38,554	23,940	14,864	9,230	5,731	3,558	2,209
11%	59,345	35,218	20,900	12,403	7,361	4,368	2,592	1,538
12%	56,743	32,197	18,270	10,367	5,882	3,340	1,894	1,075
13%	54,276	29,460	15,989	8,678	4,710	2,557	1,388	753.12
14%	51,937	26,974	14,010	7,276	3,780	1,963	1,019	529.43
15%	49,718	24,718	12,289	6,110	3,040	1,510	750.89	373.32
16%	47,611	22,683	10,792	5,139	2,447	1,165	554.59	264.05
17%	45,611	20,804	9,489	4,329	1,974	900.38	410.67	187.31
18%	43,711	19,107	8,352	3,651	1,596	697.49	304.88	133.27
19%	41,905	17,560	7,359	3,084	1,292	541.49	226.91	95.10
20%	40,188	16,151	6,491	2,610	1,048	421.27	169.30	68.04
21%	38,554	14,864	5,731	2,209	851.85	328.43	126.62	48.82
22%	37,000	13,690	5,065	1,874	693.43	256.57	94.93	35.12
23%	35,520	12,617	4,482	1,592	565.42	200.84	71.34	25.34
24%	34,112	11,635	3,969	1,354	461.80	157.52	53.72	18.33

TABLE 6
APPROXIMATE ANNUAL INVESTMENT REQUIRED TO EQUAL $100,000 AT VARYING RATES

Rate of Return	End of Year							
	5	10	15	20	25	30	35	40
5%	17,236	7,572	4,414	2,880	1,966	1,433	1,054	788
6%	16,736	7,157	4,053	2,565	1,720	1,193	847	610
7%	16,254	6,764	3,719	2,280	1,478	989	656	468
8%	15,783	6,392	3,410	2,024	1,267	817	537	357
9%	15,332	6,039	3,125	1,793	1,083	673	425	272
10%	14,890	5,704	2,861	1,587	924	552	335	205
11%	14,467	5,388	2,618	1,403	787	453	263	155
12%	14,055	5,088	2,395	1,239	670	370	206	116
13%	13,658	4,805	2,190	1,070	569	302	168	87
14%	13,270	4,536	2,001	964	482	246	126	65
15%	12,898	4,283	1,828	849	409	200	99	49

APPENDIX II

TAX RATE SCHEDULES

Income Tax Table (1988)
For Residents of Provinces* Other Than Quebec

(note 4) Taxable income $	(note 5) Federal tax $	Federal surtax $	Combined federal/provincial income tax and surtax (note 1) (note 3) — (notes 2 & 3) —										
			Nfld. $	N.S. $	P.E.I. $	N.B. $	Ont. $	Man. $	Sask. $	Alta. $	B.C. $	N.W.T. $	Yukon $
2,000	0	0	0	0	0	0	0	0	0	0	0	0	
4,000	0	0	0	0	0	0	0	0	0	0	0	0	
6,000	0	0	0	0	0	0	0	0	0	0	0	0	
8,000	340	10	554	542	537	547	520	563	440	350	525	496	503
10,000	680	20	1,108	1,085	1,074	1,095	1,040	1,157	990	875	1,051	993	1,006
12,000	1,020	31	1,663	1,627	1,612	1,642	1,561	1,750	1,641	1,492	1,576	1,489	1,510
14,000	1,360	41	2,217	2,169	2,149	2,190	2,081	2,344	2,291	2,109	2,101	1,986	2,013
16,000	1,700	51	2,771	2,712	2,686	2,737	2,601	2,938	2,841	2,702	2,627	2,482	2,516
18,000	2,040	61	3,325	3,254	3,223	3,284	3,121	3,532	3,391	3,230	3,152	2,978	3,019
20,000	2,380	71	3,879	3,796	3,760	3,832	3,641	4,126	3,941	3,758	3,677	3,475	3,522
25,000	3,230	97	5,265	5,152	5,103	5,200	4,942	5,571	5,317	5,079	4,990	4,716	4,780
30,000	4,305	129	7,017	6,866	6,801	6,931	6,586	7,358	7,036	6,736	6,651	6,285	6,371
35,000	5,605	168	9,136	8,940	8,855	9,024	8,575	9,599	9,100	8,729	8,659	8,183	8,295
40,000	6,905	207	11,255	11,013	10,909	11,117	10,564	11,840	11,171	10,723	10,668	10,081	10,219
45,000	8,205	246	13,374	13,087	12,963	13,210	12,553	14,081	13,322	12,741	12,676	11,979	12,143
50,000	9,505	285	15,493	15,160	15,017	15,303	14,542	16,322	15,473	14,783	14,685	13,877	14,067
55,000	10,805	324	17,612	17,234	17,071	17,396	16,543	18,563	17,624	16,825	16,693	15,775	15,991
60,000	12,255	368	19,975	19,546	19,362	19,730	18,784	21,040	20,013	19,097	18,934	17,892	18,137

(note 4) Taxable income $	(note 5) Federal tax $	Federal surtax $	Combined federal/provincial income tax and surtax (note 1) (note 2)										
			Nfld. $	N.S. $	P.E.I. $	N.B. $	Ont. $	Man. $	Sask. $	Alta. $	B.C. $	N.W.T. $	Yukon $
65,000	13,705	411	22,339	21,859	21,653	22,065	21,024	23,516	22,402	21,368	21,174	20,009	20,283
70,000	15,155	455	24,702	24,172	23,944	24,399	23,264	25,993	24,792	23,640	23,414	22,126	22,429
75,000	16,605	498	27,066	26,485	26,235	26,734	25,504	28,469	27,181	25,912	25,654	24,243	24,575
80,000	18,055	542	29,429	28,797	28,526	29,068	27,745	30,946	29,571	28,183	27,895	26,360	26,721
85,000	19,505	585	31,793	31,110	30,817	31,403	29,985	33,422	31,960	30,455	30,135	28,477	28,867
90,000	20,955	629	34,156	33,423	33,108	33,737	32,225	35,899	34,350	32,727	32,375	30,594	31,013
95,000	22,405	672	36,520	35,736	35,399	36,072	34,465	38,375	36,739	34,998	34,615	32,711	33,159
100,000	23,855	716	38,883	38,048	37,690	38,406	36,706	40,852	39,129	37,270	36,856	34,828	35,305
120,000	29,655	890	48,337	47,299	46,854	47,744	45,667	50,758	48,687	46,357	45,817	43,296	43,889
140,000	35,455	1,064	57,791	56,550	56,018	57,082	54,628	60,664	58,245	55,444	54,778	51,764	52,473
160,000	41,255	1,238	67,245	65,801	65,182	66,420	63,589	70,570	67,803	64,530	63,739	60,232	61,057
180,000	47,055	1,412	76,699	75,052	74,346	75,758	72,550	80,476	77,361	73,617	72,700	68,700	69,641
200,000	52,855	1,586	86,153	84,303	83,510	85,096	81,511	90,382	86,919	82,704	81,661	77,168	78,225

1. Above figures do not take into account various federal and provincial tax reductions (dividend tax credit, foreign tax credit, etc.) Combined tax payable includes federal tax and surtax (as shown in the second and third columns) plus provincial tax and any applicable surtax.
   *Provincial rates used are those in effect at the date of publication and apply to a lower federal tax base in 1988 resulting from Tax Reform measures. Subsequent provincial budget announcements in 1988 may affect the rates and calculations for particular provinces.
2. In Manitoba and Saskatchewan a flat tax is applied to net income while in Alberta a flat tax is applied to taxable income. For the purposes of the flat tax calculations net income is assumed to equal taxable income in 1988 since the elimination of personal exemptions and certain deductions in the computation of taxable income under Tax Reform has generally reduced the differences between these two numbers. The Manitoba 2% surtax has been applied based on the single taxfiler's threshhold of $30,000.
3. Certain tax reductions for low income taxpayers have been applied.
4. Taxable income is not generally comparable for 1987 and 1988. The conversion of certain exemptions and deductions to tax credits under Tax Reform results in a difference in the tax base.
5. For purposes of computing the federal tax it is assumed that only the basic credit of $1,020 applies.

Income Tax Table (1987)
For Residents of Provinces* Other Than Quebec

(note 4) Taxable income $	(note 5) Federal tax $	Federal surtax $	Nfld. $	N.S. $	P.E.I. $	N.B. $	(note 3) Ont. $	(notes 2 & 3) Man. $	Sask. $	Alta. $	B.C. $	N.W.T. $	Yukon $
2,000	188	6	306	300	297	302	193	193	193	193	290	274	278
4,000	21	16	850	832	824	839	798	749	733	537	806	761	772
6,000	869	26	1,416	1,386	1,373	1,399	1,329	1,334	1,294	1,141	1,342	1,268	1,286
8,000	1,230	37	2,004	1,961	1,943	1,980	1,881	1,940	1,876	1,794	1,900	1,795	1,820
10,000	1,610	48	2,624	2,567	2,543	2,591	2,463	2,577	2,488	2,481	2,487	2,350	2,382
12,000	1,990	60	3,243	3,173	3,144	3,203	3,044	3,214	3,199	3,094	3,074	2,905	2,945
14,000	2,378	71	3,875	3,792	3,757	3,828	3,638	3,863	3,923	3,695	3,673	3,471	3,519
16,000	2,778	83	4,527	4,430	4,389	4,472	4,250	4,531	4,565	4,313	4,291	4,055	4,111
18,000	3,178	95	5,179	5,068	5,021	5,116	4,862	5,199	5,207	4,931	4,909	4,639	4,703
20,000	3,624	109	5,906	5,780	5,725	5,834	5,544	5,939	5,919	5,617	5,598	5,290	5,363
25,000	4,798	144	7,821	7,653	7,581	7,725	7,341	7,833	7,791	7,423	7,413	7,005	7,101
30,000	6,048	181	9,859	9,647	9,556	9,738	9,254	9,981	9,779	9,342	9,345	8,830	8,951
35,000	7,298	219	11,896	11,641	11,531	11,750	11,166	12,128	11,796	11,261	11,276	10,655	10,801
40,000	8,700	261	14,182	13,877	13,747	14,008	13,312	14,531	14,110	13,451	13,442	12,703	12,877
45,000	10,200	306	16,627	16,270	16,117	16,423	15,610	17,098	16,579	15,799	15,760	14,893	15,097
50,000	11,700	351	19,072	18,662	18,487	18,838	17,927	19,665	19,048	18,147	18,077	17,083	17,317
55,000	13,200	396	21,517	21,055	20,857	21,253	20,245	22,232	21,517	20,496	20,395	19,273	19,537
60,000	14,700	441	23,962	23,447	23,227	23,668	22,562	24,799	23,986	22,844	22,712	21,463	21,757

Taxable income $	Federal tax $	Federal surtax $	Nfld. $	N.S. $	P.E.I. $	N.B. $	Ont. $	(note 2) Man. $	Sask. $	Alta. $	B.C. $	N.W.T. $	Yukon $
65,000	16,267	488	26,515	25,946	25,702	26,190	24,983	27,478	26,561	25,294	25,133	23,750	24,075
70,000	17,967	539	29,286	28,657	28,388	28,297	27,609	30,380	29,348	27,949	27,759	26,232	26,591
75,000	19,667	590	32,057	31,369	31,074	31,664	30,236	33,283	32,135	30,604	30,386	28,714	29,107
80,000	21,367	641	34,828	34,080	33,760	34,401	32,862	36,186	34,922	33,259	33,012	31,196	31,623
85,000	23,067	692	37,599	36,792	36,446	37,138	35,489	39,088	37,709	35,913	35,639	33,678	34,139
90,000	24,767	743	40,370	39,503	39,132	39,875	38,115	41,991	40,496	38,568	38,265	36,160	36,655
95,000	26,467	794	43,141	42,215	41,818	42,612	40,742	44,893	43,283	41,223	40,892	38,642	39,171
100,000	28,167	845	45,912	44,926	44,504	45,349	43,368	47,796	46,070	43,878	43,518	41,124	41,687
120,000	34,967	1,049	56,996	55,772	55,248	56,297	53,874	59,406	57,218	54,496	54,024	51,052	51,751
140,000	41,767	1,253	68,080	66,618	65,992	67,245	64,380	71,017	68,366	65,115	64,530	60,980	61,815
160,000	48,567	1,457	79,164	77,464	76,736	78,193	74,886	82,627	79,514	75,734	75,036	70,908	71,879
180,000	55,367	1,661	90,248	88,310	87,480	89,141	85,392	94,238	90,662	86,353	85,542	80,836	81,943
200,000	62,167	1,865	101,332	99,156	98,224	100,089	95,898	105,848	101,810	96,972	96,048	90,764	92,007

1. Above figures do not take into account various federal and provincial tax reductions (dividend tax credit, foreign tax credit, etc.). Combined tax payable includes federal tax and surtax (as shown in the second and third columns) plus provincial tax and any applicable provincial surtax.
2. In Manitoba and Saskatchewan a flat tax is applied to net income while in Alberta a flat tax is applied to taxable income. For purposes of the flat tax calculations it is assumed that net income is $5000 greater than taxable income. This difference represents a little more than the 1987 basic personal exemption of $4,220.
3. Certain tax reductions for low income taxpayers have been applied.

Income Tax Table (1987)
Quebec Residents

Taxable income (note 2) $	Federal tax $	Federal surtax $	Federal abatement (note 3) $	Quebec tax (note 4) $	Total tax $
2,000	188	6	31	273	436
4,000	521	16	86	595	1,046
6,000	869	26	143	952	1,704
8,000	1,230	37	203	1,336	2,400
10,000	1,610	48	266	1,743	3,135
12,000	1,990	60	328	2,170	3,892
14,000	2,378	71	392	2,615	4,672
16,000	2,778	83	458	3,076	5,479
18,000	3,178	95	524	3,541	6,290
20,000	3,624	109	598	4,018	7,153
25,000	4,798	144	792	5,231	9,381
30,000	6,048	181	998	6,479	11,710
35,000	7,298	219	1,204	7,740	14,053
40,000	8,700	261	1,436	9,009	16,534
45,000	10,200	306	1,683	10,318	19,141
50,000	11,700	351	1,931	11,628	21,748
55,000	13,200	396	2,178	12,937	24,355
60,000	14,700	441	2,426	14,247	26,962
65,000	16,267	488	2,684	15,589	29,660
70,000	17,967	539	2,965	16,947	32,488
75,000	19,667	590	3,245	18,305	35,317
80,000	21,367	641	3,526	19,663	38,145
85,000	23,067	692	3,806	21,021	40,974
90,000	24,767	743	4,087	22,379	43,802
95,000	26,467	794	4,367	23,737	46,631
100,000	28,167	845	4,648	25,095	49,459
120,000	34,967	1,049	5,770	30,527	60,773
140,000	41,767	1,253	6,892	35,959	72,087
160,000	48,567	1,457	8,014	41,391	83,401
180,000	55,367	1,661	9,136	46,823	94,715
200,000	62,167	1,865	10,258	52,255	106,029

1. Above figures do not take into account various federal and provincial tax deductions and credits (dividend tax credit, foreign tax credit etc.).
2. Taxable income for Quebec tax purposes will normally vary from federal figures due to differences in deductions and exemptions.
3. An abatement equal to 16.5% of basic federal tax is available for Quebec taxpayers.
4. Quebec tax is net of a 3% reduction calculated on provincial tax after taking into account certain tax credits.

Income Tax Table (1988)
Quebec Residents

Taxable income (note 2) $	Federal tax $	Federal surtax $	Federal abatement (note 3) $	Quebec tax (note 4) $	Total tax $
2,000	0	0	0	273	273
4,000	0	0	0	595	595
6,000	0	0	0	952	952
8,000	340	10	56	1,336	1,630
10,000	680	20	112	1,743	2,331
12,000	1,020	31	168	2,170	3,053
14,000	,360	41	224	2,615	3,792
16,000	1,700	51	281	3,076	4,546
18,000	2,040	61	337	3,541	5,305
20,000	2,380	71	393	4,018	6,076
25,000	3,230	97	533	5,231	8,025
30,000	4,305	129	710	6,479	10,203
35,000	5,605	168	925	7,740	12,588
40,000	6,905	207	1,139	9,009	14,982
45,000	8,205	246	1,354	10,318	17,415
50,000	9,505	285	1,568	11,628	19,850
55,000	10,805	324	1,783	12,937	22,283
60,000	12,255	368	2,022	14,247	24,848
65,000	13,705	411	2,261	15,589	27,444
70,000	15,155	455	2,501	16,947	30,056
75,000	16,605	498	2,740	18,305	32,668
80,000	18,055	542	2,979	19,663	35,281
85,000	19,505	585	3,218	21,021	37,893
90,000	20,955	629	3,458	22,379	40,505
95,000	22,405	672	3,697	23,737	43,117
100,000	23,855	716	3,936	25,095	45,730
120,000	29,655	890	4,893	30,527	56,179
140,000	35,455	1,064	5,850	35,959	66,628
160,000	41,255	1,238	6,807	41,391	77,077
180,000	47,055	1,412	7,764	46,823	87,526
200,000	52,855	1,586	8,721	52,255	97,975

1. Above figures do not take into account various federal and provincial tax deductions and credits (dividend tax credit, foreign tax credit etc.).
   *Quebec has deferred its decision on whether or not to adopt personal tax rate changes similar to the federal reductions. An announcement on the 1988 Quebec rates is expected when the provincial budget is presented later in 1988.
2. Taxable income for Quebec tax purposes will normally vary from federal figures due to differences in certain deductions and exemptions. The difference may be narrowed if Quebec decides to adopt the federal measures to convert many deductions and exemptions to credits beginning in 1988.
3. An abatement of 16.5% of basic federal tax is available for Quebec taxpayers.
4. Quebec tax is net of a 3% reduction calculated on provincial tax after taking into account certain tax credits.

CALCULATION OF NET TAX PAYABLE FOR 1988

CALCULATION OF NET TAX PAYABLE FOR 1988

Taxable Income (per Form 11 or 14) $ _____

Federal Tax
   17% on first $27,500 $ _____
   26% on next $27,500   _____
   29% on balance   _____

   Total $ _____

Tax Credits (federal portion only)
   UI/CPP contributions credit   _____
   Tuition credit   _____
   Education credit   _____
   Dividend tax credit ($13\frac{1}{3}\%$ of the taxable amount of
     Canadian dividend income received).   _____
   Medical expenses credit   _____
   Charitable donations credit   _____
   Pension income credit   _____
   Basic credit   _____
   Married credit   _____
   Equivalent to married credit   _____
   Dependant credit   _____
   Age 65 and older credit   _____
   Disability credit   _____
   Credits transferred from spouse   _____
   Credits transferred from other dependants   _____

   Total federal tax credits $ _____

Total Federal Tax Before Surtax
   (total federal tax previously calculated
   minus total federal tax credits)   _____

Add federal surtax – 3%   _____
Less child tax credit   _____
Less federal sales tax credit   _____

Total Federal Tax $ _____

Provincial Tax*   _____

Total Taxes Payable $ _____

*Use 50% to give you an approximate provincial tax amount, or refer to your last
 year's return for a more accurate percentage.

Note: This worksheet does not include a calculation of alternative minimum tax. If
       this tax applies, your total taxes payable will be higher than the amount
       calculated here.

YOUR PERSONAL FINANCIAL PLANNER

File under PERSONAL DATA   Date: _____

FORM 1 PERSONAL AND FAMILY DATA

1   YOU
     Name: _____   Birth Date: _____

     Social Insurance Number: _____

2   YOUR SPOUSE
     Name: _____   Birth Date: _____

     Social Insurance Number: _____

3   YOUR PRESENT HOME
     Address: _____

4   YOUR OCCUPATION
        Business Address: _____

        Employer's Name: _____

              Address: _____

                Phone: _____

        Your Job Title: _____

5   SPOUSE'S OCCUPATION
        Business Address: _____

        Employer's Name: _____

              Address: _____

                Phone: _____

     Spouse's Job Title: _____

Touche Ross Canadian Guide to Personal Financial Management. © 1988 Touche Ross & Co.

6   CHILDREN

Name	Birth Date	Social Insurance Number
_____	_____	_____
_____	_____	_____
_____	_____	_____
_____	_____	_____
_____	_____	_____
_____	_____	_____
_____	_____	_____
_____	_____	_____
_____	_____	_____
_____	_____	_____

7   GRANDCHILDREN

Name	Birth Date	Social Insurance Number
_____	_____	_____
_____	_____	_____
_____	_____	_____
_____	_____	_____
_____	_____	_____
_____	_____	_____
_____	_____	_____
_____	_____	_____
_____	_____	_____
_____	_____	_____

Touche Ross Canadian Guide to Personal Financial Management. © 1988 Touche Ross & Co.

8   OTHERS DEPENDENT ON YOU

Name	Relationship	Social Insurance Number	Amount of Annual Support
_____	_____	_____	_____
_____	_____	_____	_____
_____	_____	_____	_____
_____	_____	_____	_____
_____	_____	_____	_____
_____	_____	_____	_____
_____	_____	_____	_____
_____	_____	_____	_____
_____	_____	_____	_____
_____	_____	_____	_____

File under FINANCIAL DOCUMENTS   Date: _____

FORM 2 FINANCIAL DOCUMENTS

USE THE FOLLOWING LOCATION CODE:

SD   Safe deposit box located at _____
HF   At home in fireproof file cabinet
HD   At home in desk
HS   At home in safe
LA   Lawyer's office
BR   Broker's office
      Other (describe below)

—   _____

—   _____

—   _____

	DESCRIPTION	LOCATION
Your Will	_____	_____
Spouse's Will	_____	_____
Trust Agreements	_____	_____
Mortgages	_____	_____
	_____	_____
	_____	_____
Loans	_____	_____
	_____	_____
	_____	_____
Property Deeds	_____	_____
	_____	_____
	_____	_____
Car and other Vehicle Titles	_____	_____
	_____	_____
	_____	_____

Touche Ross Canadian Guide to Personal Financial Management. © 1988 Touche Ross & Co.

Stock Certificates   _____   _____

_____   _____

Stock Options   _____   _____

Stock Purchase Plan   _____   _____

Bonds   _____   _____

_____   _____

Canada Savings Bonds   _____   _____

Term deposit
Certificates   _____   _____

_____   _____

Real Estate Contracts   _____   _____

_____   _____

_____   _____

Chequing Accounts   _____   _____

_____   _____

_____   _____

Savings Passbooks   _____   _____

_____   _____

_____   _____

Life Insurance
Policies   _____   _____

_____   _____

Insurance Policies   _____   _____

RRSP Agreements   _____   _____

Employer Pension Plans   _____   _____

DPSP Agreements   _____   _____

Birth Certificates   _____   _____

_____   _____

_____   _____

Touche Ross Canadian Guide to Personal Financial Management. © 1988 Touche Ross & Co.

Marriage Contracts _____   _____

Marriage Licences _____   _____

Divorce Papers _____   _____

Notes Receivable _____   _____

Notes Payable _____   _____

Employment Contracts _____   _____

Income Tax Returns _____   _____

_____   _____

_____   _____

_____   _____

Financial Surveys _____   _____

Insurance Surveys _____   _____

Safe Deposit Keys _____   _____

Who has access to your safe deposit box? _____

In whose name is the safe deposit box registered? _____

Other Records and
    Valuables

_____   _____   _____

_____   _____   _____

_____   _____   _____

_____   _____   _____

Touche Ross Canadian Guide to Personal Financial Management. © 1988 Touche Ross & Co.

File under FINANCIAL DOCUMENTS   Date:_____

FORM 3   FINANCIAL ADVISORS

List advisors who currently assist you in your financial affairs.

LAWYER
    Name: _____   Street: _____

    Firm: _____   City, Province: _____

                                                           Phone: _____

    Name: _____   Street: _____

    Firm: _____   City, Province: _____

                                                           Phone: _____

BANKING OFFICER
    Name: _____   Street: _____

    Firm: _____   City, Province: _____

                                                           Phone: _____

    Name: _____   Street: _____

    Firm: _____   City, Province: _____

                                                           Phone: _____

BROKER
    Name: _____   Street: _____

    Firm: _____   City, Province: _____

                                                           Phone: _____

    Name: _____   Street: _____

    Firm: _____   City, Province: _____

                                                           Phone: _____

C.A.

Name: _____ Street: _____

Firm: _____ City, Province: _____

Phone: _____

Name: _____ Street: _____

Firm: _____ City, Province: _____

Phone: _____

INSURANCE AGENT

Name: _____ Street: _____

Firm: _____ City, Province: _____

Phone: _____

Name: _____ Street: _____

Firm: _____ City, Province: _____

Phone: _____

INVESTMENT ADVISOR

Name: _____ Street: _____

Firm: _____ City, Province: _____

Phone: _____

Name: _____ Street: _____

Firm: _____ City, Province: _____

Phone: _____

OTHERS

Name: _____   Street: _____

Firm: _____   City, Province: _____

Phone: _____

Name: _____   Street: _____

Firm: _____   City, Province: _____

Phone: _____

To which of these would you turn to discuss a serious business problem or an important financial decision? _____

Touche Ross Canadian Guide to Personal Financial Management. © 1988 Touche Ross & Co.

File under FINANCIAL PROFILE   Date: _____

FORM 4   STATEMENT OF NET WORTH

WHAT YOU OWN	ESTIMATED CURRENT VALUE	% OF TOTAL ASSET VALUE
1 LIQUID ASSETS		
Cash (chequing, savings accounts):	_____	_____
Short-Term Investments Treasury Bills:	_____	_____
Short-Term Deposits:	_____	_____
Money Market Funds:	_____	_____
Cash Surrender Value of Life Insurance	_____	_____
TOTAL Liquid Assets	_____	_____
2 INVESTMENT ASSETS		
Canada Savings Bonds	_____	_____
Term Deposits	_____	_____
Marketable Securities Stocks:	_____	_____
Bonds:	_____	_____
Mutual Funds:	_____	_____
Real Estate (investment)	_____	_____
Tax Incentive Investments	_____	_____
Other Investment Assets (describe below)		
a. _____	_____	_____
b. _____	_____	_____
c. _____	_____	_____
d. _____	_____	_____
Retirement Funds RRSPs	_____	_____
Employer Pension Plan	_____	_____

Touche Ross Canadian Guide to Personal Financial Management. © 1988 Touche Ross & Co.

DPSPs _____ _____

Other _____ _____

TOTAL Investment Assets _____ _____

3 PERSONAL ASSETS

Residence _____ _____

Vacation Property _____ _____

Art, Antiques _____ _____

Furnishings _____ _____

Vehicles _____ _____

Boats _____ _____

Other _____ _____

TOTAL Personal Assets _____ _____

TOTAL ASSETS _____ _____

WHAT YOU OWE	ESTIMATED CURRENT VALUE	INTEREST RATE	INTEREST DEDUCTIBLE
4 SHORT-TERM OBLIGATIONS			
Consumer Credit Obligations	_____	_____	_____
Personal Loans	_____	_____	_____
Installment Loans	_____	_____	_____
Borrowings on Life Insurance	_____	_____	_____
Accrued Income Taxes	_____	_____	_____
Other Obligations (describe below)			
a. _____	_____	_____	_____
b. _____	_____	_____	_____
c. _____	_____	_____	_____
d. _____	_____	_____	_____
TOTAL Short-Term Obligations	_____	_____	_____

Touche Ross Canadian Guide to Personal Financial Management. © 1988 Touche Ross & Co.

5 LONG-TERM OBLIGATIONS	ESTIMATED CURRENT VALUE	INTEREST RATE	INTEREST DEDUCTIBLE
Mortgage on personal residences	_____	_____	_____
Loans to purchase investment assets	_____	_____	_____
Loans to purchase personal assets	_____	_____	_____
TOTAL Long-Term Obligations	_____	_____	_____
TOTAL LIABILITIES	_____	_____	_____

TOTAL ASSETS   _____

− TOTAL LIABILITIES   _____

= NET WORTH   _____

Touche Ross Canadian Guide to Personal Financial Management. © 1988 Touche Ross & Co.

File under FINANCIAL PROFILE   Date: _____

FORM 5   ANALYSIS OF NET WORTH

LIQUIDITY   AMOUNT   PERCENT

    1   Total Liquid Assets   _____

    2   Total Short-Term Obligations   _____

    3   Excess (Deficiency) of Liquid Assets   _____   _____

INVESTMENT ASSETS

    4   Total Investment Assets   _____

    5   Total Long-Term Investment Loans   _____

    6   Total Equity in Investment Assets   _____   _____

PERSONAL ASSETS

    7   Total Personal Assets   _____

    8   Total Long-Term Personal Loans   _____

    9   Total Equity in Personal Assets   _____   _____

    10   TOTAL NET WORTH   _____

Touche Ross Canadian Guide to Personal Financial Management. © 1988 Touche Ross & Co.

File under FINANCIAL PROFILE

Date: _____

FORM 6   INCOME SOURCES

1 INCOME FROM EMPLOYMENT	YOU	SPOUSE	TOTAL
Gross Salary	_____	_____	_____
Commissions	_____	_____	_____
Self-Employment	_____	_____	_____
Other	_____	_____	_____
TOTAL Employment Income	_____	_____	_____

2 INVESTMENT INCOME	YOU	SPOUSE	TOTAL
Interest	_____	_____	_____
Dividends	_____	_____	_____
Rents (net of cash expenses)	_____	_____	_____
Annuities	_____	_____	_____
Old Age Security	_____	_____	_____
Canada/Quebec Pension Plan Benefits	_____	_____	_____
Other Pension Income	_____	_____	_____
Trust Fund	_____	_____	_____
Other	_____	_____	_____
TOTAL Income from Investments	_____	_____	_____
TOTAL Income from All Sources	_____	_____	_____

Investment Income as Percentage of Total Income   _____

Touche Ross Canadian Guide to Personal Financial Management. © 1988 Touche Ross & Co.

File under FINANCIAL PROFILE   Date: _____

FORM 7 BASIC LIFESTYLE EXPENDITURES

		AMOUNT	PERCENT
1	HOUSING		
	Mortgage or Rent	_____	_____
	Property Taxes	_____	_____
	Insurance	_____	_____
	Utilities	_____	_____
	Other Housing Costs	_____	_____
	TOTAL Housing Costs	_____	_____
2	FOOD	_____	_____
3	CLOTHING	_____	_____
4	TRANSPORTATION		
	Loan Payments	_____	_____
	Insurance	_____	_____
	Fuel	_____	_____
	Maintenance	_____	_____
	Other Transportation	_____	_____
	TOTAL Transportation Expenditures	_____	_____
5	PHONE	_____	_____
6	HOUSEHOLD PURCHASES AND SUPPLIES	_____	_____
7	HOUSE CLEANING AND HOUSEHOLD HELP	_____	_____
8	EDUCATION (not private secondary and university)	_____	_____
9	RECREATION AND CLUB MEMBERSHIP	_____	_____
10	PERSONAL CARE AND IMPROVEMENTS	_____	_____

Touche Ross Canadian Guide to Personal Financial Management. © 1988 Touche Ross & Co.

11   INSURANCE

      Medical and Dental, Health
         and Disability Insurance   _____   _____

      Life Insurance   _____   _____

      Liability Insurance   _____   _____

      Other Insurance   _____   _____

   TOTAL Insurance Expenditures   _____   _____

12   YARD MAINTENANCE   _____   _____

13   DEBT REDUCTION (exclude home and autos)   _____   _____

14   CHARITABLE CONTRIBUTIONS   _____   _____

15   OTHER BASIC LIFESTYLE COSTS   _____   _____

   TOTAL Basic Lifestyle Expenditures   _____   _____

   Average Monthly Amount   _____   _____

Touche Ross Canadian Guide to Personal Financial Management. © 1988 Touche Ross & Co.

File under FINANCIAL PROFILE   Date: _____

FORM 8   DISCRETIONARY EXPENDITURES

		AMOUNT	PERCENT
1	EDUCATION (private secondary schools and university)	_____	____
2	ENTERTAINMENT AND EATING OUT	_____	____
3	REGULAR VACATIONS	_____	____
4	EXTRAORDINARY CHARITABLE EXPENDITURES	_____	____
5	HOBBIES	_____	____
6	PERSONAL GIFTS	_____	____
7	SUPPORT OF RELATIVES AND OTHERS		
	Name _____	_____	____
	Name _____	_____	____
	Name _____	_____	____
8	HOME IMPROVEMENTS	_____	____
9	PURCHASE OF AUTOMOBILES, BOATS, ETC.	_____	____
10	RETIREMENT PLANS		
	Type _____	_____	____
	Type _____	_____	____
	Type _____	_____	____
11	DEBT REDUCTIONS	_____	____
12	OTHER		
	_____	_____	____
	_____	_____	____

Touche Ross Canadian Guide to Personal Financial Management. © 1988 Touche Ross & Co.

TOTAL Discretionary Expenditures   _____   _____

AVERAGE Monthly Amount   _____   _____

Touche Ross Canadian Guide to Personal Financial Management. © 1988 Touche Ross & Co.

File under FINANCIAL PROFILE   Date: _____

FORM 9 INCOME TAXES AND OTHER DEDUCTIONS

1   TAXABLE INCOME   _____

2   FEDERAL INCOME TAX   _____

3   PROVINCIAL INCOME TAX   _____

4   OTHER DEDUCTIONS

         Canada/Quebec Pension Plan   _____

         Unemployment Insurance   _____

         Provincial Hospital Insurance
         (if applicable)   _____   _____

5   TOTAL INCOME TAXES AND OTHER DEDUCTIONS   _____

Touche Ross Canadian Guide to Personal Financial Management. © 1988 Touche Ross & Co.

File under FINANCIAL PROFILE   Date: _____

FORM 10   ANALYSIS OF EARNED INCOME AND EXPENDITURES

		AMOUNT	PERCENT OF TOTAL INCOME
1	TOTAL INCOME FROM EMPLOYMENT	_____	100%
2	EXPENDITURES		
	Basic Lifestyle	_____	_____
	Discretionary	_____	_____
	Income Tax and Other Deductions	_____	_____
3	TOTAL EXPENDITURES	_____	_____
4	EXCESS (Deficiency)	_____	_____

Touche Ross Canadian Guide to Personal Financial Management. © 1988 Touche Ross & Co.

File under TAX PLANNING   Date: _____

FORM 11   INCOME TAX PLANNING WORKSHEET

	LAST YEAR	CURRENT YEAR
1. TOTAL INCOME		
(a) (i) Income from employment	_____	_____
(ii) Less employment expense deduction (1987 only)	_____	_____
(iii) Less other allowable expenses	_____	_____
(iv) Net employment earnings	_____	_____
(b) Pension Income		
(i) Old Age Security and Canada or Quebec Pension Plan benefits	_____	_____
(ii) Other pension income	_____	_____
(c) Income from other sources		
(i) Family Allowance payments	_____	_____
(ii) Unemployment Insurance benefits	_____	_____
(iii) Taxable amount of dividends from Canadian companies	_____	_____
(iv) Interest and other investment income	_____	_____
(v) Rental income (loss)	_____	_____
(vi) Taxable capital gains	_____	_____
(d) Self-employed income		
(i) Business income	_____	_____
(ii) Professional income	_____	_____
(iii) Commission income	_____	_____
(iv) Farming or fishing income	_____	_____
(e) Total income	_____	_____

	LAST YEAR	CURRENT YEAR

2. DEDUCTIONS FROM TOTAL INCOME

    (a) Canada or Quebec Pension Plan payments
           (1987 only)

    (b) Unemployment Insurance payments
           (1987 only)

    (c) Registered pension plan contributions

    (d) Registered Retirement Savings Plan
           contributions

    (e) Union and professional dues

    (f) Tuition fees (1987 only)

    (g) Child care expenses

    (h) Allowable business investment losses

    (i) Other deductions

    (j) Total deductions

3. NET INCOME

4. PERSONAL EXEMPTIONS

    (a) Basic personal exemption (1987 only)

    (b) Age exemption (1987 only)

    (c) Married exemption (1987 only)

    (d) Exemption for dependent children
           (1987 only)

    (e) Additional personal exemptions
           (1987 only)

    (f) Total personal exemptions

5. OTHER DEDUCTIONS FROM NET INCOME

    (a) Interest and dividend deduction
           (1987 only)

    (b) Pension income deduction (1987 only)

    (c) Medical expenses (1987 only)

Touche Ross Canadian Guide to Personal Financial Management. © 1988 Touche Ross & Co.

	LAST YEAR	CURRENT YEAR
(d) Charitable donations (1987 only)	_____	_____
(e) Disability deduction (1987 only)	_____	_____
(f) Education deduction (1987 only)	_____	_____
(g) Deductions transferred from spouse (1987 only)	_____	_____
(h) Non-capital losses of other years	_____	_____
(i) Net Capital losses of other years (1972-1985)	_____	_____
(j) Taxable capital gains exemption	_____	_____
(k) Total other deductions	_____	_____
6. (a) TAXABLE INCOME	_____	_____
(b) Tax bracket	_____	_____
7. (a) TARGETED TAXABLE INCOME		_____
(b) Targeted Tax Bracket		_____

File under TAX PLANNING   Date: _____

FORM 12   TAX-SAVING IDEAS

TAX-SAVING IDEA

Tax-Free Income: _____

_____

Tax-Favoured Income: _____

_____

Tax-Deferred Income: _____

_____

Tax-Sheltered Income: _____

_____

Shifting Income to Dependents: _____

_____

Tax-Deductible Expenditures: _____

_____

Action	Action Date	Funds Needed	Reduction of Taxable Income
Tax-Free Income	_____	_____	_____
	_____	_____	_____
Tax-Favoured Income	_____	_____	_____
	_____	_____	_____
Tax-Deferred Income	_____	_____	_____
	_____	_____	_____
Tax-Sheltered Investments	_____	_____	_____
	_____	_____	_____

Touche Ross Canadian Guide to Personal Financial Management. © 1988 Touche Ross & Co.

Shift Income
to Dependents

————————   ————————   ————————

————————   ————————   ————————

Tax Deductible
Expenditures

————————   ————————   ————————

————————   ————————   ————————

TOTALS

————————   ————————

Touche Ross Canadian Guide to Personal Financial Management. © 1988 Touche Ross & Co.

File under TAX PLANNING   Date: _____

FORM 13A   CAPITAL GAINS AND LOSSES REALIZED TO DATE

Number of Units	Investment Type	Date Acquired	Adjusted Cost Base	Date Sold	Net Proceeds	Gain (Loss)
_____	_____	_____	_____	_____	_____	_____
_____	_____	_____	_____	_____	_____	_____
_____	_____	_____	_____	_____	_____	_____
_____	_____	_____	_____	_____	_____	_____
_____	_____	_____	_____	_____	_____	_____
_____	_____	_____	_____	_____	_____	_____
_____	_____	_____	_____	_____	_____	_____
_____	_____	_____	_____	_____	_____	_____
_____	_____	_____	_____	_____	_____	_____
_____	_____	_____	_____	_____	_____	_____

Capital Gains Dividends
    (received from mutual funds)   _____

Capital Loss Carry-overs*
    (full amount of loss--not two-thirds)   (_____)

Total   _____

Taxable Capital Gains (Allowable
    Capital Losses)--two-thirds X Total   _____

Cumulative <u>Taxable</u> Capital Gains
    exemption available (two-thirds of Cumulative
    Capital Gains exemption available)   _____

Taxable Capital Gains (Allowable Capital
    Losses) to be included in Taxable income   _____

* Up to $2,000.00 of allowable capital losses realized before
  May 23, 1985 can be claimed to reduce taxable income from any
  source. Capital losses realized after May 22, 1985 cannot be used
  to reduce taxable income other than capital gains.

File under TAX PLANNING   Date: _____

FORM 13B   UNREALIZED CAPITAL GAINS OR LOSSES IN CURRENT INVESTMENTS

Number of Units	Investment Type	Date Acquired	Adjusted Cost Base	Current Market Value	Unrealized Gain (Loss)
____	_____	_____	_____	_____	_____
____	_____	_____	_____	_____	_____
____	_____	_____	_____	_____	_____
____	_____	_____	_____	_____	_____
____	_____	_____	_____	_____	_____
____	_____	_____	_____	_____	_____
____	_____	_____	_____	_____	_____
____	_____	_____	_____	_____	_____
____	_____	_____	_____	_____	_____
____	_____	_____	_____	_____	_____

Total Unrealized
    Capital
Gains and Losses   _____

Touche Ross Canadian Guide to Personal Financial Management. © 1988 Touche Ross & Co.

File under TAX PLANNING   Date: _____

FORM 14   YEAR-END TAX PLAN

	ACTUAL TO DATE	ESTIMATES TO YEAR END	ESTIMATES TOTAL

1. TOTAL INCOME

(a) (i) Income from employment _____ _____ _____

   (ii) Less other allowable expenses _____ _____ _____

   (iii) Net employment earnings _____ _____ _____

(b)   Pension income

   (i) Old Age Security and Canada or Quebec Pension plan benefits _____ _____ _____

   (ii) Other pension income

(c)   Income from other sources _____ _____ _____

   (i) Family Allowance payments _____ _____ _____

   (ii) Unemployment Insurance benefits _____ _____ _____

   (iii) Taxable amount of dividends from Canadian companies _____ _____ _____

   (iv) Interest and other investment income _____ _____ _____

   (v) Rental income (loss) _____ _____ _____

   (vi) Taxable capital gains _____ _____ _____

(d)   Self-employed income

   (i) Business income _____ _____ _____

   (ii) Professional income _____ _____ _____

   (iii) Commission income _____ _____ _____

   (iv) Farming or fishing income _____ _____ _____

(e)   Total income _____ _____ _____

Touche Ross Canadian Guide to Personal Financial Management. © 1988 Touche Ross & Co.

	ACTUAL TO DATE	ESTIMATES TO YEAR END	ESTIMATES TOTAL YEAR
2. DEDUCTIONS FROM TOTAL INCOME			
(a) Registered pension plan contributions	_____	_____	_____
(b) Registered Retirement Savings Plan contributions	_____	_____	_____
(c) Union and professional dues	_____	_____	_____
(d) Child care expenses	_____	_____	_____
(e) Allowable business investment losses	_____	_____	_____
(f) Other deductions	_____	_____	_____
(g) Total deductions	_____	_____	_____
3. NET INCOME	_____	_____	_____
4. OTHER DEDUCTIONS FROM NET INCOME	_____	_____	_____
(a) Non-capital losses of other years	_____	_____	_____
(b) Net capital losses of other years (1972-1985)	_____	_____	_____
(c) Taxable capital gains exemption	_____	_____	_____
(d) Total other deductions	_____	_____	_____
5. (a) TAXABLE INCOME	_____	_____	_____
(b) Tax bracket	_____	_____	_____
6. (a) TARGETED TAXABLE INCOME			_____
(b) Targeted Tax bracket			_____

Touche Ross Canadian Guide to Personal Financial Management. © 1988 Touche Ross & Co.

File under TAX PLANNING   Date: _____

FORM 15   YEAR-END TAX ACTION

Estimated Taxable Income Current Year   _____
   (from Form 14, line 6a)

Targeted Taxable Income Current Year   _____
   (from Form 14, line 7a)

Reduction in Taxable Income Required   _____

YEAR-END TAX-PLANNING ACTIONS	CASH REQUIRED	REDUCTION IN TAXABLE INCOME CURRENT YEAR
_____	_____	_____
_____	_____	_____
_____	_____	_____
_____	_____	_____
_____	_____	_____
_____	_____	_____
_____	_____	_____
_____	_____	_____
_____	_____	_____
TOTALS	_____	_____

File under FINANCIAL OBJECTIVES   Date: _____

FORM 16   FINANCIAL SECURITY

1   What does financial security mean to you?

_____

_____

_____

                                                        AMOUNT

   Annual Income (today's dollars)   _____

   Investment Assets   _____

   Net Worth   _____

   Debt Level   _____

   Other

   _____   _____

   _____   _____

   _____   _____

2   When (how many years from now) would you like to achieve financial security?

   _____

3   List the three greatest obstacles to your achieving financial security (as
     you defined it in Question 1):

_____

_____

_____

Touche Ross Canadian Guide to Personal Financial Management. © 1988 Touche Ross & Co.

File under FINANCIAL OBJECTIVES   Date: _____

FORM 17   INCOME AND EXPENDITURE OBJECTIVES

1   Estimate employment income for each year:

	CURRENT YEAR	NEXT YEAR	THIRD YEAR
Your Income	_____	_____	_____
Spouse's Income	_____	_____	_____

2   By what percentage could you reduce your basic lifestyle expenditures if you
     really wanted to? _____

3   By what percentage could you reduce your discretionary expenditures if you
     really wanted to? _____

4   What major discretionary expenditures other than education do you plan to
     incur in the next three years?

	AMOUNT	YEAR
Cars	_____	_____
Boat	_____	_____
Extended Travel	_____	_____
Major Home Improvements	_____	_____
Major Charitable Contributions	_____	_____
Other		
_____	_____	_____
_____	_____	_____
_____	_____	_____

Touche Ross Canadian Guide to Personal Financial Management. © 1988 Touche Ross & Co.

File under FINANCIAL OBJECTIVES   Date: _____

FORM 18   EDUCATION AND OTHER SUPPORT OF CHILDREN

1   PRIVATE ELEMENTARY AND SECONDARY SCHOOLS

CHILD	AGE	YEARS OF SCHOOLING	YEAR BEGINNING	YEARLY COST	TOTAL COST
_____	____	_____	_____	_____	_____
_____	____	_____	_____	_____	_____
_____	____	_____	_____	_____	_____
_____	____	_____	_____	_____	_____
_____	____	_____	_____	_____	_____
_____	____	_____	_____	_____	_____
_____	____	_____	_____	_____	_____

TOTAL Estimated Cost   _____

2   COLLEGE AND UNIVERSITY EDUCATION

CHILD	AGE	YEARS OF SCHOOLING	YEAR BEGINNING	YEARLY COST	TOTAL COST
_____	____	_____	_____	_____	_____
_____	____	_____	_____	_____	_____
_____	____	_____	_____	_____	_____
_____	____	_____	_____	_____	_____
_____	____	_____	_____	_____	_____
_____	____	_____	_____	_____	_____
_____	____	_____	_____	_____	_____

TOTAL Estimated Cost   _____

3   ASSETS SET ASIDE FOR EDUCATION

CHILD	TYPE OF ASSET	AMOUNT	HOW HELD
_____	_____	_____	_____
_____	_____	_____	_____
_____	_____	_____	_____
_____	_____	_____	_____
_____	_____	_____	_____
_____	_____	_____	_____
_____	_____	_____	_____

4   OTHER SUPPORT OF CHILDREN

CHILD	REASON FOR SUPPORT	NUMBER OF YEARS	YEARLY COST	TOTAL COST
_____	_____	_____	_____	_____
_____	_____	_____	_____	_____
_____	_____	_____	_____	_____
_____	_____	_____	_____	_____
_____	_____	_____	_____	_____
_____	_____	_____	_____	_____
_____	_____	_____	_____	_____

TOTAL Estimated Cost   _____

Touche Ross Canadian Guide to Personal Financial Management. © 1988 Touche Ross & Co.

File under FINANCIAL OBJECTIVES   Date: _____

FORM 19   RETIREMENT PLANNING

1   When do you plan to retire? _____

    Your age at retirement? _____

    Number of years from now? _____

2   Do you or your spouse have any health problems that might make you retire at an earlier date?

    Explain: _____

    _____

    _____

3   If you retired tomorrow, with all educational expenditures behind you, and no one depended on you financially, how much spendable after-tax income would you and your spouse need for one year at today's prices? _____

4   Estimate your retirement income from various sources.

SOURCE	ESTIMATED ANNUAL AMOUNT AT RETIREMENT AGE
Retirement plan from company	_____
Retirement benefits from previous employer(s)	_____
Old Age Security	_____
Canada/Quebec Pension Plan	_____
Registered Retirement Savings Plan(s)	_____
Spouse's Retirement Plan	_____
Deferred Compensation	_____
Investment Assets	_____
Other Sources	_____
_____	_____
TOTAL	_____

Touche Ross Canadian Guide to Personal Financial Management. © 1988 Touche Ross & Co.

5   What do you estimate your investment assets will be worth at retirement age? _____

6   When you retire, will you sell your home? _____
If yes, will you

        Buy another? _____

        Rent? _____

        Relocate? _____

Based on your anticipated retirement age and housing arrangements, would your housing expenditures, at present prices, be higher or lower in retirement than they are today?

      _____% higher   _____% lower

Why? _____

File under INVESTMENT STRATEGY   Date: _____

FORM 20   INVESTMENT OBJECTIVES

Indicate the relative importance you attribute to the following considerations by placing the appropriate number after each statement.

```
                 NOT IMPORTANT -- 1
          MARGINALLY IMPORTANT -- 2
          REASONABLY IMPORTANT -- 3
          DEFINITELY IMPORTANT -- 4
                MOST IMPORTANT -- 5
```

Diversification   How important is it for you to hedge against big
                  losses by spreading your risks?   _____

Liquidity   How important is it that you have cash available
                  for emergencies or investment opportunities?   _____

Safety   If we went into a deep economic depression, how
                  important would it be for you to sell your invest-
                  ments at about the price you paid for them?   _____

Current Income   How important is it that you get maximum income
                  from your investments this year and next?   _____

Future   How important is it that your investment dollars
Appreciation   keep pace with inflation or do better than inflation? _____

Tax   How important is it that you get all the tax relief
Advantage   that may be available to you?   _____

Leverage   How important is it for you to use borrowed money
                  in hopes of reaping a higher return on your
                  investment?   _____

Ease of   How important is it for you to have investments
Management   you do not have to watch or worry about?   _____

Touche Ross Canadian Guide to Personal Financial Management. © 1988 Touche Ross & Co.

File under INVESTMENT STRATEGY   Date: _____

FORM 21 REVIEW OF YOUR PRESENT INVESTMENTS

TYPE OF ASSET COL. 1	CURRENT VALUE COL. 2	% OF TOTAL COL. 3	INVESTMENT OBJECTIVES COL. 4	CURRENT INCOME COL. 5	APPR'N (LOSS) COL. 6	ANNUAL RATE OF RETURN COL. 7
_____	_____	_____	_____	_____	_____	_____
_____	_____	_____	_____	_____	_____	_____
_____	_____	_____	_____	_____	_____	_____
_____	_____	_____	_____	_____	_____	_____
_____	_____	_____	_____	_____	_____	_____
_____	_____	_____	_____	_____	_____	_____
_____	_____	_____	_____	_____	_____	_____
_____	_____	_____	_____	_____	_____	_____
_____	_____	_____	_____	_____	_____	_____
_____	_____	_____	_____	_____	_____	_____
TOTAL	_____	_____				

File under INVESTMENT STRATEGY   Date: _____

FORM 22   YOUR INVESTMENT STRATEGY

1   What investment objectives (see Form 20) will be most important for you
     during the next three years? _____

     _____

     _____

2   What do you assume the inflation rate will be during the next three years?

     _____

3   What overall annual pre-tax return on your investments do you want to achieve
     in the next three years? _____

4   What specific changes do you have to make in your present investments to
     achieve your objectives and overall rate of return in the next three years?

     _____

     _____

5   What annual amount do you believe you can set aside for investment during
     the next three years? _____

6   What investments will you make with your additional investment dollars?

     _____

     _____

     _____

Touche Ross Canadian Guide to Personal Financial Management. © 1988 Touche Ross & Co.

File under EDUCATIONAL FINANCING   Date: _____

FORM 23   UNIVERSITY, GRADUATE SCHOOL AND COLLEGE COSTS

1   Children's Names   _____   _____   _____

2   Ages of Children   _____   _____   _____

3   Number of Years
    until University   _____   _____   _____

4   Estimated Number of
    Years in University
    and Graduate School   _____   _____   _____

5   Number of Years for
    Inflation Adjustment   _____   _____   _____

6   Estimated Annual Inflation
    Rate between Now and End
    of Education   _____   _____   _____

7   Inflation Factor   _____   _____   _____

8   Estimated Annual
    University Costs in
    Today's Dollars   _____   _____   _____

9   Estimated Annual Costs
    Adjusted   _____   _____   _____

10 Estimated TOTAL Costs
    Adjusted   _____   _____   _____

11 Estimated After-Tax
    Rate of Return on
    Educational Funds   _____   _____   _____

12 Compound Factor for
    Rate of Return on
    Line 11   _____   _____   _____

13 Present Value of Funds
    Set Aside for Education   _____   _____   _____

14 Future Value of Funds
    Set Aside   _____   _____   _____

15 Annual Amount to be
    Invested for Education   _____   _____   _____

Touche Ross Canadian Guide to Personal Financial Management. © 1988 Touche Ross & Co.

File under RETIREMENT PLANNING   Date: _____

FORM 24   ESTIMATED BASIC LIFESTYLE EXPENDITURES AT RETIREMENT

		CURRENT YEAR	AT RETIREMENT
1	**Housing**		
	Mortgage or Rent	_____	_____
	Property Taxes	_____	_____
	Insurance	_____	_____
	Utilities	_____	_____
	Other Housing Costs	_____	_____
	TOTAL Housing Costs	_____	_____
2	**Food**	_____	_____
3	**Clothing**	_____	_____
4	**Transportation**		
	Loan Payments	_____	_____
	Insurance	_____	_____
	Fuel	_____	_____
	Maintenance	_____	_____
	Other Transportation	_____	_____
	TOTAL Transportation Expenditures	_____	_____
5	**Phone**	_____	_____
6	**Household Purchases and Supplies**	_____	_____
7	**House Cleaning and Household Help**	_____	_____
8	**Education (not secondary and university)**	_____	

9   Recreation and Club Membership   _____   _____

10   Personal Care and Improvements   _____   _____

11   Medical and Dental, Health and Disability   _____   _____

12   Life Insurance   _____   _____

13   Liability Insurance   _____   _____

14   Other Insurance   _____   _____

15   Yard Maintenance   _____   _____

16   Debt Reduction (exclude home and autos)   _____   _____

17   Charitable Contributions   _____   _____

18   Other Basic Lifestyle Costs   _____   _____

19   TOTAL Basic Lifestyle Expenditures   _____   _____

20   Number of Years to Retirement   _____

21   Average Annual Rate of Inflation   _____

22   Inflation Factor
     (from Table 1 in Appendix 1)   _____

23   TOTAL of Projected Annual Basic Lifestyle
     Expenditures Adjusted for Inflation   _____

Touche Ross Canadian Guide to Personal Financial Management. © 1988 Touche Ross & Co.

File under RETIREMENT PLANNING   Date: _____

FORM 25   ESTIMATED DISCRETIONARY EXPENDITURES AT RETIREMENT

		CURRENT YEAR	AT RETIREMENT
1	Education (Private Secondary Schools and University)	_____	_____
2	Entertainment and Eating Out	_____	_____
3	Regular Vacations	_____	_____
4	Extraordinary Charitable Expenditures	_____	_____
5	Hobbies	_____	_____
6	Personal Gifts	_____	_____
7	Support of Relatives and Others:		
	_____	_____	_____
	_____	_____	_____
	_____	_____	_____
8	Home Improvements	_____	_____
9	Purchase of Automobiles, Boat, etc.	_____	_____
10	Retirement Plans	_____	_____
11	Debt Reductions	_____	_____
12	Other:		
	_____	_____	_____
	_____	_____	_____
	_____	_____	_____
13	TOTAL	_____	_____
14	Inflation Factor _____		
15	TOTAL Projected Annual Discretionary Expenditures Adjusted for Inflation		_____

Touche Ross Canadian Guide to Personal Financial Management. © 1988 Touche Ross & Co.

File under RETIREMENT PLANNING   Date: _____

FORM 26 ESTIMATED RETIREMENT NEEDS, INCLUDING TAXES

ANNUAL AMOUNT

1   Estimated Basic Lifestyle Expenditures   _____

2   Estimated Discretionary Expenditures   _____

3   TOTAL   _____

4   Tax Factor (Percentage)   _____

5   TOTAL Retirement Expenditures
     Including Taxes   _____

File under RETIREMENT PLANNING   Date: _____

FORM 27   RETIREMENT INCOME

Projected Retirement Age: _____   Number of Years to Retirement: _____

1   Estimated Annual Retirement Needs   _____

2   Estimated Annual Income from Retirement Plans
     (other than lump-sum distributions)

  a. Old Age Security and Canada or Quebec
      Pension Plan   _____

  b. Company Retirement Plan   _____

  c. Deferred Compensation   _____

  d. Other Retirement Plans   _____

3   TOTAL Annual Income from Retirement Plans   _____

4   Annual Income Gap   _____

5   Retirement Capital Required to Fill Gap

  a. Estimated Pre-Tax Rate of Return   _____

  b. Retirement Capital Required   _____

6   Sources of Retirement
     Capital

	INVESTMENT ASSETS	LUMP SUMS FROM RETIREMENT PLANS	RRSPs	TOTAL
a. Value of Present Investment Assets and Retirement Accounts	_____		_____	_____
b. Estimated Rate of Return from Now until Retirement	_____		_____	
c. Years until Retirement	_____		_____	
d. Compound Factor from Table 1 (in Appendix I)	_____		_____	
e. Estimated Value of Your Investment Assets and Retirement Accounts at Retirement	_____	_____	_____	_____

Touche Ross Canadian Guide to Personal Financial Management. © 1988 Touche Ross & Co.

	INVESTMENT ASSETS	RRSPs	OTHER	TOTAL
7 Additional Capital from Annual Investments You Are Planning to Make				
a. Annual Amount to Be Invested Between Now and Retirement	_____	_____	_____	_____
b. Estimated Rate of Return on Annual Investment	_____	_____	_____	_____
c. Years until Retirement	_____	_____	_____	_____
d. Compound Factor from Table 2 (in Appendix I)	_____	_____	_____	_____
e. Estimated Value of Additional Capital from Your Annual Investments	_____	_____	_____	_____
8 TOTAL Estimated Retirement Capital				_____
9 Additional Capital Needed, if Any, to Provide Retirement Income				_____
10 Additional Annual Investment Needed to Provide Capital on Line 9				
a. Estimated Rate of Return from Now until Retirement			_____	
b. Years until Retirement			_____	
c. Compound Factor from Table 2 (in Appendix 1)			_____	
d. Annual Amount Required				_____

Touche Ross Canadian Guide to Personal Financial Management. © 1988 Touche Ross & Co.

File under INSURANCE   Date: _____

FORM 28   YOUR PRESENT LIFE INSURANCE COVERAGE

INSURANCE ON YOUR LIFE

Name of Insurance Company	Policy Number	Beneficiary	Type of Policy	Face Value	Cash Surrender Value	Loan on Policy	Owner of Policy
_____	_____	_____	_____	_____	_____	_____	_____
_____	_____	_____	_____	_____	_____	_____	_____
_____	_____	_____	_____	_____	_____	_____	_____
_____	_____	_____	_____	_____	_____	_____	_____
_____	_____	_____	_____	_____	_____	_____	_____
_____	_____	_____	_____	_____	_____	_____	_____
_____	_____	_____	_____	_____	_____	_____	_____
_____	_____	_____	_____	_____	_____	_____	_____
			TOTAL	_____	_____	_____	

INSURANCE ON SPOUSE'S LIFE

Name of Insurance Company	Policy Number	Beneficiary	Type of Policy	Face Value	Cash Surrender Value	Loan on Policy	Owner of Policy
_____	_____	_____	_____	_____	_____	_____	_____
_____	_____	_____	_____	_____	_____	_____	_____
_____	_____	_____	_____	_____	_____	_____	_____
_____	_____	_____	_____	_____	_____	_____	_____
_____	_____	_____	_____	_____	_____	_____	_____
_____	_____	_____	_____	_____	_____	_____	_____
_____	_____	_____	_____	_____	_____	_____	_____
			TOTAL	_____	_____	_____	

Touche Ross Canadian Guide to Personal Financial Management. © 1988 Touche Ross & Co.

File under INSURANCE   Date: _____

FORM 29   TOTAL LIFE INSURANCE REQUIRED

1   Cash Required Immediately

   a.   Funeral   _____

   b.   Current bills   _____

   c.   Administrative   _____

   d.   Emergency fund   _____

   e.   Taxes on death   _____

   f.   TOTAL   (_____)

2   Cash Available Immediately

   a.   Insurance proceeds   _____

   b.   Death benefits from retirement
      programmes or group life insurance
      plan   _____

   c.   Liquid assets   _____

   d.   Other   _____

   e.   TOTAL   _____

3   Net Cash Available (or Required)   _____

4   Assets Required for Mortgage and Children's Education

   a.   Mortgage outstanding   _____

   b.   Education   _____

   c.   TOTAL   (_____)

5   Assets Available for Mortgage and Children's Education

   a.   Investment assets   _____

   b.   Personal assets convertible into
        cash   _____

   c.   Other   _____

   d.   TOTAL   _____

6   Net Resources Available (or Required)   _____

7   Total Resources Available (or Required)   _____

8   Annual Living Expenses   _____

9   Annual Income Available for Living Expenses

    a.   Income from assets   _____

    b.   Employment income of spouse   _____

    c.   Other   _____

    d.   TOTAL   _____

10   Annual Income Excess (or Deficiency)   _____

11   Additional Insurance Required

    a.   Negative amount from line 7   _____

    b.   Negative amount from line 10
        divided by 10%   _____

    c.   TOTAL   _____

Touche Ross Canadian Guide to Personal Financial Management. ©1987 Touche Ross & Co.

File under INSURANCE

Date: _____

FORM 30   WHOLE-LIFE POLICY INSURANCE COST PER $1000

PRESENT POLICY

1   Face Amount   _____

2   Cash Surrender Value (your savings
       element)   (_____)

3   Net Insurance Protection   _____

4   Present Premium   _____

5   Cash Value Increase for Current Year   (_____)

6   Current Dividend   (_____)

7   Lost Earnings on Cash Value at 5%   _____

8   Earnings on Borrowed Cash Value at 5%   (_____)

9   Total Cost   _____

10 Cost Per Thousand   _____

File under ESTATE PLANNING

Date: _____

FORM 31 POTENTIAL INCOME TAX LIABILITY ON
ASSETS OWNED AT DEATH

NON-DEPRECIABLE CAPITAL ASSETS (UNLESS LEFT TO SPOUSE OR SPOUSAL TRUST)

Number of Units	Description of asset	Adjusted cost base	Current market value	Accrued gain (loss)
_____	_____	$ _____	$ _____	$ _____
_____	_____	$ _____	$ _____	$ _____
_____	_____	$ _____	$ _____	$ _____
_____	_____	$ _____	$ _____	$ _____
_____	_____	$ _____	$ _____	$ _____
_____	_____	$ _____	$ _____	$ _____
_____	_____	$ _____	$ _____	$ _____

Sum of accrued gains (losses) _____

Less unused lifetime capital
gains exemption (_____)

TOTAL _____

Two-thirds of Total _____ 1

Current value of funds and investments held in unmatured
RRSPs (unless spouse or, in certain circumstances,
dependent children or grandchildren, are designated
beneficiaries) _____ 2

Potential income to be added to final tax return (Line 1 + 2) $ _____ 3

Estimated marginal tax rate in year of death _____ 4

Estimated tax liability on assets owned at death (Line 3 x 4) $ _____ 5

Note: This form does not include income that may result on death from
ownership of other types of assets such as depreciable property,
eligible capital property, resource properties, etc. You should
consult a tax expert to estimate your potential tax liability on
death, if you own significant amounts of such properties.

Touche Ross Canadian Guide to Personal Financial Management. © 1988 Touche Ross & Co.

File under ESTATE PLANNING   Date: _____

FORM 32   AFTER-TAX VALUE OF ESTATE

1   Total net worth excluding insurance $ _____

2   Present life insurance coverage   _____

3   Potential income tax liability on assets owned
        at death   (_____)

4   Funeral expenses   (_____)

5   Administrative expenses   (_____)

6   After-tax value of your estate
        (Line 1 + line 2 - line 3 - line 4 - line 5) $ _____

File under ACTION

Date: _____

FORM 33   INCOME AND EXPENDITURE PROJECTION

Amount desired for long-term objectives:	LAST YEAR	NEXT YEAR
1 Education and Support of Children	_____	_____
2 Retirement	_____	_____
3 Investments	_____	_____
4 Other	_____	_____
5 TOTAL	_____	_____

What's available for long-term objectives:		
6 Income		
a. From Employment	_____	_____
b. From Investments and Other Sources	_____	_____
c. TOTAL	_____	_____
7 Basic Expenditures	_____	_____
8 Discretionary Expenditures	_____	_____
9 Income Taxes and Other Deductions		
a. Income Tax	_____	_____
b. Other Deductions	_____	_____
c. TOTAL	_____	_____
10 TOTAL Expenditures and Taxes	_____	_____
11 Amount Available for Long-Term Goals	_____	_____

Touche Ross Canadian Guide to Personal Financial Management. © 1988 Touche Ross & Co.

File under ACTION   Date: _____

FORM 34   ACTION STEPS

List 10 specific steps you will take during the next year to implement
your personal financial plan.

_____

_____

_____

_____

_____

_____

_____

_____

_____

_____

Index

NOTES

NOTES

NOTES

NOTES

NOTES

NOTES

NOTES

NOTES

NOTES

NOTES